Also by Erin Skye Kelly

Get the Hell Out of Debt: The Proven 3-Phase Method That
Will Radically Shift Your Relationship to Money

NAKED MONEY MEETINGS

Ending Money Fights
with Your Partner Forever

ERIN SKYE KELLY

Post Hill
PRESS

A POST HILL PRESS BOOK
ISBN: 978-1-63758-779-9
ISBN (eBook): 978-1-63758-780-5

Naked Money Meetings:
Ending Money Fights with Your Partner Forever
© 2023 by Erin Skye Kelly
All Rights Reserved

Post Hill Press
New York • Nashville
posthillpress.com

Published in the United States of America
1 2 3 4 5 6 7 8 9 10

Dedication

Before we said goodbye, we plopped down on the returned couch in the As-Is section.

He had met me there because it was a two-birds-with-one-stone scenario. The birds were that I needed to pick up furniture for a rental and that we hadn't had a visit in a long time. The stone was IKEA.

I think we saw at least half a dozen romantic relationships die in the warehouse that day, all while we were unknowingly building ours up from friendship to love.

Our conversation flowed freely while I interrupted with measurements or photographs of things named "Knullruffs" or "Läderlappen" or maybe "Svenskkock."

Either I had to be somewhere or I pre-lied and said I had to be somewhere in case he wanted to visit longer, because time just wasn't a luxury for me then. But when we completed the maze, we sat down briefly to wrap up whatever story one of us was in the middle of telling. Somehow, on that KLIPPAN sofa, everything shifted.

In the years that have followed, we've built more than just furniture, but there have been times when I wanted to take advantage of Ikea's very generous return policy and drop him off with receipts. Certainly he would have exchanged me for something that came with clearer instructions and wasn't missing parts.

I don't know exactly how we got from there to here, but it involved a lot of taking apart and putting back together.

But we reminded ourselves that we are called to love As-Is.

And that has been our commitment ever since.

Disclaimer

This book is an invitation to healing. Because of that, there are instances in the book where we look at pain, and for you, that might feel triggering. I share this because in my own life, avoiding my own triggers did not make me stronger. If now is the time for you to heal, then you'll be walking into a book that invites you to explore previous experiences that may have been traumatic for you in order to gain awareness and ultimately transform the outcome of your life.

This does not take into account any systemic issues that may affect you. It also might not be an appropriate time to read this if you are currently experiencing emotional, physical, or financial abuse or coercive control. Please contact the domestic violence hotline in your area for guidance.

From a content perspective, this book contains language and concepts that might make your grandmother blush. (Not my grandmother though. She considered herself to be a proper lady, and she had a wicked sense of humor and epic timing that could slay in the right company.) If you are turned off by abrupt, adult, or offensive language, then you'll miss the heart and the love behind the teachings in these pages.

The information provided in this book is for informational, educational, and entertainment purposes only and does not constitute legal or financial advice for your unique circumstances. It is always advisable to contact a financial professional to determine what may be best for your individual needs. The publisher and the author are providing this book and its contents on an "as-is" basis. Your use of the information in this book is conducted at your own risk.

This work stems from over two decades of working with couples and their finances. Whether I was facilitating a mortgage or helping with budgets and net worth statements, I have walked with singles and couples through the events of marriage, divorce, reconciliation, children, grandchildren, and more.

I am not a licensed therapist, and this book is not meant to replace personal, individualized therapy with a licensed family therapist.

I do believe that individual and couples' therapy is one of the greatest returns on investment you can make.

Table of Contents

Chapter One: What Is a Naked Money Meeting?.....................1

Chapter Two: Why Aren't We Budgeting and Why Is it Necessary?.........3

Chapter Three: What Is a Money Block?.................6

Chapter Four: The Quiz.....................12

Chapter Five: Accepting Your Own Money Blocks.................24

Chapter Six: Specific Healing For Your Own Blocks.................32

Chapter Seven: Your Partner's Money Blocks.................52

Chapter Eight: Where Your Money Blocks Intersect.................64

Chapter Nine: Bare-Naked Budgeting.................94

Chapter Ten: Ways to Manage Cash Flow as a Couple 98

Chapter Eleven: Net Worth.................111

Chapter Twelve: Building Wealth as a Couple.................116

Chapter Thirteen: Goals.................132

Chapter Fourteen: Financial Boundaries.................140

Chapter Fifteen: Financial Identity.................145

Chapter Sixteen: Financial Intimacy.................151

Chapter Seventeen: Naked Budget Meeting Agendas.................156

Chapter Eighteen: Turning the Blocks Into Stepping Stones.................180

Chapter Nineteen: Naked Money Meetings Forever.................262

Recommended Reading.................265

Acknowledgments.................269

About the Author.................275

Chapter One

WHAT IS A NAKED MONEY MEETING?

I joked in *Get the Hell Out of Debt* that one of the ways you can initiate those first conversations about money with your partner is to call a "naked budget meeting" because attendance is always good, and nobody can argue when the jubblies are out. But what a real *naked money meeting* entails is a complete willingness to be vulnerable and honest when it comes to your money. This applies whether you are solo, shacked up, or signed-on-the-dotted-lined.

When you were younger, you had a series of experiences with money that you gave meaning to. You could have had the exact same experiences as your siblings or classmates or neighbors had, but how you interpreted those money experiences formed part of your identity.

And now, you are responding to money as it relates to your identity. The need to be right is one of the strongest traits of the human personality, and, therefore, even when your partner screws up with money and you know they are wrong, they remain committed to that pattern.

That's why you bought this book: so that I can be the one to tell them they are wrong. You're welcome. Happy to be of service.

The nature of human relationships is changing. When it comes to Gen Zers and marriage, we know that they are more likely than any demographic in history to avoid the altar and say, "I don't."

They are not interested in the institution of marriage as a business arrangement, as it was often about historically. And they are highly likely to have been raised by parents who regularly fight about money or who divorced because of it.

I'm not here to argue for or against marriage. I'm here to help you find peace.

After working with couples and their money and mortgages for decades, I've learned a few things, and one of them is this: there are ways to handle money that will help you financially succeed. And, when you master the techniques in *this* book, your home life will have more harmony as well.

Chapter Two

WHY AREN'T WE BUDGETING AND WHY IS IT NECESSARY?

For most of us, the word *budget* sends us screaming into the void. Statistics tell us that a third of us *actually* budget, but we know that the majority of that third also say lots of swear words, fight with our partners for not following the budget, and often give up for a few months before desperately starting again.

The reason why most budgets fail is that we are foolishly doing two things:

1. We are trying to make our lives fit into a math equation.
2. We keep thinking that we have to get everything to work exactly right or else we are a colossal money failure.

It is no wonder the majority of humanity hates budgeting. Even super nerdy accountants who have found themselves in the depths of debt come to me secretly for help because they know how to make other people's numbers make sense, but they struggle to understand their own. This can sometimes evoke deep shame in people who think they ought to "know better."

Well. Breaking news: This happens because numbers are not the issue.

I mean, truly, if you are reading this book, odds are you can add or subtract. Or, if you are listening to the Audible version, the odds are good that you have a tiny pocket computer that comes with a free calculator. We all know *what* to do. The issue lies in that we can't seem to get ourselves to do the things we know we need to do.

This book is going to change a few things that will radically alter the way you see money and the way you interact with it.

The first rule is that you must completely accept that your budget will never balance perfectly. You are a living, breathing human being full of amazing emotions who goes on wonderful daily adventures, and all those layers of complexity cannot be perfectly planned for and executed in a spreadsheet. Sometimes your daily adventure might be a trip to the laundry room, where you discover you are out of detergent and your son has ripped the knees of every pair of pants he owns. Sometimes your daily adventure might mean Sarah Millican is performing in your hometown and there is only one seat left and it's in the front row and it's your birthday and this feels like a once-in-a-lifetime opportunity, so you splurge, dammit.

We need to get over the idea that we only succeed when the budget balances. I went through this phase when I asked every financially successful person I knew how many times their budgets went perfectly according to plan, and every single one of them said, "Zero times."

ZERO TIMES.

The budget's job is not to be perfect. The budget's job is to make your net worth go up.

I need to say that again because there are a lot of words in this book still to come, and I do not want you to forget that. If that is the only sentence you remember, you will radically improve your finances, and your purchase of this book will ultimately be your largest return on investment.

The budget's job is to make your net worth go up.

We'll get into that net worth later, too, but what you need to know right now is that, more importantly than working out to the penny, the budget needs to find the money to buy assets or pay down liabilities. When that happens, you get richer.

The budget is simply goal-setting for your income.

It acts as a boundary for your wealth.

It protects you from making dumb decisions you will later regret, like that time I absolutely thought I needed that paint-by-numbers kit during the pandemic. It would have been wiser to put those fifty dollars into almost any stock that week in March 2020.

(Also, if you are interested, I have a paint-by-numbers kit available for sale. Barely used. Ten dollars.)

You are going to do dumb things with your money. But you also are going to do brilliant things with your money. I know this because you are reading this book, telling me you are committed to making a change.

But as you are already figuring out, numbers are not the main issue. The reason your budget hasn't been working has nothing to do with numbers. The reason you haven't built the wealth you desire is because there are deep money blocks driving your behaviors.

And once we identify your specific money blocks, it will be so much easier for you to manage your cash flow and make that budget do what it is supposed to: increase that net worth.

Chapter Three

WHAT IS A MONEY BLOCK?

When I talk about money blocks, I'm referring to the unconscious beliefs you have that limit your ability to receive. Money is an exchange. There is a giver and a receiver, and often, when we are blocked from this exchange, we are prevented from building wealth. Your money blocks evolved because of a set of experiences you had in your life.

There was an event.

The event evoked an emotion.

You assigned some sort of meaning to that event and emotion.

It became a pattern.

Patterns arise because human beings learn to anticipate. We also learn to react. We learn what to expect, and we decide what to accept. This is all necessary for survival. The challenge in adulthood results from whether we assigned meaning that was empowering or disempowering. Because, when that pattern is repeated often enough, it forms part of our identity, or how we see ourselves. And this becomes a deeply ingrained and unconscious way of being. We can walk around as fully functioning adults with jobs and responsibilities while believing deep down that we don't deserve any of it. Without even consciously trying, we are ultimately sabotaging our own happiness.

In the financial realm, this is a money block.

If you think back to some of your earliest experiences with money, the events that you remember likely evoked some kind of emotion at the time. Maybe it was joy, but it might have been embarrassment or frustration, or something painful. It's likely you have more than one memory, and often they are attached to different emotions. It would be worth it to stop and take a moment right now to recall your earliest positive memory with money. Write that down. Capture as much detail as you can. Where were you? Was there anyone with you? What happened? How did you feel? Capture the smells and sounds and as much as you can remember.

Now do it again, but this time try to recall your earliest negative money memory. Write that down. Capture as much detail as you can. How did you feel? What was happening? Was there anyone there? What decisions did you make as a result of that moment? What did you make it mean in your mind?

Boom. There you go. You likely just described two money patterns you have been living out on autopilot.

These are the eight most common money blocks:

The Lack Block
I never have enough. This mentality blocks the flow of wealth to your life because you struggle with receiving.

The Spend Block
I can't control my spending, or the minute I receive money I repel it and give it away. This mentality blocks the flow of wealth because you are consistently taking action that opposes financial accumulation.

The Worthiness Block
I'm not good enough to be wealthy. This mentality blocks the flow of wealth because life doesn't give us what we need; it gives us what we believe we deserve. And if we don't believe that we are deserving, then we won't plant the seeds of success in our life today so that we can reap the harvest later.

The Intelligence and Skill Block
I'm not smart enough to be wealthy. This mentality blocks the flow of wealth because you often live in the land of, "When I [get a job/get

a bonus/win the lottery], then I…," meaning that, for you, money always exists only in the future.

The Hard Work Block
In order to make money, I have to work really hard. If it comes easily, it's not worth it. This blocks the flow of wealth because we are trading time for money, and unless we learn how to leverage that time, we will spend our one precious life exhausted and overworked.

The Stress Block
Money is stressful. Finances are stressful. This blocks the flow of wealth to our lives because we believe that money circumstances are outside of our control, and we are now at the mercy of what happens to us.

The Procrastination Block
I am afraid of both success and failure. I delay taking action on things that bring me more income. This blocks the flow of wealth because we are losing out on time, which is one of the most powerful factors that allows money to compound.

The Money Guilt Block
I feel guilty when I have money and other people are struggling. It feels greedy or unfair if I have money while other people are hurting financially. This blocks the flow of wealth because we believe that there is a finite amount of abundance.

When these patterns stop us from reaching our full financial potential, we call them "money blocks." What is most interesting about immersing myself in this work for many years is that often when people dissolve a money block in one area, it improves their life in other areas too.

You will likely find that you have a primary money block, but you might also have a couple that compete for the top spot. This is OK. You might find that you have all the money blocks. That's OK too. You're just going to figure out which one feels like it might be your primary block, and you're going to use a combination of the words on these pages and your own gut instinct to determine which that might be. Later, you'll be able to see how your primary block has been affecting the way you handle (or don't handle!) finances and how that affects your relationship.

You'll first become aware of the blocks, and then you'll work to dissolve them by interrupting old patterns and consciously creating new ones. If you have a partner committed to doing the work with you, they will work at dissolving their own blocks too.

Here's some of the nitty gritty about money blocks:

1. As mentioned, you can have more than one. In fact, you probably do.
2. Your money blocks may change. As we encounter people and situations and come up against our own growth and constriction patterns, we might heal certain blocks only to find out that we have others. Check in with this book every six to twelve months to see how you are doing.
3. Your partner will also have a primary money block or two. And some of the most incredible work you will ever do will be shutting the hell up. You do not need to remind your partner about this. You do not need to point it out. You don't need to be right, and you are not the money-block police. Let your partner have their own growth experience (even if it means they aren't!), and you can focus on yours.
4. Your partner's money blocks may change. One of the kindest gifts we can give another human being is to not hold them to an older version of themselves.
5. Do your very best not to say, "This is my money block." Don't own it. Make it the money block you *used* to have.
6. The goal is not to get rid of the money blocks completely. That is almost impossible. The goal is to take away the power they have over us. That way, we can recognize the blocks when they show up and still make conscious, healthy choices.
7. Have lots of grace with yourself and others. Love is the most transformational power in the universe.

I have a dear friend from high school who contacted me on social media and reminded me of an event I barely remembered. Kenneth and I went to the 1997 movie *Anaconda*, and I thought I was so funny, sneaking up on the people in the row in front of us, grabbing their shoulders, and yelling, "Anaconda!" to scare the hell out of them. I grew up in a small town, so odds are I knew those people, but my reaction to this conversation taking place on Twitter was sheer embarrassment. I said, "That's *terrible*! I'm terrible. That was terrible."

I would never do that now! I have latent embarrassment for myself. The first half of my life was entirely embarrassing, and now it's thankfully only marginally so. But that's how I will be remembered by my friend Ken: as a sh*t-disturbing, mischievous troublemaker. It doesn't matter that I was acting out because of a series of things that were going on in my life that desperately made me want to escape. It doesn't matter that I hadn't yet learned respect for other people or their space.

It's critical that we allow people to grow and that we give them the space to do so. I am grateful I don't define myself by the (almost entirely dumb) decisions I made in my younger years. And the good thing about being connected to people who happen to have been there is that it reminds us of how far we've come. But imagine that you make a mistake early in a relationship, and your partner *constantly* and *relentlessly* brings it up, and every time you make progress and fail, they say, "Of *course* you did," because they cannot imagine you ever breaking the pattern of how they choose to see you. It is going to be infinitely more difficult for you to change.

When our children are learning to walk and they wobble and fall down, we don't say, "Can't you do *anything* right? You are an *idiot*." No matter how many times they fall, we softly say, "You can do it! I'm proud of you! I love you!" That's the kind of energy this work needs. I am not trying to infantilize you or your partner, but I am saying let us give ourselves and the people we love some space to grow. Change is absolutely possible. And while it's happening, we are allowed to screw up. Because we will, on account of being human.

I also know that by telling you that story (if you've missed the point), when you see me in public now, you will sneak up behind me and grab my shoulders and yell, "Anaconda!" And I will scream and drop my chai latte, and I will deserve it.

It's like when JLo sings that she's still "Jenny from the Block." She used to have a little now she has a lot. And she knows where she came from. But Jenny ain't still living there, you know? She's not "*Jenny in* the Block." She's "*Jenny from* the Block." And it's important that we don't make these money blocks part of our identity now. Make them the blocks you come *from*, and let's move toward something else.

Chapter Four

THE QUIZ

To help you assess which block might be your main money block, you can answer each of these questions on a scale of 1–10, 1 being "nope, not me," and 10 being "heck yes." Then add up your totals.

This is not a scienterrific quiz, and you are not diagnosing anything about yourself or your partner. You are simply gaining clarity.

If you find this process worrisome, I highly recommend that you find a great licensed therapist with whom to work things through, and you'll be pleased to know that even your therapist will have a money block (on account of being human).

Don't treat this like how I treated the "Cosmo Quiz" I found in my grandmother's magazines in the '90s, when I tried to assess if I was Good-Girl Hot or Bad-Girl Hot. I forget which Hot I was, but I remember I wanted to be the Other Hot so I just went back and changed my answers to be the Right Kind of Hot.

(Spoiler: I could get one half of my bangs to stand straight in the air by spraying the hair with Aussie spray as my hair sizzled on my curling iron while the other half of my bangs was slicked down with Dep, so it's no wonder I was confused.)

Once you've assessed a number for each line, come back and journal on the ones that invoke feelings in you. Take some time to fully process and lay out where these blocks might have originated and what patterns they've set in motion for you.

Here you go:
1 is for "nope, not me."
10 is for "yes, I identify with this."
And you can choose any number in between that feels right.

The Lack Block

I am scared that I am going to run out of money.

I tend to react to financial stress instead of anticipating and dissipating it.

I don't like to be around people who are "bigger thinkers" than I am.

Even though I fear I will run out of money, I still spend all my money or resources.

I tend to feel resentful of other people's success.

If I don't know something, I feel stupid.

I tend to focus on what is not working financially.

I compare myself to other people who have more financial resources.

I am often afraid of change.

I often feel financially helpless or hopeless.

I compare myself to others frequently, and not just financially.

I have a mental list of things I wish I could afford to buy.

I often wonder how other people seem to have so much because I just don't get it.

When I dream about my future, I have no idea how I will get there.

The idea of having wealth seems so hard that I don't even try to achieve it.

I often feel that "positive thinking" is a waste of time and not for me.

It is easy for me to focus on what I don't have.

I am used to having very little money.

When I do have more money than I'm used to having, I usually feel stressed about it.

I have been described as "cheap."

The Spend Block

I can't control my spending easily.

Money doesn't stay in my bank account for very long.

I often feel the urge to cash out my investments to pay off debt or buy things.

I make good money, but I am still living paycheck to paycheck.

I spend money to look as though I have money or status.

Even if I go into a store to purchase one thing, I will leave with more.

I can look through my bank statements and still be unsure of what I spent money on.

I spend money to meet an emotional need.

When money comes into my life, I instantly think of things to spend it on.

I often feel as though I must justify or explain purchases to other people.

I have a hard time saying no to myself.

I will spend recklessly but then underestimate what I've done, and I'm surprised when I add it up.

I will buy more items than I intend to because they are on sale or a "good deal."

If you were to ask me randomly what was in my bank account, I'd have no idea.

I feel a tiny little high when I buy things.

I probably have things in my closet with the tags still attached.

When I can't find something, I'll just buy a new one.

I purchase things I don't need "just in case" I might need them one day.

I often won't bother returning something if it's not suitable.

Sometimes I feel as though I'm drunk or not thinking clearly when I spend.

The Worthiness Block

I'm not good enough to be wealthy.

I treat other people better than I treat myself.

People like me never succeed financially.

I struggle to say no.

I haven't done enough to deserve financial freedom.

I put a lot of pressure on myself to do things perfectly.

I struggle to ask for help.

If I am with a financial professional or someone who I think knows more than me, even if I disagree with them, I will not speak up.

I struggle to keep promises I've made to myself.

There are people in my life who often criticize me.

I buy from discount shops and rarely treat myself to luxury items.

I often have feelings of inferiority.

I lack confidence when it comes to money and other areas of my life.

I can be a people pleaser.

I often look for external validation.

There have been times in my life when I've had or wondered if I had depression or anxiety or struggled with mental wellness.

I'm known for putting other people's needs ahead of my own.

I have used money or resources to get people to like me.

My credit score can dictate how I feel about myself.

I have a hard time speaking up in the moment.

The Intelligence and Skill Block

I'm not smart enough to be wealthy.

I often think that when I hit my financial goals my life will be easier.

I fear looking foolish around people.

I secretly feel resentful of wealthy people.

I would be embarrassed if other people knew my financial situation.

I avoid situations where money or finances will be discussed.

I am afraid that if I make a lot of money, I will lose it.

I behave immaturely with money, or I act rebellious with it.

Because I have delayed taking care of myself financially, I often look for opportunities to build wealth quickly.

I feel shame around money and finances.

I'm often looking in the rear-view-mirror at my life and wishing I'd started learning earlier.

I start reading money books, but I rarely finish them.

It would be easier if someone just took over my finances for me or told me what to do.

I won't ask questions of wealthy people because I don't want to look dumb.

I have exaggerated my financial circumstances before so that I look smarter to people.

I don't trust myself to make smart decisions, so I often outsource my decision-making.

I worry that I am managing my money "wrong."

When I do invest money, I ignore it because I don't know what to do from there.

I assume rich people must be smarter than me.

I'm just not good at math.

The Hard Work Block
To make money I must work really hard.

If it comes easy it's not worth it.

When I need more money, I must work more hours.

I judge people who appear to be rich and lazy.

I feel constantly distracted by work, even when I'm not working.

I am scared to slow down in case money dries up.

I may be using work to avoid other areas of my life (including finances).

If money comes into my life easily, I assume there must be a catch.

Wealthy people probably did something unethical to get their money.

When I have free time, I can feel guilty that I'm unproductive or like I "should" be working.

I am working or have worked multiple jobs at the same time to get by.

When I need more money, I instantly think of ways to work.

Burnout is a very real concern of mine.

I often feel I am the hardest working person I know.

I have a hard time relaxing if work or chores are not finished.

People have told me, "You work too much/you work too hard."

I will often overcomplicate things.

It feels like I have worked hard all my life and I don't have much to show for it.

I seem to be surrounded by a lot of drama.

When I work more hours to make more money, it seems like my expenses go up, too.

The Stress Block

Money is stressful.

Dealing with finances overwhelms me.

I can lose sleep over my finances.

Thinking about money takes up a huge part of the real estate in my brain.

I find it hard to dream about things if I don't have the money.

I constantly think about money or the lack thereof.

I am unclear on how I will retire.

I feel financially disorganized.

I tend to get into black/white or all/nothing thinking when it comes to my money.

I have created financial chaos by missing payments, hitting overdraft, or making little mistakes that have bigger consequences.

I avoid conversations about finances because they stress me out.

I find it hard to trust others when it comes to money.

I have physical stress symptoms when I deal with money (headaches, tummy troubles, anxiety, sweatiness, loss of focus, moodiness, short emotional fuse, insomnia, clenched jaw, poor judgement, etc.).

When I am stressed financially, I notice an increase in my use of alcohol, drugs, cigarettes, or food to cope.

I often feel caught between the feeling of losing control and the need to take control.

I have had sudden angry outbursts because of money.

Dealing with money has caused me to cry at least once in the past year.

I have had relationship problems because of finances.

I often think, "If only I had more money, then these problems would go away."

I sometimes wish I could start all over financially.

The Procrastination Block

I am afraid of financial success.

I am afraid of financial failure.

I delay taking action on things that would bring me more income.

I avoid hard or important conversations about money.

I can feel paralyzed by indecision.

I am continually saying, "I'll do it tomorrow."

I will often file my taxes or hand in forms just under a deadline or late.

I often find excuses for not dealing with my finances.

I will needlessly delay doing things even if they are important to me.

I can sometimes overcommit or overbook myself and set myself up to fail.

I often feel as though I am in "financial crisis."

When I can't do something perfectly, I will often avoid it.

I often can't figure out how to break down big goals into smaller pieces, so I get lost not knowing what to do next.

I think finances are boring, therefore, I don't like to spend time on them.

When I don't have clear deadlines or dire consequences for not doing something, I just keep putting it off.

I underestimate how long things will take.

A lot of financial tasks feel like a waste of my time.

I take on too many things and then get overwhelmed and do none of those things.

There are small financial to-do items that I've been meaning to do for a long time that I still haven't done (enroll in my 401(k) at work, buy life insurance, start an emergency fund, and so on).

If I were not a procrastinator, I would be much wealthier by now. I've wasted a lot of time by not taking action.

The Money Guilt Block

I feel guilty when I have money and other people are struggling.

It feels greedy or unfair if I have money while other people are hurting financially.

I didn't earn money the way I had anticipated, so I feel bad having it.

I can worry about things that aren't in my control.

I often find that I'm trying to "pour from an empty cup," or give what I don't have.

I often spend time thinking about what life would be like if my circumstances were different.

I will make decisions today based on things that happened in my childhood, sometimes unconsciously.

I am comfortable feeling negative about money.

I will give money to other people, charities, or causes before I spend on myself.

I can feel upset that other people don't care as much about the world as I do.

I am uncomfortable when people I know talk about their possessions.

I have a hard time enjoying life and luxuries.

Sometimes I mentally punish myself to ward off feelings of guilt.

I feel very sensitive to financial injustice.

Sometimes I feel all consumed by guilt, and it cuts me off from experiencing a full range of emotions.

Guilt has kept me from being truly successful.

I tend to think in terms of "right" and "wrong" when it comes to finances.

I have acted against either my personal beliefs about money or what society has deemed acceptable financial behavior.

I have used my spending to demonstrate my moral beliefs.

Money has divided family members or people close to me.

I have felt bad about some of the thoughts I've had about people and their money.

CONGRATULATIONS! YOU DID IT!

That was the hardest part of this whole process.

Now, this quiz is not meant to be definitive. For instance, if you once wondered whether you might have had depression, that doesn't mean you absolutely struggle with worthiness. Worthiness and depression might be linked, but you can also feel very worthy and struggle with mental wellness. When answering these questions, we aren't looking for absolute certainty— we're looking for patterns to see if we can gain better awareness as to why you might do the things you do when it comes to money. This is also not a diagnostic tool, though many mental-health-care professionals have incorporated this work on a clinical level with their clients.

But none of this has any meaning unless you feel that something resonates with you. *You* determine what it means and how you'd like to release the blocks.

You might also have only one block in a category, but you read it and it hit you with such force that you thought, "Whoa, this one runs deep!" You can choose to focus on that block as opposed to several less-significant blocks, if you prefer. You are in control of your life.

OK, SO, LIKE, NOW WHAT?

These money blocks will interrupt the flow of money to and from your life by interfering with your ability to give and/or receive. If you struggle with debt, you most likely struggle to receive.

In the first book in this series, *Get the Hell Out of Debt*, you read that I believe people who struggle with consumer debt are not selfish over-shoppers like the world would have you believe. They are often people who are much more generous with others than with themselves. They are often amazing at taking care of others and putting others' needs ahead of their own. Yes, we want to learn to budget and increase our net worth and manage those dollars, but unless we take a look at what is *driving* those behaviors, and at the deep-seated beliefs we hold about who we are, we won't ever effectively take care of the problem, and either it will manifest in other ways or we will keep repeating the cycle of paying off debt and racking it back up again. Teaching how to master money behaviors is what made *Get the Hell Out of Debt* so successful.

Additionally, sometimes these money blocks affect our ability to give. We each absolutely must create and reinforce our money boundaries, but living with abundant generosity is also important. The difference between giving with abundance and giving recklessly stems from the position from which we give. In the example above, people who struggle to receive often give from a place of lack, meaning that they will give even when they don't have much to give. We often herald this behavior and see it as selfless, but in actuality it can be harmful if the giver is putting themselves in a precarious financial position, going into debt, or making themselves not able to properly plan for their own retirement in order to help someone else. This is not abundant giving. When a person *is* in a position of abundance but doesn't know how to properly give, they can interrupt the flow of someone else's receiving. Society will often treat these people as greedy or as hoarders when, in actuality, they can be people who have been hurt or rejected by giving in the past and have their own work to do in order to heal.

When the channel between giving and receiving is opened, the incredible subsequent flow leads to greater connection between human beings. You cannot force this. For instance, if you are giving from a place of lack or with the expectation of receiving something in return, you are not creating an open channel. The same goes for if you are receiving because you feel that you are owed something.

An open channel of giving and receiving will feel energetic, free, positively charged, and loving. It will feel safe, and your body will feel at home.

You can do this quiz online at NakedMoneyMeetings.com and share with a friend!

Chapter Five

ACCEPTING YOUR OWN MONEY BLOCKS

It is your job to heal your own money blocks. It'll be important not to shove this chapter in your partner's face and tell them how to fix their lives. You won't actually fix anything. They're not going to fix anything. The only person you need to worry about is you. Let the results in your own life be motivation for somebody else. Or not. Sometimes when we learn something new, we can get zealous and excited, and we want to tell everybody what they need to do.

One of the comments I hear from people who take personal development seriously is how frustrated they are that they are growing and their spouse is not, and so they want to know what they can do to make their partner grow. My internal response that I never say out loud is: "You actually haven't grown at all. You're just starting your journey. Because if you had grown to the level that you claim you have, you wouldn't be at all concerned with your partner's progress."

Ouch, right? My inner response is a cheeky bugger.

The truth is that you would only be concerned with your own growth, and you would love your partner entirely for who they are. Just because you have started to grow and develop does not make you *better than*. In fact, one of the things you'll discover is that the more you grow and the more you know…the less you *actually* know. Wisdom is both knowledge and curiosity, and the best posture you can have in a relationship with somebody who doesn't have a desire to grow is love and curiosity. Just get to know and understand them. Let them feel seen and heard and loved. The end.

Now let's dive into what *you* came here to learn, and then you can share with your partner what you learned about *you*.

It's important to know that the work is never really done. Everything is always a work in progress; you might find you have blocks that diminish throughout your life, and yet other ones could still crop up based on conversations you have with others or triggering situations you experience. This is true for relationships as well, because it's not as though you create a perfect relationship and then never have to work on it.

Throughout your life, there will be times when your person challenges you, or when you're causing emotional injury to the other accidentally. Those things need to be healed, and you can often grow through them together.

UNDERSTANDING YOUR MONEY STORY

To really heal your money story, you must remove blame.

The story is the thing we tell ourselves to justify emotions or behaviors in response to an event. This can eventually cause a money block.

When we dive into the challenges we experienced in childhood, it can be easy to see ourselves as an innocent victim. I'm going to encourage you to rewrite the ending of the story by seeing yourself no longer as the victim but as someone who has learned to overcome the thing that was blocking you. It can feel comfortable to blame others because doing so justifies our hurt. But it also keeps us in the hurt when what we want to do is grow. And growth is almost always uncomfortable. It requires us to do things we don't always feel like doing. It requires us to see things in a new way.

Perhaps you can see how these events brought you incredible teaching moments and became the catalyst for your own growth and change. Even more astounding is that many people can learn to be thankful for their hardships because those experiences created unbelievable opportunities for love, connection, and growth, or because they made you the incredible, beautiful, inspiring person you are today.

There are five key concepts that I need you to pinky swear you will abide by and adhere to, no matter how tempting it might be to veer into your partner's lane:

- ✓ You must focus on healing your own blocks.
- ✓ You are not responsible for your partner's blocks.
- ✓ You are not responsible for healing your partner's blocks.
- ✓ It is not your job to point out your partner's blocks.
- ✓ Being tempted to tell your partner what they need to do is a sign that you have more work to do on you.

Sometimes we think we are helping our partner by bringing their blocks, flaws, or challenges to their attention. It would be far better to put that energy into dying a thousand ego deaths and focusing on how we can better show up for our partners in love.

Before we even begin to look at our partner's money blocks, let's look at our own. If you are single, know how blessed you are to be able to do this work at this moment in time!

The keys to healing any block are the following:

- ✓ Presence and Awareness
- ✓ An Energetic Shift
- ✓ Leaning into the Things You Want to Avoid
- ✓ Consciously Making New Choices
- ✓ Celebration and Conditioning
- ✓ Compassion for Self and Others

PRESENCE AND AWARENESS

This involves being present to *what is* happening in the moment and not thinking about what you want to happen.

The lack is in the want. The struggle is in the want. The poor decisions are in the want.

When we remove "the want" and we focus on "what is" with radical acceptance, we are freed to be truly naked to the experience.

One of the behaviors I've noticed in people who carry a lot of consumer debt is a level of beautiful and horrific hopefulness that allows them to believe there will be more money tomorrow than there is today; so, they keep outspending their income now and then trying to out-earn their spending later. The honesty that comes when they can truly be present to what is happening right now holds so much healing power. As long as we keep trying to pretend things are not what they are, we delay our healing and potentially cause ourselves more harm.

AN ENERGETIC SHIFT

Years ago, I was backstage at an event, and I was nearly in tears. I had been placed on a team with a person—who has since been referred to as the "twatwaffle"—who was intent on lighting little fires everywhere she went. She delighted in driving people mad, making others cry, causing drama, and getting attention. I do not believe she was a bad person, but somewhere along the way someone must have spiked her water with some toxic radio-active sludge because she emanated this life-draining energy all the time. On this particular day, she had offended nearly every other core team member to the point of tears, frustration, or numbness. People who took time away from their jobs and families to volunteer that day were walking out, and I didn't try to stop any of them. How on earth do you convince people to stay to be verbally abused? I was ready to leave, too.

I was appearing to function on the outside but having an internal level-ten nuclear meltdown on the inside when my friend Jenny McKinney asked me, "What could be your lesson here?" And thus began an energy-shifting process that changed my life.

Initially I was annoyed. Like, "What is *my* lesson? I'll school *her* alright." My first thought was a very wounded one, but then I pulled myself together and had some profound shifts in thought that ultimately ended up changing my life for the better.

But that's just it, isn't it? Sometimes the lessons come years later, when you look back and think, "Thank goodness I met that twatwaffle, and thank goodness she shook me to my core." In the moment, however, you need to shift your energy.

Jenny is a certified EFT tapping practitioner, and I encourage you to seek one out if you feel like you keep getting stuck, energetically speaking. EFT stands for "emotional freedom technique." It's considered an alternative treatment for physical pain or emotional distress.

Tapping is a healing technique that involves gently tapping on different acupressure or acupuncture points on your body.

As someone who used to say, "I eat cortisol for breakfast," I know that whenever I experience a stressful or traumatic event, my body dumps cortisol into my bloodstream (or wherever stress hormones swim to). This creates a disruption in the system that can lead to illness or injury, physical or emotional pain—or, because of the way cortisol can create memories of painful events, it can affect our psychology and be a factor in our participation in negative relationships, our financial problems, or our low self-worth.

And this is studied extensively. It's been proven to help war veterans with PTSD. When I learned how tapping heals those factors listed above, I had to see for myself how it could help people with financial problems.

Sometimes math is not the primary solution to your financial struggles.

I decided to put this woo stuff to the test and had Jenny come into the *Get the Hell Out of Debt* community for eight weeks to see if we could remove these money blocks with EFT tapping.

We divided the participants into two groups:

1. The control group: people who submitted their net worth on day one, did not participate in EFT tapping or money-block work, and then submitted their net worths again at the end of the eight sessions.
2. The tapping group: people who submitted their net worth on day one, participated in eight sessions designed to help them dissolve their money blocks, and then submitted their net worths again at the end of the eight sessions.

After eight weeks, the participants in the control group for *Get the Hell Out of Debt*'s experiment had increased their net worth by $4,753.71 on average.

The group that participated in a weekly ETF tapping session had increased their net worth by $32,202.39 on average. After eight weeks!

Sometimes shifting your relationship with money is simply about shifting the way you show up in the world.

LEANING INTO THE THINGS YOU WANT TO AVOID

You don't need me to give you all the analogies about how when an obstacle shows up the only thing you can do is find a way around it or through it or over it. You know this already, but I need to point out that that's exactly how money blocks work as well. When we notice we have one, we have to find a way around it. We must consciously take action on the thing we don't feel like doing in order to practice a different pattern or a different response to the block.

Having a money block doesn't make you bad, and it doesn't mean there's anything wrong with you. It was created to serve a purpose at one point in your life. Something painful was happening, and to protect yourself and alleviate or avoid the pain, you unconsciously created this energy block, which we now refer to as a money block.

So, see? You did a good thing.

Now, however, you might notice that the block isn't serving you, and yet it is still there. I wish I could tell you with full confidence that once you heal a money block it's gone forever, but it doesn't quite work like that. The good news is that once you have *awareness* of your block, when you notice it from that point on it acts as a constant and gentle reminder to make a new choice.

CONSCIOUSLY MAKE A NEW CHOICE

This is easier said than done. Our money blocks have kept us locked in an old pattern for so long that we got comfortable. And even if you can't think of anything worse than repeating the same old money habits you've already developed, there will be a deep pull within you to continue the pattern because it's what you know. It's where you feel safe.

We have to get uncomfortable for a bit. We have to make a new choice that will lead to a new outcome. It's not going to feel great.

Have you ever gone to the gym after a long hiatus? And the next morning you got out of bed and walked around like a cowboy who has mounted an invisible horse?

That first gym visit is uncomfortable. But the first gym visit is necessary to get to the next one, to get to the next one, to get to the five hundredth one.

CELEBRATION AND CONDITIONING

Don't think of this as a one-shot deal—think of it as practice. Eventually, when you have made the new choices over and over, you will have conditioned yourself to this new, healthy financial normal.

If you only ever make a good financial decision once in a while...well, then you'll have yourself some bowlegged financial consequences. But if you *condition* yourself to be uncomfortable for a while, and you repeat these great financial decisions over and over, then you'll eventually start to see progress.

Much like if you go to the gym consistently. Those first few times were awkward and uncomfortable, and you probably thought about quitting. But if you persisted for a while, you probably built yourself a fabulous bulgy bicep.

It's the same principle when it comes to money. If you want some money guns, you are going to have to condition some new money patterns over and over again until it's your new normal.

COMPASSION FOR SELF AND OTHERS

All the while you are healing, you need to practice compassion. I used to think I was a compassionate person because I would feel moved by holiday commercials or by kitten videos on the internet. It wasn't until I realized how I was selectively compassionate that I knew where I had to grow.

It's really easy for me to be compassionate with myself or others when I feel that people or circumstances are *deserving* of compassion. (Ugh. That damn ego.)

But I found that I was lacking in compassion if people had different values or beliefs than me. If someone was struggling financially, had a ton of credit card debt, and kept trying to pay it off every month by insisting that they were getting free trips with points and that they needed to keep their credit score high even though they might not have a penny saved for retirement—well, you can see where our beliefs differed.

But the truth is that almost every human being on earth deserves compassion on some level. And when we can approach life with this perspective, our own relationship with money will change for the better.

....
Chapter Six
....

SPECIFIC HEALING FOR YOUR OWN BLOCKS

HEALING THE LACK BLOCK: *"I never have enough."*

This block might show up for you as the following:

- ◆ I am scared that I am going to run out of money.
- ◆ I tend to react to financial stress instead of anticipating and dissipating it.
- ◆ I don't like to be around people who are "bigger thinkers" than I am.
- ◆ Even though I fear I will run out of money, I still spend all my money or resources.
- ◆ I tend to feel resentful of other people's success.
- ◆ If I don't know something, I feel stupid.
- ◆ I tend to focus on what is not working financially.
- ◆ I compare myself with other people who have more financial resources.
- ◆ I am often afraid of change.
- ◆ I often feel financially helpless or hopeless.
- ◆ I compare myself to others frequently, and not just financially.
- ◆ I have a mental list of things I wish I could afford to buy.

- I often wonder how other people seem to have so much because I just don't get it.
- When I dream about my future, I have no idea how I will get there.
- The idea of having wealth seems so hard that I don't even try to achieve it.
- I often feel that "positive thinking" is a waste of time and not for me.
- It is easy for me to focus on what I don't have.
- I am used to having very little money.
- When I do have more money than I'm used to having, I usually feel stressed about it.
- I have been described as "cheap."

This block is healed mostly with gratitude. It will require a constant redirection of focus and attention to abundance. There are plenty of gratitude practices you can do, formally or informally, but essentially the healing comes from noticing and being grateful for all life's blessings, even when they are not obvious.

Sometimes when I talk about this, people assume that it means they have the block because they are an ungrateful cow. That is not true. You can be a very grateful person and have this block, but there is always room to increase gratitude to release the block. Some people think of gratitude as a bit of a wish list—they ask for something, and then spiritual Alexa makes it come true. However, we also must be grateful for the things we maybe haven't asked for but that still bless our lives.

We can also practice something called "effective blaming," which I learned from Tony Robbins. Essentially, this is the process of being grateful for all the obstacles and challenges you've had that have made you the courageous, brilliant, and resilient person you are. Sometimes in the moment the challenges we experience justify not being grateful. But when we can be grateful for life anyway, we begin to heal this block and experience tremendous growth. So, sometimes we have to be thankful for things that are painful. Like the twatwaffles among us.

This is very different than "spiritual bypassing," which consists of pretending everything is OK when it's not. Clinical psychologist John Welwood came up with this phrase in the 1980s. It describes being overly idealistic or overly detached. It's overemphasizing the positive and minimizing the negative instead of embracing the feelings that are actually real, and then choosing what to focus on. It's the equivalent of sweeping an elephant under a rug and then pretending the rug isn't lumpy.

Effective blaming is different than spiritual bypassing. Blaming effectively empowers you to live your most authentic and free life. Blaming effectively allows you to release the pain of your past and to use it as a springboard to your future. It allows you to focus on the growth, not the pain itself. It allows you to move forward, or past the obstacle, and keeps you from feeling stuck.

Blaming effectively is essentially releasing the elephant back into the wild while being grateful that it gave you the elephant-management skills you needed in the meantime.

HEALING THE SPEND BLOCK: *"I can't control my spending, or the minute I receive money I repel it and give it away."*

This block might show up for you as the following:

- I can't control my spending easily.
- Money doesn't stay in my bank account for very long.
- I often feel the urge to cash out my investments to pay off debt or buy things.
- I make good money, but I am still living paycheck to paycheck.
- I spend money to look as though I have money or status.
- Even if I go into a store to purchase one thing, I will leave with more.
- I can look through my bank statements and still be unsure what I spent money on.
- I spend money to meet an emotional need.

- When money comes into my life, I instantly
  think of things I can spend it on.
- I often feel as though I have to justify or
  explain purchases to other people.
- I have a hard time saying no to myself.
- I will spend recklessly but then underestimate what
  I've done, and I'm surprised when I add it up.
- I will buy more items than I intend to because
  they were on sale or a "good deal."
- If you were to ask me randomly what is in
  my bank account, I'd have no idea.
- I feel a tiny little high when I buy things.
- I probably have things in my closet
  with the tags still attached.
- When I can't find something, I'll just buy a new one.
- I purchase things I don't need "just in
  case" I might need them one day.
- I often won't bother returning something if it's not suitable.
- Sometimes I feel as though I'm drunk or
  not thinking clearly when I spend.

This block is usually caused by an emotional void or by feeling that you're "not enough" as you are.

Healing this block requires you to take full inventory of yourself, your life, who you are, and how you show up.

Here's how you take a personal inventory:

Spend time writing (give yourself a couple of uninterrupted hours if you can) an objective assessment of your life. Be so honest in this assessment that you want to light it on fire afterwards. You'll include all your character defects (so, basically the opposite of a Bumble profile), all your strengths and weaknesses, and a look at the hurt you've caused yourself and other people—*without* writing the reasons why or pointing out where the blame lies. It's basically a full responsibility-taking. If you had to accept full responsibility without involving any other human being, could you do it?

Would your ego want to come up with a justification or an excuse for your behavior in order to protect its fragile self?

I'm not suggesting for a minute that this is intended to bypass anything that happened *to* you. Certainly, experiencing abuse of any kind is not something you take responsibility for.

But in your recovery from abuse, there may be behaviors or choices or actions you made that you could consider taking responsibility for, even if in the moment you didn't feel as though you had another choice.

The big things to watch for here are selfishness, dishonesty, resentment, and fear.

When we do not feel healthy or whole, this struggle often shows up in our finances as a spend leak. Sometimes we are trying to fill an emotional hole with a Mastercard-shaped solution, and, as you know, those don't fit.

If gift giving is your love language and you also feel unloved, you might be on the fast track to Spend Town. Be really mindful of engaging in proactive self-care so that you are managing your state instead of letting your emotions dictate your behaviors.

HEALING THE WORTHINESS BLOCK: *"I'm not good enough to be wealthy."*

This block might show up for you as the following:

- I'm not good enough to be wealthy.
- I treat other people better than I treat myself.
- People like me never succeed financially.
- I struggle to say no.
- I haven't done enough to deserve financial freedom.
- I put a lot of pressure on myself to do things perfectly.
- I struggle to ask for help.
- If I am with a financial professional or someone who I think knows more than me, then, even if I disagree with them, I will not speak up.
- I struggle to keep promises I've made to myself.
- There are people in my life who often criticize me.

- I buy from discount shops and rarely treat myself to luxury items.
- I often have feelings of inferiority.
- I lack confidence when it comes to money
  and other areas of my life.
- I can be a people pleaser.
- I often look for external validation.
- There have been times in my life when I've had
  or wondered if I had depression or anxiety, or
  when I've struggled with mental wellness.
- I'm known for putting other people's needs ahead of my own.
- I have used money or resources to get people to like me.
- My credit score can dictate how I feel about myself.
- I have a hard time speaking up in the moment.

This block is in nearly every person to some degree. And for a large percentage of us, this lack of feeling worthy turns into a huge need to be perfect. According to recent research conducted by the Hardin Group, 92 percent of people struggle with some form of perfectionism.

If somehow as a child you developed the idea that if you behave perfectly, you will be worthy of love, then you created a belief that can wreak havoc on your adult-life results. Given that part of being human is to be so messy and imperfect, it's easy to constantly feel as though you are failing at perfection simply by existing.

One of the ways we help heal this financial block is by working at being "goodish." My friend Karissa Kouchis will often talk about the importance of taking imperfect action. When we can make motion toward our goals, we build up our confidence. When we are starting, we don't need to add pressure on ourselves to get it perfect the first time.

Our self-esteem is built by mastering our personal integrity. When we can trust ourselves to do what we say we are going to do, we will naturally build self-confidence. This will show up in our skills, abilities, accomplishments, and other performance-based activities.

Our self-worth, or worthiness, is separate and distinct from our self-esteem, though the two are woven together. Self-worth is the understanding that you do not have to do anything or achieve anything to be loved. You are worthy as is. You deserve to take up space. You deserve to be loved and cared for. And even if you are surrounded by people who cannot show up for you, you can show up for yourself and care for yourself in this deeply intimate way. You deserve it.

Unfortunately, we are surrounded by advertising that points out our flaws and offers a solution—if we pay for it. Our education system points out all our wrongs and tells us that the closer we are to right or perfect, the better off we are. Our society points out all our awkwardness and uniqueness and tells us that in order to fit in, we have to behave a certain way, talk a certain way, and appear a certain way, or else we risk not being loved or included.

It's no wonder we have no idea who we are; we've forever performed to try and fit all the molds that are set out for us, and that makes it more difficult for us to feel that we deserve love and connection just as we are.

One of the most essential ways you can start to feel more worthy is to stop outsourcing your decisions to other people. We often look to other people to affirm our decisions, but in essence, when you do that, you are telling your heart you don't trust yourself.

Making decisions you know to be right for you, and then looking for outside advice on how to best act on those decisions, is different than leaving your life up to other people's choices.

Getting back to the heart of who you are and listening to and loving that version of yourself will help you heal this block, and likely many other life wounds too as a result.

HEALING THE INTELLIGENCE AND SKILL BLOCK:
"I'm not smart enough to be wealthy. "When I [get a job/get a bonus/win the lottery], then I..."

This block might show up for you as the following:

- I'm not smart enough to be wealthy.
- I often think that when I hit my financial goals, my life will be easier.
- I am scared of looking foolish around people.

- I secretly feel resentful of wealthy people.
- I would be embarrassed if other people knew my financial situation.
- I avoid situations where money or finances will be discussed.
- I am afraid that if I make a lot of money, I will lose it.
- I behave immaturely with money, or I act rebelliously with it.
- Because I have delayed taking care of myself financially, I often look for opportunities to build wealth quickly.
- I feel shame around money and finances.
- I'm often looking in the rearview mirror at my life and wishing I'd started learning earlier.
- I start reading money books, but I rarely finish them.
- It would be easier if someone just took over my finances or told me what to do.
- I won't ask questions of wealthy people because I don't want to look dumb.
- I have exaggerated my financial circumstances so that I look smarter to others.
- I don't trust myself to make smart decisions, so I often outsource my decision-making.
- I worry that I am managing my money "wrong."
- When I do invest money, I ignore it because I don't know what to do from there.
- I assume rich people must be smarter than I am.
- I'm just not good at math.

We need to stop believing in the idea that there is a right answer for everything. Even when we look at facts, we have to acknowledge that science changes all the time because, thank goodness, scientists are curious enough to ask questions.

One of the best ways to heal this block of feeling as though you aren't smart enough is to get curious.

There is not one right answer to everything, even though school might have trained you to believe otherwise.

There is not one way to get rich. In Phase Three (the wealth-building phase) of *Get the Hell Out of Debt*, people will often ask, "What should I invest in?" as though there is one thing they've been missing all this time that they can access now that they aren't in the consumer-debt club. There are many different ways to get wealthy. Even if real-estate investing became your method of choice, there are thousands of ways within real estate itself to get rich (and, frankly, thousands of ways to go broke). There isn't "a right thing" or "a wrong thing" when it comes to finances.

The key is to get curious, ask questions, make the best decision you can in the moment, stay curious, ask more questions, and adjust the plan as needed.

This is also an important approach to model for children. Don't let your children think that you are always right when it comes to life. You'll fall off that pedestal really fast one day anyway. Stay curious. Even if you know the answer to "What is an erection?" your best parenting work will come from saying, "Well, I have an idea, but what do *you* think an erection is?" Then, you can read age-appropriate educational books together and say, "Wow! I thought that was fascinating. What did you think?" All the while you'll be protected just in case your child was actually asking, "What is an election?" but somehow mispronounced it.

HEALING THE HARD WORK BLOCK: *"In order to make money, I must work really hard. If it comes easy, it's not worth it."*

This block might show up for you as the following:

- In order to make money, I must work really hard.
- If it comes easily, it's not worth it.
- If I need more money, I must work more hours.
- I judge people who appear to be rich and lazy.
- I feel constantly distracted by work, even when I'm not working.

- I am scared to slow down in case money dries up.
- I may be using work to avoid other areas of my life (including finances).
- If money comes into my life easily, I assume there must be a catch.
- Wealthy people probably did something unethical to get their money.
- When I have free time, I can feel guilty that I'm being unproductive or that I "should" be working.
- I am working or have worked multiple jobs at the same time to get by.
- When I need more money, I instantly think of ways to work to get it.
- Burnout is a very real concern of mine.
- I often feel that I am the hardest-working person I know.
- I have a hard time relaxing if work or chores are not finished.
- People have told me, "You work too much," or "You work too hard."
- I often overcomplicate things.
- It feels as though I have worked hard all my life, and I don't have much to show for it.
- I seem to be surrounded by a lot of drama.
- When I work more hours to make more money, it seems that my expenses go up too.

The way we heal the hard work block is to truly understand compound interest and how it works. You need to make sure you are tracking your net worth weekly to watch it grow. You'll focus intently on staying out of the red column (the liabilities section) of your net worth, and you'll actively grow the green column (or purchase assets).

In the *Get the Hell Out of Debt* program, we reference how important it is to watch your "money bunnies" grow. You know how bunnies breed, and debt and wealth compound the same way!

When you see that there are ways to grow money and wealth that don't involve working from sunup 'til sundown, you will expand the possibilities for your own life. What's important to remember, though, is that often these kinds of investment or passive income opportunities do require some learning or hard work up front—but at least they have the potential to allow you to earn back some of your time.

The other important part of this healing is to make sure that you are surrounded by people who understand this concept and are implementing it within their own lives. When we are surrounded by people who believe the only way to gain wealth is to work arduously, we are likely to give up on our dreams simply because the people around us don't believe it's possible to achieve them. Consider spending time with people who have accomplished what you hope to accomplish, and don't let that intelligence/skill block prevent you from asking questions and staying curious. It's OK not to know everything, but it's not OK to pretend that you do.

HEALING THE STRESS BLOCK: *"Money is stressful."*

This block might show up for you as the following:

- Money is stressful.
- Dealing with finances overwhelms me.
- I can lose sleep over my finances.
- Thinking about money takes up a huge amount of the real estate in my brain.
- I find it hard to dream about things if I don't have the money to achieve them.
- I constantly think about money or the lack thereof.
- I am unclear on how I will retire.
- I feel financially disorganized.
- I tend to get into black-and-white or all-or-nothing thinking when it comes to my money.
- I have created financial chaos by missing payments, hitting overdraft, or making little mistakes that have big consequences.

- ◆ I avoid conversations about finances
  because they stress me out.
- ◆ I find it hard to trust others when it comes to money.
- ◆ I have physical stress symptoms when I deal with money
  (headaches, stomach troubles, anxiety, sweatiness, loss
  of focus, moodiness, short emotional fuse, insom-
  nia, clenched jaw, poor judgement, and so on).
- ◆ When I am stressed financially, I notice an increase in my
  consumption of alcohol, drugs, cigarettes, or food to cope.
- ◆ I often feel caught between the feeling of los-
  ing control and the need to take control.
- ◆ I have had sudden angry outbursts because of money.
- ◆ Dealing with money has caused me to
  cry at least once in the past year.
- ◆ I have had relationship problems because of finances.
- ◆ I often think, "If only I had more money,
  then these problems would go away."
- ◆ I sometimes wish I could start all over financially.

One of the ways we overcome the stress block is to instead find the joy and fun in money obstacles. Years after I went through my personal financial hell, the government would send me letter after letter, wanting to verify everything from charitable receipts to whether my children were real. It used to be the case that I would be stressed whenever those brown envelopes from the taxman appeared. Then, I started to pretend that the tax-revenue office was madly in love with me and would write me long love letters. I would roll my eyes when I'd open the mailbox and whisper, "Why are you so obsessed with me?" and make myself laugh.

Obstacles are always an invitation to our own growth. You are not meant to be stressed by money, and, if you find that you still are, it might mean that there is an invitation to growth that you just keep passing up!

Belief in the idea that money is stressful is a learned behavior. You picked it up from somewhere and believed it so deeply that now your emotional system is activated by money. If you didn't have this belief, how would life feel? What if money were a fun game you were playing and you might have failed a few levels, so you need to go back and pass them in order to level up again?

What if you made your experience with money enjoyable? What if you loved looking at your net worth and finding ways to make it grow?

To heal this block, we need to believe that money is not stressful. We need to behave as though this is true, and we need to reinforce that belief through new actions. If you can intentionally believe that building wealth is fun, you might choose to see buying investments as fun. Then, when those investments produce gains, you'll see that as fun. Then you might eventually see wasteful spending as not fun because it takes you away from the fun of growing your money through investments.

You can choose to link money to other things you find enjoyable. If you love the outdoors, spend time budgeting under a beautiful tree in the park on Sunday afternoons. If you love health and fitness, consider enjoying freshly squeezed celery juice while you reconcile for five minutes in the mornings. If you love long, luxurious baths, perhaps listen to amazing financial podcasts while you soak with candles and bubbles.

Here's the mistake most people make: we think our feelings are a reaction to something outside of ourselves. But the truth is that our feelings live in us all the time. Happiness is in there. Sadness is in there. Stress is in there. Silliness is in there. They simply get activated by the things that happen to us, and then we react. But we can train ourselves to react in different ways.

Let's imagine that you and your coworkers are looking outside during a freak snowstorm, and someone slips on the ice, banana-peel style, where their feet whoosh right out from under them. It's likely that one of you laughs hysterically, one of you worries, one of you runs out to see if the person is OK, and one of you physically feels the pain of falling. You all saw the same incident, but your reactions to it were entirely different. This is all because of patterns!

Here's the part that is hard to hear. Money isn't stressful. *You* stress. You are the cause of your stress. You choose stress. And just as you've chosen to decide that money is stressful, you can also choose to decide that it is fun.

HEALING THE PROCRASTINATION BLOCK:
"I am afraid of both success and failure. I delay acting on things that bring me more income."

This block might show up for you as the following:

- I am afraid of financial success.
- I am afraid of financial failure.
- I delay taking action on things that would bring me more income.
- I avoid hard or important conversations about money.
- I can feel paralyzed by indecision.
- I am continually saying, "I'll do it tomorrow."
- I will often file my taxes or hand in forms just under a deadline or late.
- I often find excuses for not dealing with my finances.
- I will needlessly delay doing things even if they are important to me.
- I can sometimes overcommit or over-book myself and set myself up to fail.
- I often feel as though I am in "financial crisis."
- When I can't do something per-fectly, I will often avoid doing it.
- I often can't figure out how to break down big goals into smaller pieces, so I get lost not knowing what to do next.
- I think finances are boring AF; therefore, I don't like to spend time on them.
- When I don't have clear deadlines or dire consequences for not doing something, I just keep putting it off.
- I underestimate how long things will take.
- A lot of financial tasks feel like a waste of my time.
- I take on too many things and then get over-whelmed and do none of those things.
- There are small financial to-do items that I've been meaning to do for a long time that I still haven't

done (enroll in my 401(k) at work, buy life insurance, start an emergency fund, and so on).

- If I were not a procrastinator, I would be much wealthier by now. I've wasted a lot of time by not taking action.

Your comfort zone must have been really cozy and doing its job to keep you feeling safe. You probably have a space heater in there, one of those beanbag lounge chairs you can just plop into, and probably the new Taylor Swift album on vinyl.

But because we are wired for growth, even comfort feels uncomfortable after a while. You'll get these emotional bedsores and start to feel restless. When we don't have a clear direction for our lives, we can feel stuck and uncertain about which direction to take. And then, even when we have clarity about the direction, we can be uncertain about the first steps as we haven't been on that journey before, and now everything feels uncertain and uncomfortable. Most of us will retreat back into the zone of comfort, roll right onto that beanbag chair, and put our headphones on to drown out the world. The brave few of us will take imperfect action and learn from the things that go well as well as the things that do not.

Some of the reasons people procrastinate include the following:

- You're trying to avoid negative emotions, like anxiety and fear.
- You're overwhelmed.
- You have a neurodiverse condition, such as ADHD.
- You struggle with impulse control.
- You are surrounded by many general distractions.
- The new season of *Love Is Blind* has been released on Netflix.
- You're feeling uncertain about what life will look and feel like when you've finished procrastinating.
- You view the task as aversive.
- You are generally rebellious.
- And, frankly, so many more reasons!

Look at all the reasons you have to *not* do something! When you consider all these reasons, you can see how miraculous it is that we do anything at all!

If you are a true procrastinator, anything I say in the following paragraphs will only serve as a reminder of what you already know because you *know* what you need to do. It's the doing it part that trips you up.

But if we want to get back into alignment and overcome any all-or-nothing/black-and-white thinking, we need to look at all the ways we can celebrate little victories in order to increase our momentum.

The hardest thing to do when you aren't doing anything is to do something. Inertia is the killer here. You've certainly procrastinated doing something before that you then chastised yourself for taking so long to do after finally doing it because it didn't take nearly as long as you thought it would.

Taking small, imperfect steps will be your starting point. If you have an underlying concern, such as ADHD, you will need to get impeccable and innovative care for this first. If you are neurotypical, consider chunking tasks together. If you have a few financial things to do that involve going to the bank, make a list and handle them at once, treating yourself to your fav coffee (if it's in the budget) on your way home. Make it fun. Celebrate your consistency.

When JC completed the *Get the Hell Out of Debt* program during the pandemic, the very next thing she wanted to tackle was her health. She put a sticker on the calendar for every day she was consistent with her health goals. About halfway through the year, she started waking up and putting a sticker on the calendar every morning because she *knew* she could trust herself to take action. She rewarded herself with a trip where she celebrated her amazing, active, beautiful body and all the miracles it could accomplish, with long hikes, walking up flights of stairs with suitcases, and turning heads because she looked like fire.

Make sure you are managing your energy and treating your body well. It's difficult to accomplish much financially if you are staying up late, crashing into a pile of Cheetos dust, hitting snooze, and then jolting yourself awake with coffee, cream, and sugar. In the short term you can power through, but, in the long term, you are headed for an expensive health crash.

All emotions are important. Life is about feeling and experiencing them all. Avoiding the emotion (which already lives inside you, remember?) means cutting off parts of yourself. Feelings are valuable bits of information meant to guide and direct us, so make sure you are moving through the feeling and not pretending it's not there when it tries to visit.

HEALING THE MONEY GUILT BLOCK: *"I feel guilty when I have money and other people are struggling. It feels greedy or unfair if I have money while other people are hurting financially."*

This block might show up for you as the following:

- I feel guilty when I have money and other people are struggling.
- It feels greedy or unfair if I have money while other people are hurting financially.
- I didn't earn money the way I had anticipated, so I feel bad having it.
- I often worry about things that aren't in my control.
- I often find that I'm trying to "pour from an empty cup," or giving what I don't have.
- I often spend time thinking about what life would be like if my circumstances were different.
- I make decisions today based on things that happened in my childhood, sometimes unconsciously.
- I am comfortable feeling negative about money.
- I will give money to other people, charities, or causes before I spend on myself.
- I can feel upset that other people don't care as much about the world as I do.
- I am uncomfortable when people I know talk about their possessions.
- I have a hard time enjoying life and luxuries.

- Sometimes I mentally punish myself to ward off feelings of guilt.
- I feel very sensitive to financial injustice.
- Sometimes I feel all consumed by guilt, and it cuts me off from experiencing a full range of emotions.
- Guilt has kept me from being truly successful.
- I tend to think in terms of "right" and "wrong" when it comes to finances.
- I have acted against either my own personal beliefs about money or what society has deemed acceptable financial behavior.
- I have used my spending to demonstrate my moral beliefs.
- Money has divided family members or people close to me.
- I have felt bad about some of the thoughts I've had about people and their money.

This block will prevent you from doing as well as you could do financially because you are trying to avoid taking away from someone else.

We are funny creatures. We feel guilt and shame when we don't have enough. We feel guilt and shame when we have too much. What if we decide to give these feelings a new meaning and instead make them signify that you are a deeply caring person who doesn't like seeing others struggle?

To heal this block, we must recognize that to properly help someone else, you need to be in a position of abundance from which you can give. It's admirable that you can give a couple of dollars at the grocery store, or to a friend's GoFundMe, or even to tithe your 10 percent. But what if you could give scobs and scobs of money away that could make massive impacts on society and humanity? Here's what is true: there are lots of people who are extremely wealthy. Don't you owe it to humanity to be one of them if you can be trusted to care about others?

You'll need to connect to a cause that matters to you and set financial goals with those causes in mind. So, if you know you can earn $100,000 per year and hit all your financial targets, and if you subsequently create $140,000 in after-tax income, doesn't that allow you to do $40,000 worth of good in the world that wouldn't happen otherwise? You not earning money doesn't make other people better off.

At the same time, we have to look at the truth that you are not responsible for all the suffering in the world. Certainly, if you are reading this book, then it is likely you have experienced privilege. You are able to afford a book (or the Audible version) or you have access to a library in your area. And with that opportunity comes extra responsibility, not extra opportunities for avoidance. Feeling guilty is rather self-indulgent. It makes something that is happening to someone else all about you. Instead, it's entirely possible that you can properly care for others with empathy, not guilt.

I had this incredible opportunity as an Oprah Insider to interact with Oprah Winfrey and one of her guests, Jeff Weiner, who was presenting the idea of compassion plus empathy.

I learned empathy is feeling what someone else feels. Compassion is empathy plus action. When you align your financial goals with a cause that can actually help others, you eliminate the selfishness of guilt and make a radical shift into an abundant state of life.

It is true for both relationships and finances: everything comes down to giving and receiving.

When we have money blocks in our lives, it affects our ability to receive. When we have been hurt, it can impact our ability to give. Giving is a posture of vulnerability. Giving is asking, "Please receive me and accept me. Please don't reject me."

Receiving is claiming your worth. Receiving is saying, "Thank you for loving me, and I receive your thoughtfulness."

We've somehow turned giving into a sign that you are a generous person. You are selfless and thoughtful and "better than." You pour out onto others. We assume generosity kills our self-centeredness.

Our culture has equated receiving with greed. When you receive you are perceived as a taker, a label that presumes you are "less than."

We've got all kinds of ancient sayings to back up this thinking. "'Tis better to give than to receive." This is taken out of context, and it presupposes that you have to make a choice between the two. But in order for you to give, there has to be a receiver.

In some relationships, it is going to feel as though one person is a giver, and one person is a receiver. Be mindful not to label each other as such. Giving and receiving is a cycle, and we want to ensure that our relationship is itself a whole cycle, that each partner is regularly doing both. Rather than seeing yourself as either a giver or a receiver, try seeing yourself as neutral and the act of giving as flowing through you just as the act of receiving flows through you. You and your partner are not the acts themselves, but rather participants who allow the energy of abundance to flow through you all the time. Think of it as a posture or way of being rather than an adjective.

If we are going to have money conversations with our partner, we need to come at them with extreme vulnerability. The mistake many couples make is coming at money conversations armed with numbers and facts, where they are trying to figure out who is right when it comes to the great math equations in their lives.

But love is energy. Money is energy. And when we come at the conversation with the energy of needing to be right, we come at the conversation from a place of ego.

If you've ever had a knock-'em-down, emotional-punch-fest argument with your partner about money, it's because your egos showed up to the fight, and egos are fragile. When we show up with our hearts, we show up with the strongest and kindest parts of ourselves. Our hearts have the ability to hold everything: pain, joy, fear, sadness, frustration, love…all of it. The heart-space allows room for our relationship to grow. The ego only has space to hold what it wants to see.

OK. I feel that you are ready, friend. Let's have a look at your partner's blocks. Let's do this with love and compassion.

Chapter Seven

YOUR PARTNER'S MONEY BLOCKS

My single readers, you are welcome to jump right through to the next sections if you want. But given that you are likely in relationships with friends, family members, or other people that may have money blocks, not only will reading through these pages give you a depth of awareness that most coupled-up people wish they had before entering into their commitments, but it will help you have greater compassion and awareness for how people are showing up financially in the world. It will also give you new awareness if you are dating and, perhaps, allow you to have healthy money conversations while you are meeting prospective partners, if that's of interest to you!

SHOWING UP FOR YOUR PARTNER IN LOVE

Before we enter into any sort of serious conversation with our partner, we have to make sure it's really safe. Many of us grew up in homes where difficult discussions were not had. Or, we've been in relationships where hard conversations were not handled well, or not allowed. If somebody were invited to share something real and personal and vulnerable, what was revealed was sometimes used as a weapon later on. We must promise ourselves to never do this.

If your partner trusts you with their deepest fears and their biggest emotional challenges, you have formed a sacred bond. Nothing is for discussion with the girls at coffee the next day. Nothing is for screenshotting and texting with your friends. Nothing is for conversation on the phone with your mother.

Emotional safety is an absolute requirement for the financial health of your relationship.

And it absolutely requires that you go first.

Relationships have become transactional. This means that often we don't want to do something unless somebody has done something for us first. This type of score-keeping sounds as though it is about giving and receiving, but it is not. It is absolutely about giving in order to get.

This is a very dangerous emotional response in a relationship because it makes love very conditional. It will never be fully acceptable for you to be wholly and completely you, and your partner will never be accepted wholly and completely for who they are—because you are expecting a certain level of performance out of them.

When we are called to love, we are called to love unconditionally. This concept is easier to understand theoretically than in practice, especially if you've not experienced unconditional love yourself.

This is sometimes referred to as loving without measure. There's no scoreboard. Your partner is not responsible for your happiness, and you are not responsible for theirs. You both show up to the relationship happy because you've taken proper care of yourself, and your enjoyment of each other increases your joy. Furthermore, if your partner has a bad day, you are comfortable with all their emotions.

Now, just a little note for our friends reading this that are in unhealthy or abusive relationships: unconditional love means that you also have it for yourself. Some partners will expect that you love them unconditionally, and they think it means they can treat you badly. There are only two conditions, but they always exist: both partners must be safe, and both partners must feel safe.

Before you talk to your partner about finances, run through these five checkpoints with yourself to ensure that you are in the right framework to be talking about money. This, frankly, will help you in many areas of your relationship, if you want to substitute *money* for *parenting* or *health* or *nookie*:

- ✓ Am I able to be patient with my partner, even if they are handling money differently than me? Am I able to cultivate patience and grace when they slip up from their own financial goals, or do I expect perfection every time?
- ✓ Am I able to be a strong supporter of my partner when things are difficult? When they lose a job, when money is tight, when they share their big dreams and ideas with me, am I able to put my own needs aside and listen to and encourage them, or do I let my fears about hard times influence my level of support?
- ✓ Am I able to be honest with my partner in a loving and kind way, or do I alter the truth in order to get a certain outcome? Am I open to hearing feedback when my partner is honest and kind with me, or do I let my ego shut out the lesson I could be learning?
- ✓ Am I able to verbally express how much I love, cherish, admire, and respect my partner without expectations? Am I able to speak openly about my love for them, or do I feel the need to hold back? Do I wait for the words to be reciprocated? Does my partner know daily how important they are to me?
- ✓ While I am not entirely responsible for my partner's happiness, does my presence make their life better? Am I showing up to the relationship having taken care of myself so that I can be fully present? Do I have unfair expectations that my partner is responsible for my happiness?

I once saw this hilarious video on TikTok @Girawrd had taken from a Ring doorbell camera. Standing at the door was a pregnant woman, Jules Girawrd, carrying a tray of sodas, and her husband was standing behind her. Suddenly a ladybug flew over and landed on her arm, and she freaked out, yelled an expletive. "#%$& DAVID! *COME ON!*" and David was just standing there. He had nothing to do with the ladybug.

The caption of the video? "Do better, David." I laughed for a long time.

Sometimes what we think is our partner's fault has absolutely nothing to do with them. We are often unconsciously looking for someone to blame. The couple in the TikTok video are obviously in love and happily married, but they reminded me that in many partnerships we can be walking around slightly disconnected from our partners. You might have had a bad day at work. You might be frustrated that your partner said she'd pick up groceries on her way home, but she forgot. You might not have had a good and proper orgasm in a long time. You might be worried about an ailing friend or relative. And then a ladybug lands on your arm in the dark, and you freak the eff out. It wasn't about the ladybug. The ladybug simply reminded your nervous system that you are a little on edge, and there is some work to do.

We have to start paying better attention to how we show up in a relationship and dropping the expectations of the people we are called to love the most. In the meantime, David, get your sh*t together.

In all seriousness, we need to remember that in a relationship we are a combination of elements. I need to bring my whole self to the partnership, and my husband also needs to bring his whole self.

If my husband and I were chemicals, on our own, we'd be fairly benign. Together we have a relatively easy, fluid, and happy relationship. If we were actual physical elements, I might be hydrogen and he would be oxygen, and together we'd combine to create water.

Previously, I dated a fellow who was more like uranium. When we combined, it was as though hydrogen bombs would detonate randomly. It wasn't that he is a bad element or that I am a bad element. It was the combination of the two of us that was deadly and destructive. No matter how much we worked at it or how hard we tried, we were lethal. The relationship was stressful, and I felt that I was trying to quietly tiptoe through life so as to not set off a bomb.

Hopefully, Mr. Uranium has found a lovely heavy metal to bond with.

I'm not ever going to tell you to leave your partner or that the two of you are not compatible. That's your work to do. What I am saying is that sometimes, in a relationship, the combination of two people is unworkable no matter what.

This idea will show up in so many other areas of your life aside from finances.

If, by and large, you have a healthy relationship, then this book will help you to figure out the framework you need to make the relationship even better or stronger. This book will not save a relationship that is on the brink. And no amount of work or personal growth or prayer will help you if your relationship is fundamentally unsafe, or if there is abuse. Get to safety first, and pray along the way.

In *Get the Hell Out of Debt*, I talk more specifically about financial abuse, but in the meantime, if you are being controlled with money, or if your money situation is volatile, financially unsafe, or erratic for emotional reasons, this is an abusive relationship, and you will need radical and specific care to remove yourself from the situation. That is a domestic issue that cannot be fixed with conversation or grace.

Let's proceed, assuming you are safe. This section will be about coming to a better understanding of your partner and what they might be experiencing. Remember that you are not going to diagnose your partner's block or give them the tools to fix themselves. Your job is simply to love them as they are while gaining the awareness as to how they are affected by their block.

YOUR PARTNER'S LACK BLOCK

If your partner primarily has a lack block, the solution is not to simply tell them that they have enough, that they are enough, that everything will be OK. You are going to have to listen—really listen—to their deep fears. What they are telling you is that they worry there are limited opportunities, resources, relationships, love, and wealth. They might not *want* to believe this, but, unconsciously, their brain will default to find the lack. This is actually a very profound survival strategy because it allows them to think about and prepare for all the threats and all the worst-case scenarios in life. If your partner were a zebra and they found themselves in a lion's den, the lack thinking would be a very useful, proactive problem-solving tool; however, because we have evolved, this lack mentality isn't as helpful in daily suburban life as it is in the savanna.

When you have a partner that experiences a lack block, the best thing you can do is to keep your own focus on abundance without being annoying about it and pointing it out at every turn. You need to do this for you because being around lack or lack thinking consistently can shift your focus easily. After all, there's the part of your brain that wants to keep you safe too.

YOUR PARTNER'S SPEND BLOCK

If your partner has a spend block, your tendency might be to try to help them with budgeting. I went to college with a woman named Willa who used to give her husband Mack an allowance. *Shudder.* She felt that her way of handling money was the right way because she seemed to be able to save her money and, to her, he was wasting money recklessly on frivolous things, like buying coffee while out with his coworkers. She would send him to work with coffee from home in a thermos.

I asked her if it was possible that his spending on the coffee might be not about the coffee and more about the community and conversation with the coworkers. I asked if it was possible for Willa to work the budget another way to give him the ability to have coffee with his work pals and more freedom in his spending. She was convinced that the reason they had met so many financial milestones was because of her genius budgeting skills, and she believed that left to his own devices, they would be in financial ruin because of his reckless caffeination. My ghasts had never been so flabbered.

Sometimes the spending isn't about the spending. Sometimes it's about needing to feel in control. Sometimes people spend recklessly because they don't trust themselves with money, and so the minute it hits the bank account they unconsciously feel the need to get rid of it. They'll pay bills, buy things, and give money to family and friends, and they feel uncomfortable if there is a lot of money in the account. My grandma (and yours too, probably) used to say that "money is burning a hole in your pocket" when this happens. But it's not the money that is causing the destruction. It's an inner unhealed money block.

YOUR PARTNER'S WORTHINESS BLOCK

If your partner has a worthiness block, you must tread carefully. Truly, every human being at their core has a worthiness issue because the two most common fears are: "Will I be loved?" and "Am I worthy?" (I know—you thought they were public speaking and spiders.) But, on a deeper level, we all need to know we belong.

Remember that while we can heal our blocks, they never truly go away. When worthiness is your own block, it will be your life's work to challenge this block with new thoughts, new patterns, and new beliefs that won't eradicate the worthiness block but will diminish it.

The key in a relationship with someone who has this as their primary block will be to remember that you are not responsible for making your partner feel worthy. Your partner simply *is* worthy. If you make it your job to help them feel worthy, you will end up in Codependency Town. Codependency shows up as people pleasing, caretaking, dependency, lack of self-image, or a need to be in a relationship to reinforce your identity and/ or avoid the fear of being alone.

When you have a partner that struggles with worthiness, your focus and energy will be wasted if you spend your time trying to prove to them all the ways they are worthy. It's an exhaustive practice. Instead, love them well, and make sure you know and treat them as the worthiest person in the world, even during the times they can't receive it. Sincerely point out your partner's amazingness when it is legitimately called for. Work on cultivating a deeply intimate relationship (more on this later!) and take good and proper care of yourself.

YOUR PARTNER'S INTELLIGENCE/SKILL BLOCK

If your partner struggles with feeling as though they're never going to be smart enough, or that money is meant entirely for rich or educated people, the key will be helping to focus on what you *can* do. You are going to have to celebrate money wins in this relationship. Every time you even make the smallest amount of progress, make sure you stop to high-five or celebrate and show that there is growth and learning. It can still be helpful to talk to people about their failures, but we want to see these as opportunities to learn. Being open to learning changes the way you grow. If you only have expectations of perfection, then there is only ever a passing or failing grade to life. Given that there isn't actually a way to achieve perfection, you will always fail. Isn't that disheartening? When we learn to love the trying, the attempting, and the experimenting (and when we learn to find the joy in the striving), we actually move closer to wealth.

This learning doesn't even need to necessarily be financial. You can read biographies or study people you admire. There is no biography that exists that doesn't have a story of a failed attempt at something before the success came. If you truly get in the practice of accepting that failure is inevitable and that you're not going to get it right the first time, you can accelerate your success because you have eliminated the obstacle of feeling foolish.

People who have an intelligence or skill block are often less concerned with learning than they are with getting something right the first time. Sometimes this happens because in school we get labeled as "not bright" early on, and this sticks with us throughout our academic career even though we might be extremely brilliant but simply learn in a different way than is traditionally taught.

It's also going to be really important to choose financial products in which to invest that you are absolutely interested in. If you choose something you don't "get," then it's going to feel complicated or hard to understand, and you're always going to feel stupid.

You can demonstrate for your partner, even by taking up something like the unicycle or the accordion, or something that has low stakes that will require a lot of practice in order to master. You can fail many times in front of your partner and then eventually become an accordion-playing, unicycle-riding freak in your neighborhood cul-de-sac.

As an example, my friend Jonathan secretly studied Welsh for no reason other than to surprise his wife. After two years of gibberish and nonsense, he started to speak fluently. It is one of the most ridiculous and yet romantic stories. She speaks fluently with her family, and one day after years of flubbering up when he practiced alone, he started to converse with her. It took her a moment to realize what was happening, but the sheer surprise was worth it. Failure can be a beautiful act of love.

YOUR PARTNER'S HARD WORK BLOCK

If your partner has a hard work block—meaning that they always think they have to work really hard in order to make anything happen—nagging them to be home more often is not the answer.

This block is not simply about money. This block is likely part of your partner's identity. Being a hard worker is seen as a virtuous character trait in most cultures. In many families, you are commended for providing for your family even if you are working a job you hate or dealing with a boss or organization that is disrespectful. Take a look at the education system. It's built on rewarding hard work, and it regularly praises students who are punctual, dependable, attentive, detail-oriented, tenacious, and committed to improvement. I agree that these are fabulous characteristics—but they are also dangerous when they become the measure of a human being. There are so many outstanding ways to contribute to humanity that don't require you to know how to sit still at a desk all day.

If your partner often spends a lot of money and time away from you or the family, learning about passive income is going to be key for this relationship. Understanding how tiny little bits of money add up over time is essential in making this relationship work, as well as regularly calculating your net worth. Both are important for financial transformation as a couple.

YOUR PARTNER'S STRESS BLOCK

If you have a partner that fears money because they are trying to avoid stress—and they like to bury their head in the sand when it comes to important financial matters—this block is going to be tricky. Your person might feel like The Notorious B.I.G. in "Mo Money Mo Problems" (good luck getting that song out of your head now). The challenge with this is that as soon as you decide money brings problems, you're going to be automatically looking for problems.

The most amazing thing about a stress money block is that it is really easy to find stress if we look for it. If you are a partner to somebody who thinks this way, it can be really helpful to create a romantic money date. Make looking into your money a beautiful, calm, sacred ritual. Light some candles and put on some great background music and spend some time dreaming of the future and all your goals while taking tiny little actions toward what it is you want. You are going to have to really mark your progress in this relationship, even when it doesn't feel very big. This shift in focus will be instrumental in reducing financial stress in the relationship.

You can also be supportive by ensuring that you've taken good care of yourself. If your partner lives in a state of stress or worry, you are less likely to be affected if you are hydrated, rested, and full of nourishment. If you haven't slept and you've been surviving on lattes and you come screeching in sideways to a financial conversation, you're likely going to make your challenges more prominent.

YOUR PARTNER'S PROCRASTINATION BLOCK

When we are in love with somebody who has a procrastination block, we have to recognize that this block is not at all about productivity and is instead mostly about how your partner feels about themselves.

One of the main enablers of procrastination is distraction, and we all have a list of things we know distract us. You may have to put your distractions away for a little while. My partner is one of the best writers I know, and he's written some phenomenal fiction books in his spare time—but to accomplish this he has had to fight distraction.

He gets up in the morning without touching his phone or any devices that would take him off course until he's written a minimum of five hundred words. Often, he can do more than that, but five hundred is the minimum because it's an easy amount to write and allows him to battle procrastination and win.

Sometimes if we wait until the *right* moment to do big things, there is never a big enough moment.

When it comes to your partner's money procrastination, you mostly need to get out of the way. Nagging a partner to do something is not as effective as we'd imagine it would be. Honestly, how have we not figured that out?

If your partner expresses that they need to call the bank, but they are avoiding it because they know they are going to be on hold for two hours, you could suggest that the two of you go for a walk while you are on hold to make use of the time together. You aren't trying to fix the problem *for* your partner, but instead you are simply showing that you are *there* for them. When we procrastinate, we also tend to judge ourselves, so simply being there for your partner when they are struggling can often act as a reminder that you are on the same team. When we nag the procrastinator we love, we end up on opposing sides.

YOUR PARTNER'S MONEY GUILT BLOCK

When you are married to somebody who has a money guilt block, you might be in a relationship with one of the kindest, most generous human beings because they care deeply and feel deeply. They are compassionate and thoughtful. It does impact your money personally, however, and it's going to be important to get those priorities realigned. (Otherwise, it will feel as though you're constantly trying to pour from an empty cup.) In this situation you're going to have to sit down together and strategize how to divide up your money. Giving is going to be a very important part of your budget, and so it's necessary that you find ways to give without depleting your resources. Giving brings true joy, when done from a position of abundance.

This can also be a great way to work with your resourcefulness to make your home budget work so that everybody is happy, and then you can get resourceful and creative together to help the causes and people you care about. You can often participate in fundraisers or charity events that allow you to leverage your time in order to potentially give or bring in more money to those causes you care about. If the guilt is about spending in terms of other family members (for example, feeling expectations about spending or not spending enough), this will be important for you to work through.

I worked with an amazing woman named Laura who has guilt about her own abundance, having grown up in a house where wealthy people were judged. She had to do a lot of work with financial boundaries, and she shifted her belief that other people's financial priorities were more important than her own. She has far more financial harmony in her life now that she isn't trying to help everyone around her first. She takes care of her family and gives money, but interestingly her charitable donations this year were higher than they'd ever been before after she looked after her family first.

To support your partner who has a guilt money block, make sure your financial conversations are about where your priorities lie. With all the suffering in the world, it can be easy to become distracted and stretched thin. Gently reminding your partner about how you can contribute while still maintaining focus on your financial goals will be important so that you don't feel derailed. It can be helpful to focus on one cause that matters to you. That doesn't mean you don't care about other causes; it simply means your dollars are focused elsewhere right now.

Chapter Eight

WHERE YOUR MONEY BLOCKS INTERSECT

Ooooh, here we go. This is where it gets real juicy.

This is where you'll clearly be able to see why you've had the money fights, the money friction, the money frustration, or the money failures.

To read this next section:

Find your block, and then find your partner's block, if they've told you what theirs is.

Figure out where your primary blocks intersect.

You can repeat this process for multiple blocks or read straight through to satisfy your own curiosity.

This will cover some of the most common themes of the relationship combinations; as always, you are two unique people who bring your unique personalities to create a unique relationship, and you might find that your financial blocks show up in unique ways.

If *you* have a Lack Block and *your partner* has a Lack Block

It's highly likely you will feel like you just scrape by. You will be more focused on expenses than on growth and expansion of income. Money stress is high in this relationship. You are likely living paycheck to paycheck. You may also experience something called "chronic dissatisfaction," which might show up as the feeling of "wanting more" (without being clear on what "more" actually is). You might also struggle to accept any emotion that isn't happiness, and when you feel emotions that aren't pleasant, you might choose to assume those emotions mean you are doing something wrong. You might be harsh on yourself or with the other because of high expectations that chronically go unmet. You might feel anxious when you or your partner isn't productive. You might live in a state where you believe things will be better/easier/happier once you hit your goals, but you aren't sure when that will ever happen because you can't seem to hit them. And you might feel a sense of constant frustration or agitation when it comes to finances. You can see how this would create a sense of unease in a relationship!

Sometimes in this partnership, if one partner starts to make strides in an area of their life, the other partner will unconsciously sabotage the progress. There also might be lots of talk in the relationship about what you don't have and a greater focus on the struggles rather than the successes. Gratitude won't come easily, or it will likely be short lived. When you look at other couples who appear wealthy or successful, you cannot fathom how they did it, and they might appear "lucky" to you. You may also find that you shoot down ideas or help from others and that you seem unconsciously committed to being stuck.

If *you* have a Lack Block and *your partner* has a Spend Block

Your relationship requires massive communication, immediately. You are likely highly stressed and feel that you need to have one hand on the emergency brake at all times while your partner drives the finances out of control. You might wonder, "Are we ever going to get out of this mess?" or, "Will we ever retire?" You might choose to avoid money conversations entirely because they lead to fights.

There will likely be high blame placed on the partner who has the spend block, though both partners contribute to the difficulty. You may need to lead conversations because the spender may have guilty feelings associated with their behaviors, especially if they feel unable to stop them. You may not be a controlling person in other areas of your life, but sometimes you may feel the need to control your partner's spending for fear you will run out of funds. This likely feels very uncomfortable for you!

You might feel embarrassed of your partner at times. You might also feel as though you are apologizing for their decisions or behaviors. You might notice that your partner justifies their spending to you, or that there seems to be a financial power differential in your relationship. You both might find it is very difficult to keep promises to yourselves, yet you might both be great at keeping promises to others.

If *you* have a Lack Block and *your partner* has a Worthiness Block

It's likely that your two major blocks are feeding off each other. Your partner gets to reinforce that they are "right" and not worthy when they are reminded of the lack, and their struggle to feel worthy will reinforce that there just is not enough.

This is a dangerous combo when it comes to self-esteem.

Because the two of you are also highly likely to put other people first, the relationship can start off feeling very caring as you'll put each other first; however, over time, we can see how this could lead to codependency, where one partner's emotions become the other partner's responsibility. This is a very unhealthy emotional dynamic and will not be a long-term strategy for financial success. Eventually, you may put other people's money needs ahead of what you need financially as a couple, and this kind of entanglement becomes very costly in the long run.

This is the ultimate combo that creates debt. You likely have carried a credit card balance or debt balance throughout your life. You might have previously tried consolidation loans or other quick fixes in moments of desperation. You may also often avoid salespeople because you feel you are easily "sold" or that you can't say no.

If *you* have a Lack Block and *your partner* has a Skill/Intelligence Block

If you are worried about never having enough and your partner is worried about not *being* good or smart enough, the not-enough-ness will be the prevailing theme in the relationship. In order to find belonging, it's likely that your partner's friend circle will be full of people who are also perceived as lacking in skills or education. Your partner may feel inadequate hanging around intelligent people. If there is ego at play, your partner may even claim disdain or dislike for people who are financially free. Growth and progress will be greatly hindered in this relationship, and this pattern not only will show up via poor financial results but it may also be affecting other areas of your relationship as well.

You might notice you frequently enable each other. This means you might be trying to protect your loved ones from experiencing the full consequences of their behavior because of your own personal fears. You may also be indirectly supporting your partner's harmful behavior. Remember that harmful behavior might not simply refer to activities that are harmful; sometimes we harm the people we love by limiting them or by not allowing them to grow to their full potential.

If *you* have a Lack Block and *your partner* has a Hard Work Block

When you are living in a lack mentality and your partner believes that in order to be successful, you have to work really hard, the relationship could be strained because your partner is never home and is always working instead. This may feel like a lack of love. Workaholism could develop.

There will be emotional strain on the relationship because there will never be enough quality or intimate time spent together when one person is always thinking about work or the lack of money. The other theme that tends to crop up in this combination is that you may feel blamed for some of the financial struggle because, as the other partner is working hard, it might be wrongly assumed that it can't possibly be their fault.

Your partner might be burned out and possibly resentful, even though you aren't making them work hard or long. You might even increase your nonessential spending out of boredom or loneliness. You might have a lot of imaginary dangling carrots, such as the belief that "when we get to this goal…then everything will be easier," even though that goal never comes.

If *you* have a Lack Block and *your partner* has a Stress Block

If you are struggling with lack and your partner believes that more money is going to cause more problems and that money equals stress, then you will both live in a constant state of stress.

You might find that you want to avoid dealing with finances to avoid the stress, so you might have unopened bills. You might also be pretending things are better than they are because you want so badly for that to be true.

The relationship will always be strained because the lack itself causes stress, but the strain increases when one partner avoids stress by avoiding money; this will obviously repel money and reinforce the lack belief system. This is a doozy! Because you are a caring person who loves your partner and wants what is best for them (and hates to see them stressed), you might be overcompensating in trying to take the pressures away, but all that happens is a little stress transference, where you start to take on all the work and, subsequently, all the stress.

This relationship may be riding the emotional roller coaster at Resentmentland, so make sure you have saltines on hand when you do the budget so that you don't get nauseous!

If *you* have a Lack Block and *your partner* has a Procrastination Block

If you are struggling with lack and your partner's main block is procrastination, then even if you are aligned on the need to talk about and work on money, it's going to be so much harder because procrastination is very demotivating.

The longer it takes you to do something, the longer you may lose belief in yourself. If your partner has been a procrastinator for a long time and is also plagued with self-doubt, sometimes the solution is simply to break tasks up into smaller pieces and build confidence through consistent competence.

However, having a lack mentality (you don't believe there will ever be enough) enables the procrastination, putting you and your partner in an endless loop—like that "Baby Shark" song. Your partner requires extra compassion because their block may be part of a bigger issue, such as attention deficit or depression, as procrastination is often a by-product of something more serious.

You might be tempted to nag, prod, or incentivize your partner to get them to take action, but you might also already know that doesn't work. Be careful not to blame your partner's procrastination for the position you are in because it can be tempting to say, "If only they did _____, then our problems would go away," but we know that Blame Town only has a population of one.

If *you* have a Lack Block and *your partner* has a Guilt Block

If you feel as though there's never enough, and if your partner is always worried about *other* people not having enough—and when you do get money, your partner feels (consciously or unconsciously) the need to get rid of the money or give it away in order to alleviate the guilt or feeling—it's going to be really difficult to ever experience abundance in this relationship. Both people need to work on their belief systems. While you feel financial uncertainty, your partner may be creating financial uncertainty in the name of doing the right thing.

The trouble is that sometimes what is the "right thing" publicly is the "wrong thing" personally because we need to be in a proper state of abundance to truly care for others. One of your challenges will be to not take on your partner's financial worries as your own, because your partner is already worrying about a heck of a lot of things.

In this scenario, both spouses are going to have to commit to working on the inside of the relationship first before trying to help anyone on the outside of it. Setting small goals here that are easy to manage and building financial trust in each other will both help and intrinsically motivate you to do more so that you can give more.

If *you* have a Spend Block and *your partner* has a Lack Block

You may feel controlled in this relationship when it comes to spending. Even if your partner doesn't explicitly say that you spend too much (because they feel as though there is never enough money), you may feel that you do in comparison. You may want to experience a bit more freedom when it comes to money, but your partner might be so worried that they are always trying to rein in your spending.

Spenders, you get blamed for much of the stress in the relationship, but it's not entirely your fault, so know that you are an easy scapegoat, but you are not the cause.

You're going to primarily work on keeping that net worth spreadsheet updated. It can be helpful in this scenario to learn about investing together because often when we can flip a spender from an interest in buying consumer goods to an interest in buying investments, the entire team will benefit. Watching your net worth increase week after week will be motivating and will compound all the inner work you do, as well as the dollars.

If *you* have a Spend Block and *your partner* has a Spend Block

The main issues here will involve justification of spending. If you feel as though your partner doesn't spend wisely—and they believe *you* don't spend wisely—it could mean your finances have turned into a game with a scoreboard. But when we keep score in a relationship, there is never a winner. Wealth may be difficult to accumulate in this relationship because there will often be more urgent things to spend money on. While wealth building is important, it doesn't always feel urgent. When everyone is spendy, it's going to require some self-discipline to focus on your own spending instead of comparing it to the wallet next to yours. This is a relationship that is going to require you to stay in your own lane because your partner cannot drive you crazy unless you hand them the keys.

This relationship is a great opportunity to do the "Yours, Mine, and Ours" method of budgeting. The household expenses can be shared from one account, but each partner can manage their own money in a separate account so that there is no scorekeeping. This relationship is definitely one that will benefit from a financial planner to help you see the big picture and keep you on track, and you absolutely must implement the "pay yourself first" philosophy as a safeguard. This means that the minute your paycheck hits your account, you siphon some off to your retirement accounts so that you don't accidentally spend it while you are building those money muscles.

If *you* have a Spend Block and *your partner* has a Worthiness Block

If you struggle to keep money in your realm and your partner feels a general lack of worthiness, sometimes you both start to equate your net worth with your actual worth. These are very different things and should not be used to determine value. Sometimes the spender (depending on their love language) can end up spending in order to make the other person feel worthy, but that is a fruitless effort. Sometimes the person who feels unworthy ends up blowing funds because they may unconsciously think, "What difference does it make? My partner overspends anyway." We hit bumpy relationship territory when you—our fearless spender—keep trying to solve the internal problems of the relationship with external resources that cost money.

Your primary work will involve connection. Because of the frenetic energy that buzzes between the two of you, stillness is the key. Watch your screen time, you two. Spending time in nature, reading, slowing down, and journaling will be key to your financial transformation.

If *you* have a Spend Block and *your partner* has an Intelligence/Skill Block

If you are a spender and your partner doesn't feel smart enough, sometimes you end up overcompensating for your partner's lack of belief in themselves.

For example, if you are not able to keep money, and your partner does not feel as though they can get ahead because they're too dumb or don't have the right skills, you might end up with a lot of student loan debt while your partner keeps taking course after course trying to get ahead, yet not actually putting things into practice. This occurs because they never feel as though they actually know enough to make anything positive or productive happen; they don't understand that tiny actions are building blocks that will support all the learning they're doing in personal development. This combination sometimes turns a couple into personal development or academic junkies, where it can be easy to justify the expense because it's an "investment in yourself," even though that investment isn't generating any tangible return.

If *you* have a Spend Block and *your partner* has a Hard Work Block

This one is tricky because, in this relationship, many fingers can be pointed at each other. While one person is spending, the other is trying to out-earn the spending, and this creates a lot of resentment and worries. While it isn't actually true that the spender is causing the partner to work more hours, it can easily seem this way if we're looking at it logistically instead of spiritually. From a spiritual perspective, we know that the person who wants to work hard would do that anyway because of their own beliefs about money; however, it's easy to blame the spender in this circumstance, so you might feel as though you are always at fault. It's important to note that your hard-working partner is contributing equally to the challenge in the relationship because one person is never entirely to blame in a two-person pattern. Regardless, you need to focus on healing your spend block so that you can feel above reproach and know in your heart that everyone in the relationship is entitled to their own experience of the relationship.

If *you* have a Spend Block and *your partner* has a Stress Block

In this situation, if you have a partner that always seems stressed about money or seems to want to repel money, and if you are constantly getting rid of money, the relationship will likely be tense. Sometimes, you won't realize how stressed you actually are until you're attempting to relax. For you, it might feel freeing, in the moment, to spend. For your partner, it might feel terrifying. This makes things like vacations or date nights particularly difficult because of how much you are *wanting* to spend versus how much your partner is *willing* to spend. You will have to be really careful not to equate this with how much love your partner has for you. In this relationship, it usually turns out that neither partner wants to deal with the finances, so it will be critical to do this work together. If both of you don't step up, your money struggles may fester into a giant, stinky emotional wound.

If *you* have a Spend Block and *your partner* has a Procrastination Block

If you are feeling overwhelmed with overdue bills and as though you're always waiting for the next paycheck to come in, but the minute it does come in it's gone, these money blocks need to be healed before you will ever find financial harmony. You may feel completely frustrated with your partner or may even see them as lazy, but that response is going to create an inappropriate power dynamic in your relationship that is both unfair and unworkable. Much as how the spend block and the hard work block intertwine, you might end up with a partner who feels that it is their responsibility to bail you out of overspending, but in this case your partner may also be frozen in inaction because they feel overwhelmed.

No matter the cause of the spending, it is going to be your responsibility to take ownership of this behavior and work through it with consistency and tenacity. Otherwise, your partner may feel as though they are drowning financially.

If *you* have a Spend Block and *your partner* has a Guilt Block

In this case, you both might be spenders—whether it is on the family or each other—and your partner may be spending on other people due to their guilt block. When your partner feels guilty about having money or privilege, they are put in a disempowering financial position. It is possible to recognize your privilege and still be able to receive money and do amazing things with it that help people affected by disparities in the system that create true lack for them (not a perceived lack driven by a lack block). One of the best ways to recognize if this is affecting your relationship is to take note if you ever feel as though your partner should be spending more money on you than on other people, and if you feel that they have terrible money boundaries. You actually do, too (*gasp!*); it's just always easier to see in other people, isn't it?

If *you* have a Worthiness Block and *your partner* has a Lack Block

Sometimes when we are dating, we unconsciously choose people who affirm what we already believe about ourselves, even though what we believe might be unhealthy. Every single person feels unworthy in a tiny piece of their spirit and sadly that's just the human experience. However, for some people, that little thread of unworthiness becomes a giant tapestry in which we wrap our hearts, and it guides most of our decision-making. When we really struggle with feeling that we are never enough, we can sometimes end up in partnerships where this is affirmed. So, even if you have an incredible partner who loves you and thinks you're amazing, if they have a lack block, you may unconsciously believe this is because you don't deserve it. That one hurt to read, didn't it?

If *you* have a Worthiness Block and *your partner* has a Spend Block

One of the reasons why you might feel absolutely certain about your lack of worth is by being in a relationship with somebody who is always giving it away. Ouch. I know. You aren't doing this on purpose, and neither is your partner; it's simply that sometimes we can't see the patterns that run our lives because they are so constant that they become unnoticeable. If I tell you to imagine you are sitting in your kitchen in silence, you won't "hear" anything. But next time you *are* sitting in your kitchen, listen for the sound of the refrigerator. You have to intentionally notice it, or it just fades into the background.

It's always running and is programmed to constantly use up energy. We often don't notice when we have a worthiness block because that feeling of not being enough becomes so normal that it gets comfortable. Your partner (hopefully!) doesn't want you to feel this way and may even try to show you or tell you that you are worthy, but it is not their job to do so. If they are spending to try and show you love, then they are trying to bail out the *Titanic* with an ice cream pail.

If *you* have a Worthiness Block and *your partner* has a Worthiness Block

These relationships can sometimes become volatile because, when you feel as though you are never enough and you're with someone who feels as though *they* are never enough, then feeling unworthy can become a self-ful-filling prophecy. You will look for ways to *be* unworthy. This is ultimately a lie because every human is worthy. Take note if the driving force in your life is to people-please or prove your worth, *or* if your driving force is trauma. If you've experienced abuse or neglect or consistent challenges to your self-es-teem, sometimes when unhealed those damaging patterns can be repeated in how you relate to other people. Even if you don't have obvious issues in your relationship, individual and couples' counselling (both, not either/or) will be a great gift you can give yourselves and the partnership. You may need to make it a priority in the budget.

If *you* have a Worthiness Block and *your partner* has an Intelligence/Skill Block

Because of your own feelings of inadequacy, sometimes you can end up undermining your partner. It's important to recognize that your partner also has feelings of inadequacy, especially when it comes to their intelligence. If these blocks go unrecognized in your partnership, you may end up feeling a general malaise about the relationship over time, or it may feel stagnant or depolarized. This means that the relationship could struggle to grow or that the passionate charge (the polarization) of the coupledom could dissipate. The solution is not buying sexy underwear and draping yourself across a chaise lounge like George Costanza. The antidote is a renewed commitment to doing the deep work required to improve both your personal and your financial circumstances, so that you can show up better for your partner and for your own life.

If *you* have a Worthiness Block and *your partner* has a Hard Work Block

When you have a partner who is constantly working, has a difficult job, and endlessly thinks about work or how to make money, and if you question whether you are worthy, it can feel as though your partner's efforts are fruitless. You would think that this would make *them* realize that working harder is not the answer and that they would work smarter and then spend more time with you. But what can often happen here is that they feel as though nothing they do can please you, and so they just bury themselves more in their work. Some partners get their identity from work, meaning they don't know who they are if they aren't working. This whole arrangement compounds if you have a primary love language of quality time, yet your partner participates in "acts of service" in order to demonstrate their love.

If *you* have a Worthiness Block and *your partner* has a Stress Block

When you feel less than and your partner feels that money is stressful, you will often internalize that the reason your partner is stressed and wants to avoid money or fixate on money is because of you, something you've done, or who you are. You will carry an extraordinary amount of blame in this relationship, even when it is unfounded (hint: it's mostly unfounded). When it comes to money, this partnership may experience bouts of hopelessness and frustration, and it can be very difficult to work toward financial goals when there isn't an absolutely clear vision of where the partnership is headed.

In this relationship it's going to be important for both partners to focus on gratitude, abundance, and paying attention to and celebrating the things that go well—no matter how small. You'll need to do it for each other, but you'll need to get in the practice of doing it for you, too.

If *you* have a Worthiness Block and *your partner* has a Procrastination Block

In some respects, procrastination can be the result of feeling unworthy because often procrastination shows up as a by-product of perfectionism. Black-and-white thinking. All-or-nothing. So, when you have somebody that doesn't think they are worthy of very much and somebody who only thinks they're worthy when something is perfectly executed, you have the perfect storm swirling in a land of wishing things would be better but not feeling capable of making them so. The cool kids would call this a "low vibe" relationship. Those of us who did not get the memo that skinny jeans are out (the uncool kids) would call this an opportunity to choose the possibility of failure in the name of growth. You are going to have to get used to struggling in the gray areas of life for a while, but the good news is that I hear there are fifty shades of them. You and your partner will need to find out what shade suits you best.

If *you* have a Worthiness Block and *your partner* has a Guilt Block

When you feel as though you don't have enough, aren't worthy of enough, or are simply not enough, and when your partner feels as though everything is too much, we have a great disparity in the way finances are viewed. Relationships are successful when both partners have a healthy belief about what the purpose of the relationship is and then (often unknowingly) work to keep that identity true.

If we are committed to a disempowering identity, even if our partner believes it exists in the name of the greater good, our relationship can erode quickly and radically because it cannot hold the weight of the financial strain. In this relationship, you might notice that one of the things that initially attracted you to your partner was the way they cared so deeply for others, but now the things that initially attracted you might annoy the ever-living heck out of you.

If *you* have an Intelligence/Skill Block and *your partner* has a Lack Block

When we think we're not smart enough to know something, we cut ourselves off from the possibility of learning. Of course, we can't possibly know everything there is to know. For some reason when we grow up, we assume that the minute we turn eighteen we're supposed to become financially literate (even though most of us have had very little exposure to money by the time we leave home). When we feel like we are not smart enough and our partner feels like there is never going to *be* enough, we create an environment where we live with very low standards. When low standards become normal, it's very difficult to find abundance and financial freedom.

If *you* have an Intelligence/Skill Block and *your partner* has a Spend Block

When you feel as though you're not smart enough and your partner receives money and then immediately spends it, whether because they feel as though they can't manage it or they have a spending problem, you can give your power away to your partner so that the money decisions and the spending is mostly in the hands of somebody who feels financially out of control. This block allows you to stay stuck so that you can "be right," which in one of those weird, twisty ways makes you feel smart. But that's just it, isn't it? It doesn't work long-term to "feel" smart. It is so much better to *be* smart.

If *you* have an Intelligence/Skill Block and *your partner* has a Worthiness Block

When you feel as though everybody else knows more than you, and when you are looking for the external solution to an internal struggle with your own intelligence, a partner with a worthiness issue can be made to feel as though they are not valued—especially if they have an opinion on what needs to be done, and you keep seeking outside advice. There are millions of smart people who are broke. It's also entirely possible to be dumb and rich. The financial healing you'll work through has nothing to do with what you actually know and everything to do with how you approach learning.

If *you* have an Intelligence/Skill Block and *your* partner has an Intelligence/Skill Block

When both partners struggle with a primary block of intelligence or lack of skill, it may often feel as though you are chasing riches. When both partners feel that what they lack is intelligence when it comes to money, you may fall pretty quickly for get-rich-quick schemes or terrible financial advice because you are putting more trust in other people than in your own critical-thinking skills. You also are cut off from your ability to hear your own gut instinct and will often try to reason or rationalize poor financial decisions rather than educate yourself. In this relationship you'll both need to be careful to avoid one-upmanship, where you try to outdo your partner in response to your own low self-esteem.

If *you* have an Intelligence/Skill Block and *your* partner has a Hard Work Block

One of the challenges associated with feeling as though you don't have the right skills or the right knowledge (and with not trusting yourself to get it) is that if you are partnered with somebody who is a very hard worker and believes hard work is the key to success, you can often undermine your partner's efforts by comparing them to other people who seem to have it all together. Comparison in a relationship can often cause its death, and we know that it certainly causes the death of joy. It is going to be critical in this relationship combination to focus on progress, no matter how small, in order to start stacking happiness.

If *you* have an Intelligence/Skill Block and *your* partner has a Stress Block

When you feel as though other people know more or are more capable than you, and when your partner finds that money in general is stressful, they may ostrich—bury their head in the sand—when it comes to finances. Because you are also not actively obtaining the right education or taking effective action, you often miss out on the compound effect of little bits of wealth building and adding up over a long period of time. The other type of thinking that can creep into this scenario is one of waiting for big rescues to happen. There may be a temptation in this relationship to consolidate debt or sell assets in order to take vacations in hopes of reducing stress; it might be tempting to look for quick fixes or big moves when, essentially, these end up being ineffective if you haven't done the inner work first.

If *you* have an Intelligence/Skill Block and *your partner* has a Procrastination Block

If you feel as though you don't know something and you are coupled with a partner who has a hard time getting started on things, you might silently view your partner as incompetent and, subsequently, feel horrible about that. In this relationship, sometimes one partner will act as a "coach" and may try to motivate the partner who has a difficult time starting or finishing things. I can't recall a time when any person ever put on their Tinder profile that they were "looking for a mate who will point out my shortcomings and teach me how to overcome them while silently seething inside." So, this relationship needs to be very mindful of any shifts in respect to power differentials.

If *you* have an Intelligence/Skill Block and *your partner* has a Guilt Block

In this particular situation, you may often feel stupid because (if you feel as though you are undeserving and your partner often feels guilty) you might create a dynamic where you reject both learning and receiving. This becomes compounded if there is other guilt in your relationship. All unfounded guilt presumes that life is fair and logical and reasonable, and it expects that there are certain predictable outcomes. A definite recipe for disappointment.

If *you* have a Hard Work Block and *your partner* has a Lack Block

This combo is tough because when you are a hard worker and feel that your financial situation will only improve if you work hard—especially when everything already feels difficult—and when you are with a partner who feels that there will never be enough, it can seem as though you are staring down the barrel of a life that will contain little joy. You might think other people who struggle financially simply need to "work harder" but that is a challenging mindset, given that you've proven already that hard work doesn't guarantee success or happiness. Your expectations of your partner may be a point of pain (for either of you!) so please tread kindly.

If *you* have a Hard Work Block and *your partner* has a Spend Block

This one can feel as though you are constantly trying to bail out a leaky boat while your partner keeps drilling holes in it. It can be particularly challenging for relationships because you might feel disrespected or that your partner doesn't value how hard you work while they can sometimes appear to be reckless. This relationship may burn out or feel exhausting quite quickly, and it is going to require a lot of compassion instead of judgment if it is to survive.

If *you* have a Hard Work Block and *your partner* has a Worthiness Block

You may feel as though you're working hard or that the solution is to work harder. Meanwhile, your partner is wallowing in "not enough-ness" and sometimes it's difficult to extend them grace when you really need to. If your solution is just to work harder—work that you give to your job and not your relationship—then it will be really challenging for you to stay motivated to remain in the relationship. The solution is not external. It's not a different partner or more work. Fixing the relationship is going to require deep accountability and honesty, and a willingness to work hard on the inside instead of just working long hours on the outside.

If *you* have a Hard Work Block and *your partner* has an Intelligence/Skill Block

Workaholism might show up in this relationship for one or both parties. The other thing that may show up at times (in addition to the physical work) is the feeling that you have to carry the emotional weight for your partner because of the doubt they have in their own abilities. Sometimes when we are stuck in a financial rut, taking some sort of action, like working hard, can feel like progress, but we need to be mindful about whether repeating this strategy day after day actually gets us where we want to be.

If *you* have a Hard Work Block and *your partner* has a Hard Work Block

This relationship might often feel like ships passing in the night. If everything feels as though it must be hard to be worth it—and if everyone feels as though there's not enough hours in the day to make ends meet or achieve the level of success you desire--it's going to be nearly impossible to emotionally connect with your partner. Sometimes people who believe they have to work hard actually *don't* need to work harder to create wealth. Often, working hard is a distraction to avoid leaning into feelings or conversations or trauma or anything that might feel difficult and can be avoided with the justification of hard work.

If *you* have a Hard Work Block and *your partner* has a Stress Block

When you feel as though the only way money should come to you or that you deserve it is if you've worked really hard for it, and if your partner feels as though everything about money is stressful, you are likely missing lots of financial opportunities as a couple because you are not open to receiving. You've got your head down working, and your partner has their arms folded across their chest stressing, and the two of you are potentially closing yourselves off to opportunities. You might be around other couples who seem to "have it all," and they work less hours and seem to have more fun. You might be romanticizing the benchmarks and creating "when I" scenarios. ("When I get the next overtime check, then I will stop working so much.") You might already know from experience that never actually changes.

If *you* have a Hard Work Block and *your partner* has a Procrastination Block

This is a really challenging combination because if one partner believes hard work is the answer to financial success, and if the other partner can only get things done if conditions are perfect or there is a deadline forcing them into action, then you have partners working on opposing sides. One partner might show up with frustration that the other isn't working as hard, and the other partner might feel completely inadequate because they aren't able to get started or aren't feeling driven. It will be crucial to watch your negative assumptions about the other person's work ethic, not just because you might be mistaken, but mostly because it lacks compassion.

If *you* have a Hard Work Block and *your partner* has a Guilt Block

If you have a hard work block and your partner feels guilty about everything money-related and wants to give it away, or if your partner has a spiritual belief system about money, often both partners can end up working much harder than they need to in order to compensate for the injustices in the world. The challenge is that no amount of hard work or guilt from one couple can solve the world's issues as much as teamwork, initiative, love, and acceptance. So, the very things you worry about in the partnership, such as time, stress, and finances, cannot be solved anyway until you heal the money blocks you each are individually experiencing.

If *you* have a Stress Block and *your partner* has a Lack Block

When you believe that having more money just means you are guaranteed to have more problems—and when your partner believes that you will never have enough—then your partner may avoid telling you about anything they do to bring in more money because they are worried about bringing you stress. And, with this money block combination, sometimes couples end up getting caught in financial infidelity because what starts off as a good intention of trying not to cause stress to a partner ends up creating secrets and, perhaps, even lies about financial circumstances in order to avoid conflict. Your primary desired outcome will be to not transfer your stress onto your partner in order to justify its existence.

If *you* have a Stress Block and *your partner* has a Spend Block

I think you can see the writing on the wall with this one. If everything financially stresses you out and your partner is overspending, then your emotional home (the place you live emotionally for most of your life) is stress a majority of the time. And then, when you are stressed all the time and you are in a relationship with somebody that has even a little bit of an emotional-spending pattern, then we know stress could possibly trigger them to spend more, in turn causing you to stress more. You can see how this pattern quickly gets out of hand.

If *you* have a Stress Block and *your partner* has a Worthiness Block

Sometimes when you stress about money, you try to avoid stress by avoiding money. When you are partnered with someone who feels unworthy when it comes to financial situations (or even financial discussions), what can sometimes occur is avoidance or neglect. In the case of somebody who already feels massively unworthy, this can contribute to a deeper wounding when it comes to their feelings of value in the relationship. You are not responsible for your partner feeling worthy, but when we are in partnership with somebody, we need to be careful to hold their heart tenderly and to not be reckless with how we treat them because of our own stresses or feelings of inadequacy. This one is a delicate dance.

If *you* have a Stress Block and *your partner* has an Intelligence/Skill Block

When finances activate your nervous system and your partner feels they do not have the ability or intelligence to figure out what action to take, the relationship can feel as though it's not getting anywhere, financially speaking. In this situation, it can even be difficult for a partner to engage in any type of learning. Often education costs money, and when one partner is very stressed and can't figure out how to get ahead, the other partner can feel as they never will. Spending on education becomes stressful, and yet not getting an education can also feel stressful, so you walk the line of indecision for a long time.

If *you* have a Stress Block and *your partner* has a Hard Work Block

When you are somebody who is stressed financially, oftentimes you worry. When you have a partner who believes that the way out of the financial stress is through hard work, the relationship becomes compounded with worry. It gets extra spicy if you worry about them when they work too much or if they aren't working enough, and then you also worry about whether you are working or contributing enough in order to make the relationship fair. It can be extremely challenging to have conversations that are deep and meaningful because so much of this relationship is focused on surface or external solutions.

If *you* have a Stress Block and *your partner* has a Stress Block

Maybe you feel stressed financially because your parents were always stressed financially, and somehow you picked up along the way that money causes tension in a relationship. In this case, you are in the perfect partnership to commiserate! If we aren't careful in this relationship, we can "one up" each other with how stressed we feel, and it can be challenging to find solutions when so much of our identity when it comes to money is found in the problem itself.

No matter where your financial stress comes from, you've learned that money activates the part of you that isn't present, that is focused on what hasn't happened yet or on all the things that could go wrong. This puts an energetic burden on both partners, who are overwhelmed already by their own stress! In this situation, you either don't take enough action toward achieving your financial goals or you are often undoing your success because you are second-guessing it.

If *you* have a Stress Block and *your partner* has a Procrastination Block

This is a great blame-y, finger-pointy relationship because you can easily claim that you are stressed because your partner procrastinates when it comes to money; however, your partner can easily claim that the reason they procrastinate is *because* you are so stressed and they don't want to make a bad or wrong decision. You also might think your stress would go away if your partner didn't procrastinate, but stress is an inside job, and your greatest self-development will come when you can manage in spite of any external circumstances.

If *you* have a Stress Block and *your partner* has a Guilt Block

In this relationship, you are usually excellent givers because the thought of having money or receiving money for you is very stressful. You likely often feel guilty because there are other people in the world who are worse off than you. The irony here is that you can help more people when you are able to receive and be good stewards of money. Even though you're giving your money away in order to relieve stress and guilt, it's not nearly as beneficial as building true wealth and giving a larger portion of a larger amount of money away.

If *you* have a Procrastination Block and *your partner* has a Lack Block

Vitale Hardin of the Hardin Group brilliantly talks about how procrastination is a form of perfectionism. When it comes to money, this is true so much of the time. Whether we want to do things right or we're overwhelmed by the number of things we have to do, procrastination allows us to have some sort of control. A partner with a lack block feels as though they are never in control, so it's interesting that you may be using procrastination to control things when there is actually nothing to control. Because there are so many things competing for your money—whether it be advertisers, other people, obligations, debts, or anything at all—you can see how quickly indecision will creep up and allow you to avoid things that need handling in order to grow your wealth.

If *you* have a Procrastination Block and *your partner* has a Spend Block

If one of the main ways procrastination manifests in your life is through control, then you might be trying to control a situation where it feels as though your partner is out of control. Now, even if your partner doesn't have a reckless spending problem and all they do is simply mishandle money that comes into your life by, for instance, immediately paying bills with it, they also might be trying to stay in control of a situation that feels reckless.

It's going to be necessary for you to come up with a prioritization plan. Compared to all the couples and combinations of blocks, you may need to automate your finances (if you both have steady incomes) to ensure that it goes where needed before you can get your hands on it.

If *you* have a Procrastination Block and *your partner* has a Worthiness Block

This relationship may feel sensitive at times because you may struggle to ask for help from your partner when you need it. Worse yet, you may not even recognize when you need help. It might feel as though the pressure to solve the financial problems in your partnership lie solely with you. You may have noticed that when you are able to complete tasks or handle things quickly and efficiently, your partner feels excited and hopeful; however, know that your struggle doesn't mean you love your partner any less and that you are trying to disappoint them. This relationship is going to require both partners to participate in and work together on handling both income/expenses and assets/liabilities. While some couples can get away with one partner handling the bulk of the finances, here you both need to be rowing the boat so that you don't go in circles.

If *you* have a Procrastination Block and *your partner* has an Intelligence/Skill Block

This is where a relationship can get caught in research hell. There's a lot of talk and thinking about doing things, but not a lot of things are actually getting done, and this can feel frustrating to both parties. Be careful not to blame your partner and be very aware of how you contribute to this cycle. If overthinking has been your pattern in the past, you will have to work on taking small action steps to increase the level of confidence and the level of accountability in your relationship.

If *you* have a Procrastination Block and *your partner* has a Hard Work Block

If you struggle to get started on things and your partner feels as though they are the one doing all the work, then this is a hard dynamic to reconcile. Even though you are partners, it might not always feel like it. Your partner may be doing a lot of work that can be seen, and it might feel to you as though you are doing a lot of emotional work, or the work that can't be seen. In this relationship, sarcasm equals death. You may have to work hard to overcome feelings of bitterness or other flavors that slowly poison a relationship. Open but kind and honest communication, coupled with empathy, is a necessary daily event if this relationship is to heal properly.

If *you* have a Procrastination Block and *your partner* has a Stress Block

In this relationship, you might easily trigger each other. If you're over-whelmed or feel as though you have the inability to get things done, this can cause your partner to feel more stressed about money. It's going to be very difficult to have calm, level-headed discussions because one of the challenges of being in a relationship with a procrastinator is that their intentions are often pure but don't always line up with their actions, and this can unfortunately breed mistrust. One of the greatest gifts you can give your partner is that of under-promising and overdelivering (and of being graceful and lighthearted when you fail). Overcoming procrastination has less to do with finishing things and more to do with improving your relationship with failure. You're going to have to lead by example with grace here.

If *you* have a Procrastination Block and *your partner* has a Procrastination Block

Relationships where both partners have procrastination blocks and heal them together become unstoppable. It is challenging to manage these relationships, however, when nobody is willing to go first. So, because you are the one whose eyeballs are hitting this page, I highly encourage you to be the one to take the first step when it comes to money. Be willing to talk about it, take action with it, and overcome the block. You're already killing this leadership thing because you are reading this book, so high five to you! Your financial future will be painful if you enable each other to procrastinate, so be the brave one. Otherwise, you will be that old couple who looks back and says, "If only we would have…."

If *you* have a Procrastination Block and *your partner* has a Guilt Block

What's really funky about this combination is that procrastination often comes with a lot of guilt (you have a lot of guilt for not earning more income or managing your finances better), and your partner also has a lot of guilt, although for not helping other people more. (And if either of you is a practicing Catholic, this is a triple-scoop sundae with guilt sauce.)

The anxiety your partner feels about the state of the world may spill into the anxiety you have about which financial decisions to make next. You're going to have to be very clear about what your inventory is (meaning what you're responsible for) and what your partner's internal inventory is, and you're going to have to do everything in your power not to take your partner's. This relationship needs extra patience and grace. Thankfully, you are two people who are naturally good at giving those things outside of the relationship. We just need to redirect it.

If *you* have a Guilt Block and *your partner* has a Lack Block

When you feel that the world is unjust or unfair, you sometimes cut off receiving blessings because you feel it's taking away from other people who deserve such blessings too. Unfortunately, this isn't how the world works, and starving yourself does not feed everyone else. Your guilt block might have been formed in your younger years, particularly if you were exposed to religion or the social sciences, and you felt a deep caring for other people. This is an important part of the human experience, but it's necessary to live from a position of strength if you are to properly impact and support people who need you. As the saying goes, you cannot pour from an empty cup, and when you have a guilt block and your partner has a lack block, you are constantly trying to do so.

If *you* have a Guilt Block and *your partner* has a Spend Block

This is another relationship combination that may experience financial infidelity because when you are trying to impart your belief system about what is fair onto your partner (who may be expressing their own financial stress by spending), it makes it difficult for them to feel as though they can safely be honest with you. They may be concerned about receiving judgment from you, or they may be worried about disappointing you. Sometimes people who have a guilt block will try to shame someone else so that they can feel justified in their guilty feelings. Be mindful to be open and loving (read ahead on the levels of intimacy) so that your partner can begin to feel safe and connected first, for safety and connection don't come after healing. Our partners must feel safe and connected *in order* to heal.

If *you* have a Guilt Block and *your partner* has a Worthiness Block

When you have a guilt block and you feel that your blessings are inappropriate, you may want to alleviate the guilt. This can mean you are often giving resources away. If you are partnered with somebody who has a worthiness challenge, this can impact them by reiterating that they are not worthy of receiving because you'll give to others first. They may feel emotionally unsafe. Financial boundaries will need to be created and reinforced to ensure that your partner feels secure financially and that you feel the freedom to give, provided it is not impacting the resources you need to experience financial calmness together.

If *you* have a Guilt Block and *your partner* has an Intelligence/Skill Block

The guilt block is often associated with negative forms of regret or stress that make you believe you are responsible for causing harm to other people. In turn, this usually means that you struggle to forgive yourself. Whether your actions are real or perceived, you'll carry this weight. The feelings you generate about yourself will limit your ability to help in the future. Guilt is very disempowering, whereas it is possible to feel a compassion for the world and a desire to help people that comes from an empowering place. In a partnership, when we feel disempowered and our partner feels as though they lack intelligence or the necessary skills in order to build wealth, we allow ourselves to stay in a state where we will never be challenged or, perhaps, will never challenge each other in order to avoid conflict. But by never challenging each other we do not allow ourselves the opportunity to grow and contribute in a way that serves people on a larger scale.

If *you* have a Guilt Block and *your partner* has a Hard Work Block

When you feel as though things are your fault most of the time (or you wonder how you could possibly deserve something when there's so much awful going on in the world), and when your partner is out working hard, neither of you will ever actually reach the end goal—because there's no such thing. It is impossible to ever feel as though you have enough success or enough wealth, so both of these blocks allow you to live in a place where you're never truly present. You are always trying to solve the future's problems, and by doing so you miss out on a lot of today's blessings. You probably already carry some of that regret.

If *you* have a Guilt Block and *your partner* has a Stress Block

When you feel as though a lot of the challenges exist because of you or because of what you have or what you are able to experience, and if you're in a partnership with somebody who has a stress block, you may be inadvertently causing them more stress because you carry the weight of the world on your shoulders. Conversations about money with your partner may already feel overwhelming because, if you are both already stressed *and* you are carrying the stress of everything else in the world, you don't live in a solution-oriented relationship. You live in a relationship where you are only ever bringing problems to each other's attention. This is a great opportunity to shift and one of the easiest things in your control.

If *you* have a Guilt Block and *your partner* has a Procrastination Block

When you have tremendous guilt about all the things that are happening in the world, and your partner struggles with a procrastination block, it can feel as though there's no end in sight. This is because there's no progress being made in this relationship. Depending on how long you've had the guilt block, you might be getting so comfortable blocking opportunities that you are like an NHL goalie in the Stanley Cup Final: all reflexes. If your guilt stems from some of the injustices in the world, it can be tempting to "educate" other people on these disparities/inequalities, but the best strategy of all is to take care of yourself first so that you are in a good position to help, and then you can inspire people with your actions and progress.

If *you* have a Guilt Block and *your partner* has a Guilt Block

Guilt is both experienced and expressed in different ways, but when you and your partner both have a primary guilt block, we have to watch that you or your partner does not try to solve your financial problems with manipulation. People who feel a tremendous amount of guilt often experience manipulation because guilt is a manipulative emotion. It doesn't allow you to see things as they actually are; it allows you to see things only in relation to yourself. Perhaps you and your partner bonded over some of the things for which you both experience guilt. This is a great opportunity to create compelling financial goals that allow you to truly serve and help others—not from a place of guilt, but rather from a place of love and service.

Chapter Nine

BARE-NAKED BUDGETING

M any people budget backward. I almost typed, "Many people budget from behind," but, given the title of this book, I'm already slightly more off-side than any other money guide out there.

We don't budget to figure out where our money went. We budget because we have to direct our money to where it needs to go in order to reach our financial goals.

People are often so surprised at the end of each month. "Oh my gosh, I couldn't believe I spent $1,800 on groceries this month!" That is budgeting backward.

Forward budgeting is pre-allocating $1,000 for groceries and then setting up financial boundaries and systems to ensure you get as close to that target as possible.

You wouldn't leave West Palm Beach to head home to New York for Thanksgiving and end up in Regina, Saskatchewan, accidentally a year later. You'd have a plan to get to New York, and you'd follow the plan. And if a plane was late, you might have to rent a car or take a different route, but you would still end up where you intended.

We have to treat a budget like a money map.

The other major mistake people make when budgeting is that they set the budget, and if the plan isn't followed exactly, they think they suck at budgeting and quit. This is like heading out on a road trip that says you'll arrive at your destination in four hours, but after you pull over to pee two hours in, you quit and go home because now there's no way you'll make it in time.

Ridiculous.

The good news is that there is no right way to budget.

The whole point of budgeting is to increase your net worth by using some of your income to buy assets. If you do this repeatedly, you will build some wealth. Ta-daaaa!

The trouble is that there are so many things competing for our dollars that if we do not allocate them, there will not be a whole lot left to retire on.

Your budget process is going to involve some facts and science, some art and improvisation. It's going to be a bit of trial and error. And then you are going to course-correct, adjusting as you go. Just as you make lifestyle adjustments to increase your *health* and performance in biohacking, some serious wallet-hacking will let you figure out your *wealth* and performance, financially speaking.

A budget simply contains the data of all your income and expenses.

A *working* budget comes about by you determining how much of your income goes to each expense, then consciously choosing to keep your word to yourself.

Most of us don't even consider budgeting until long after we realize we are running out of money. Fun fact: this is when it is harder to budget.

This is when people are often tempted to throw out the budget altogether, but this would be like deciding to let your entire house burn down because of a fire in the bedroom. In reality, you would do what you could to limit the damage and protect what you've worked so hard to create, and you'd rebuild the area of the house that is no longer functional. You must both take control and allocate your limited resources as best you can until you can increase your resources to make things happen. If things are tight, you must get ruthless with those expenses. Sometimes the things we think we need today add no additional value to our lives overall. When you think back over the last ten years, what were some purchases or monthly expenses you made that feel like a waste today? Now jump ten years in the future. When you look at today's spending through the lens of a decade from now, what are you spending on now that will seem frivolous in your future?

I remember years ago wondering if I should cancel my subscription to this membership of real-estate investors that sent out their monthly-meeting audio recordings on CDs. I probably only listened to four out of the twelve they sent each year, so I considered canceling my subscription until I realized that one of those meetings contained enough valuable resources that inspired me to do a transaction from which I made thousands of dollars. So sometimes when you are considering the expense of something, be sure to also consider the price of not having it. The subscription was ninety-nine dollars per month, but it increased my net worth by tens of thousands per year. If someone said to me, "Here, give me ninety-nine dollars, and I'll give you a thousand back," I'd do that deal over and over again.

What you are looking to *cut out* of the budget are things that you purchase to curb boredom. Boredom is an expensive pastime!

What you are looking to *cut back* in the budget are the variable expenses that change each month. Usually, a variable expense has some flexibility to it. While economics are sometimes at play (gas/fuel rates, inflation on groceries), much of the time it is in our own control, if only we can master our emotions.

You're going to play with your budget a few ways. You will list all your sources of income each month or week or pay period or however you choose to segment it. Then you'll list all your known and guessed expenses for that same period.

Then you'll play with these numbers. You'll get creative. You'll try to squeeze out a few extra dollars here and there to increase the amount of money you are putting toward assets. You'll see what happens if you pay yourself first before paying all your expenses. (This means you pay your assets first, or put a lump sum toward retirement, then pay your expenses with what is left.) You can consider playing with whether it's better to buy bulk or to simply pick up what you need as you need it. You'll figure out what works for you and what doesn't, and you'll do more of what works for you. You'll know that it works for you if you are able to contribute more each month to growing your net worth.

When dealing with a fluctuating income, you'll do the same thing, only with much higher levels of stress. (I'm mostly teasing.) One of the best parts about having a fluctuating income is that when you can learn to live off the leanest months, and you start aggressively saving and investing during the flush months, you build wealth rapidly. Most people who master budgeting on a fluctuating income are impeccable when it comes to wealth building because they don't get excessive when there is excess. When you are paying attention to the extra and using it to buy assets, your assets compound and create more money for you on the side while you are managing your active income from your job with your budget.

It's important not to get caught up in the minutiae of "how" to do this. And it's critical to focus on the result you are aiming for. Do not overcomplicate your money with fancy systems or rigid rules. As long as you are putting as much as you can toward increasing assets and decreasing liabilities, you are a budget genius.

Chapter Ten

WAYS TO MANAGE CASH FLOW AS A COUPLE

I get it. You hate budgeting. You're not good at it. It never works out for you. You want to try a new app. You need new software. You hate spreadsheets.

I promise you that all these excuses put you in good company. One of my favorite interview questions when I'm talking to a wealthy person about money is: "How many times has your budget balanced perfectly?" The answer is always the same.

"Zero."

Never.

And because we spend so much time trying to get it to go perfectly and then it doesn't, we decide there must be something wrong with the method we are using, so we want something different. Maybe a new app will help. Maybe a new system. Maybe a new haircut. I mean, you could try anything, and it's not going to work. The very best budgeting app in the world is YNAB (it stands for "You Need a Budget"), but even when you use the very best budgeting app in the world, it isn't going to work out perfectly either.

Then people think, "Well, there must be something wrong with me." There is nothing wrong with you! You are not stupid. You are not bad at math. (And if you are, it doesn't matter, I promise.)

A budget is simply a financial boundary that protects your financial goals. That retirement mansion with the infinity pool you want is much more likely to happen if you spend the next few years telling your dollars where you want them to go.

Whether you use the very best budgeting app in the world or make a list of your income and expenses each week on paper, whatever you do will simply work to keep you focused on the end goal. The cumulative or compound effect is that you are much more likely to make your goals happen.

When you are in a partnership and have two incomes, you will need to choose how you want to manage that cash flow.

There are a few different ways to handle money as a couple:

TODAY AND TOMORROW METHOD

Here, one of you takes care of daily needs, and the other takes care of the future.

One paycheck goes entirely into retirement and wealth building.

This doesn't necessarily mean that one person receives their paycheck and buys all the investments. You can combine and redistribute the funds however you want. This is simply the best way to organize learning to live on less so that you can invest.

Because the way the funds are allocated—and the way you think about the money—gets a bit tricky, it may be wise to put some sort of agreement in place so that later on someone doesn't think to themselves, "Yeah, well, I built our entire retirement," while forgetting completely that somebody else provided your toilet paper and tissues.

When choosing to live off one income, make sure you are budgeting with the after-tax dollars!

The Benefits:

If something happens to one partner's job or income stream, you know you'll be OK because you'll have some savings/investments, and you've learned to live on much less.

The Risks:

If you decide to consciously uncouple, you'll need to be clear that everything has been fifty-fifty, even though one person wasn't actively building wealth.

The person who is the future-builder of the couple *must* also build wealth in the name of the other individual, as both people need separate retirement funds, even though we know you will be together forever.

Just as one person is buying groceries for your butt, you can't just be buying investments in your name. Your partner isn't prechewing your groceries for you, so we don't want this to be a codependent thing. It's more of an asset-allocation thing. Your partner will still be involved in determining their own assets; you'll just be using one set of funds to purchase them.

ORDER AND CHAOS METHOD

One of you takes care of the fixed costs, and the other takes care of the variable expenses.

This works well if there's a reason these numbers work out based on your incomes. Sometimes there's a partner who does really well with knowing exactly what comes out of your account every month, and there's a partner who's really good at budgeting fluctuating money. You know your personalities best. If one of you is rarely wrinkled and is always neat and tucked, and if the other is sometimes a crumpled heap on the floor, you know who needs to do each role.

The Benefits:

This allows both partners to work on their strengths and then ensure that each individual partner has funds left over to manage retirement.

The Risks:

Depending on inflation and the changing costs of goods over the course of a year, this plan may need to be adjusted to ensure that it is equitable for both partners.

SMASHING IT TOGETHER METHOD

This is traditionally what couples have done—combining all finances into one account and paying all expenses out of that account. It requires a deep amount of trust and is ideal for a couple that may not have any financial trauma.

The Benefits:

Each person sees every dollar and has a say in where each dollar is spent.

The Risks:

This method doesn't allow for a lot of autonomy, and if one partner is not great with money or doesn't have a healthy relationship with it, it can drastically affect the other partner in a negative way and cause a lot of money stress or arguments.

I would never tell you that the goal is to never have an argument as a couple. A life free from friction is a life devoid of growth, and sometimes hard discussions are necessary for our own benefit. We should never try to avoid conflict when we talk about money. What we want to do is to figure out a way to have difficult money conversations in a healthy way so that we can hold our partner's heart carefully instead of doing additional damage to a heart that may already be hurting.

THE YOURS, MINE, AND OURS METHOD

I talked about this method earlier as being one of the best solutions, especially if one of the partners has experienced financial trauma in the past. Both partners have the autonomy to manage their own money, and then the two of you come up with a joint amount that gets put into a joint account to handle joint expenses.

This might sound as though it takes the romance completely out of the relationship, but it does allow the partnership to operate much like any other partnership or business arrangement when it comes to money.

The Benefits

This method allows each partner to manage their own income and finances and to spend their individual money however they choose without interference. It does put each person in charge of their own financial future, so your retirement is completely up to you. You must manage the remainder of the money wisely.

In the case of my amazing clients Lorissa and Jensen, they over-budget for what they need in the joint account and then take the remaining money at the end of every year and decide together how to spend it. Sometimes they use that money to pay down the mortgage. Sometimes they renovate or travel, or they divide the money up and each contribute to their retirement.

The Risks

You will need to decide ahead of time what happens if one partner cannot pay their deposit that month. You will also need to decide what happens if one partner starts to make more money, and you may have to frequently reevaluate the fairness of this arrangement.

EQUAL METHOD

If one partner is uncomfortable sharing full finances, then this method is necessary to explore. It would require a joint account for all shared household expenses, but each partner would be entitled to manage their own finances separately. This works really well if one partner has debt, and the other does not. If you make roughly the same amount of money, then each partner would be responsible for depositing a specific amount of money at a specific interval.

To keep it simple, we will say that each partner earns $8,000 per month after tax and that the household expenses are $5,000 a month. Each partner would then put $2,500 toward some of the shared expenses, but through their own bank account. The rent or mortgage, utilities, household groceries, and expenses like toilet paper, repairs, insurance, taxes, and so on all get divided up, and each partner takes a portion. If you have children, you might also have their expenses come out of this account for ease of budgeting. If you are planning retirement together, then you might also include those contributions in that account.

In this situation, both parties make nearly the same amount, so they feel as though they are sharing the responsibility equally. What they then decide to do with their additional $5,500 per month is up to them. Hopefully they are being wise with it, but, again, if all the agreed-upon obligations are met and one partner wants to spend $5,500 per month on manscaping, then so be it.

PERCENTAGE METHOD

If one partner makes significantly more than the other, you could decide to split the expenses based on a percentage that you agree is fair. If Bruce makes $100,000 per year, Lance makes $50,000 per year, and the household expenses are $5,000 per month, it hardly seems equitable that each partner would contribute $2,500 per month to the shared account.

Because Bruce earns 66 percent—and Lance, 33 percent—of the household income, it might make more sense for Bruce to pay something like $3,325 toward the household expenses and for Lance to contribute $1,675.

In this scenario, both partners need to be equal participants in budgeting for and managing the household expenses. It is not necessary that both partners are involved in each other's individual budgeting. This allows the freedom for each partner to spend their own money how they choose. This is great for people who have had financial trauma or are learning financial boundaries. If, as partners, you are committed to a life together and want to plan for retirement, then those conversations will need to be shared and to happen in addition to budgeting the household expenses together.

The Benefits

This method doesn't require you to talk much about money (if that is something you struggle to do) until you can learn to have healthy communication about it. This method will allow both you and your partner to focus on what you each can control.

The Risks

While it is good for a relationship that this method requires a high level of trust, it might be worthwhile to "produce receipts" for each other now and then so that you don't learn by a visit from the bailiff that your partner hasn't been paying the rent after all.

BLENDED FAMILY METHOD

If you have a new partnership but you have children from a previous relationship, it might be necessary to have a separate account for the children. This way, if you are giving or receiving child-support payments or managing child expenses, and you have to account for those with a former partner, everything is running through a single account.

If you are in this situation and you have trust concerns about your previous partner, then there's absolutely no need to share this account with them. I've seen this happen. People are in a new relationship, but they have an actual bank account shared jointly with a former spouse who is not trustworthy. This can be harmful to the new relationship as it puts your new partner's finances at risk by entangling them with a former partner.

If you want to make sure your children are properly accounted for (e.g., saving for their college education or providing extra dollars for some medical needs), you want to make sure you've got that set aside from the regular household expenses. Be mindful of who has access to the account and come up with a plan that cares not only for your children but for your new partner as well.

The Benefits:

You can be certain that the children will not be financially affected by any breakdowns in adult relationships.

The Risks:

There are only very minor risks associated with using this method, provided you are actively managing the money. Be sure to keep an eye on all bank accounts, as sometimes when we have too many accounts, we can forget about money that is stashed away.

You might even have your own unique way of managing money (and I'd love to hear about it!), so the point of this is that you have to do what works. You are allowed to try a few things and then change them as you grow or as your finances change, or simply because you want to spice it up. There isn't one right way to manage money, provided that each partner has a say and is granted access. Anything you do, you can tweak. But you can't tweak and improve the process unless you've already started.

You'll know you're headed in the right direction if your net worth is generally increasing. You'll know your budgeting needs another look if your net worth is decreasing. (Unless you can pinpoint the reason, like the market took a bit of a dive; a drastically different experience than "I bought new Stanley cups in every shade of pastel and put them on my credit card for points.")

A NOTE ABOUT FINANCIAL TRAUMA

If one partner has money trauma, you must move at the pace of the partner who is least ready to combine finances. That means not forcing or convincing a partner to combine finances if they aren't comfortable doing so.

It is not financial infidelity if one partner is not ready. Financial infidelity happens when a partner fails to disclose a debt, spends excessive money and doesn't tell the other partner (especially when it's previously been decided that certain spending will be discussed), or is lying about their use of money.

If your partner is not ready to combine finances, you must find a way to make the finances work without combining money.

The *gray* area: what if your partner is a spender, and you are squirreling away money?

This, to me, is *not* financial infidelity on your part.

After decades of working with couples, what I know to be true is that when one partner feels they need money set aside in order to have a certain level of safety because the other person's spending is out of control, the person spending out of control is the one committing the infidelity. If a partner has savings in case of financial disaster, and historically the other partner would take that money to pay off debt and then rack it back up again…the first partner is under no obligation to disclose a savings account.

You might be thinking, "Well Erin! That's a slippery slope!" And it is.

I'm a medium-bad skier, and I can navigate a slippery slope. Let's make a pizza with our skis and go through this slowly and carefully together.

If a partner has been squirreling money away in their own savings—therefore making it impossible for the other partner to make ends meet—and that partner has to take on debt in order to get the groceries, then, yes, the person who is saving the money is committing financial infidelity. Basically, financial infidelity is anything that causes harm to the financial well-being of the other partner, whether real or perceived.

If you are getting together for your first naked budget meeting and you have undisclosed savings accounts, it's not necessary to talk about those things today. But it will be in the future when trust is built.

And hear this: if you've just learned that your partner has undisclosed savings, it hasn't been putting your financial situation in jeopardy, and you feel butt hurt about this, you're going to have to take a long look in the mirror before you complain. There may be financial behaviors you are engaged in that are unsafe for your partner, and they are acting defensively in response to these behaviors. You both have to adjust here to make this really work.

Dr. Galen Buckwalter is an expert on financial trauma, and he says financial trauma interferes with a person's ability to carry out normal work and home functions. These are some symptoms of financial trauma:

1. Basic thought patterns regarding money are negative and often involve rumination on failure.
2. The ability to concentrate is interrupted by nagging thoughts of financial doom.
3. The thought that it's only a matter of time before bad or worse things happen again persists.
4. The nervous system gets stuck in overdrive, with jitteriness, insomnia, chronic nightmares, and more.

5. The use of coping mechanisms, such as avoidance or substance abuse, increase.
6. Habits such as fearing that every time the phone rings it's a bill collector or not opening financial mail start to appear.
7. Isolation from friends, or even people involved in your financial world, increases.
8. Financial behaviors are taken to the extreme, even when they first appear to be healthy, such as things like allocating to a partner a restricted amount of cash in the name of the budget, an amount that in actuality wouldn't allow the person to leave the relationship in an emergency.

Dr. Buckwalter explains that our stress system was made to help us respond to a threat to our existence, long before financial systems were developed and money existed. It's as though we are being ambushed by an animal in the wild, except back in the day, once the threat of danger disappeared, we could relax. But he says that with financial trauma, there is no downtime. Society makes money a daily consideration, and our stress system is locked on overdrive.

If this describes your relationship, one of the best ways to handle your money is to come up with a plan in the presence of a couple's therapist. You don't want the partner with financial trauma to stay stuck there, but you don't want to push them faster than they are ready. But for now, separate finances may be the best decision.

If you are a partner who feels threatened by this idea, remember that it isn't your partner's job to make you more comfortable. It is absolutely your own job to figure out why you have the need to control your partner's finances. Even if you are worried that your partner is going to get into a lot of debt by mismanaging their money, believing that they will be fine if you manage it for them is wholly untrue. An unhealthy person will have unhealthy finances, even if they don't have anything to manage. Restricting access doesn't fix the habit.

Here are some questions to ask yourself while you are dialing the number of a couple's counselor in your area:

1. Do I have a need to be needed or to rescue?
2. Am I trying to do something for my partner that they can do for themselves?
3. Will money decisions be imbalanced?
4. Am I on a journey with my partner, or am I trying desperately to get us to a destination?
5. Is my identity tied to helping others?
6. Does my partner often need people to bail them out? Is this a pattern in *their* life that I am enabling?
7. Do I get a sense of significance from being the money expert in our partnership?

WHEN YOU THINK YOU ARE HELPING, BUT YOU ARE OPERATING FROM A WOUND

Whoa, that's a painful subtitle.

I was on the phone one day with a friend of mine who was complaining that he is always bailing his girlfriend out of credit card debt. I listened to him for about twenty minutes, then finally said, "You know you don't have to do that, right?"

He legitimately thought it was his duty to bail her out. He kept getting frustrated that he was making all this money, and she would spend and accumulate more debt. He is so against credit card debt that he cannot imagine having it. For her it is normal. So, I said to him, "Why not let her be in credit card debt?"

He was not expecting that from the person who wrote a book called *Get the Hell Out of Debt*, but my book is not called *Get Your Partner the Hell Out of Debt* or *Pay Off Your Partner's Debt So You Can Be Miserable and Never Want to Make Out.*

I agree with my friend that paying interest on credit card debt is an absolute waste of money; however, I think what's more wasteful is allowing somebody else's poor decisions to take down your good ones.

The issue here was not even with her spending. That's the part we can't control. The issue was with his poor boundaries.

Because he didn't want her to have debt, *his* hard-earned money was going towards paying off her debt. And because debt was fine for *her*, she wasn't interested in managing her spending at that point in their lives. He was quickly becoming resentful.

He didn't love my solution. I think he was hoping I would show up on her doorstep with Chris Harrison and a giant pair of scissors and cut up her credit cards in some dramatic ceremony.

My solution was just to let her manage her own debt and credit cards. Obviously, I do not think they need to be joining finances in any way because he does not need to be responsible for her financially. And frankly, I thought that this misalignment would show up in other areas of their lives before they started combining other things, too. And that is important to know before you intertwine lives.

I felt that leaving her to figure out how to manage it and pay it off was critical.

She continued recklessly spending for another nine months, racking it up and paying it off, then racking it up and paying it off again on her own. It drove him bananas, but eventually he learned to focus on building his own wealth. When things got really tight for her and she realized she couldn't do all the things she wanted to do with her life, she decided to make a change and focused on increasing her net worth. This became her own success. She formulated her own relationship with money and started to heal it.

You probably know where this is going. She got the hell out of debt and started to take an interest in planning for the future. They created a vision for the future together that included owning a home, doing some adventure travel, getting married, and starting a family.

She wanted to be able to stay home with their future children, so they learned to talk openly about what that looked like from a financial perspective.

He called me out of the blue after they'd be dating for two years and said, "She's $10,000 away from being debt free. I think I'm going to tell her I will propose when she is."

I lost my ever-loving mind.

An engagement is not a carrot to be dangled. It's not a reward for hard work. He was "scoreboarding," and it again put him in the power position of "if you behave, then I will reward you."

If you want to build a life with someone, you build a life. A life doesn't start when everything is perfect. It doesn't start when someone checks the boxes you've set out as milestones. People are not commodities, and it's your job to love your partner as they are, if you are choosing to be with them. Obviously, we want to create lots of room for our partners to grow into their full potential…but that is not your work to do. You just need to provide a safe space for them by giving them a container of love in which they can grow. If you try to control or restrict, you are acting out of your own money blocks.

Of course, it's very nice to be able to do things for and with a partner. It's lovely to care for them and love them and treat them to things, but when it becomes something that we are trying to control, the power differential shifts from a partner-to-partner to a weird parent-to-child dynamic.

In all your financial dealings with your beloved, you must ask yourself questions like the following:

1. If my partner's behaviors or beliefs never change, can I love them completely anyway?
2. If my partner's financial, mental, emotional, or physical health worsens, can I love them completely anyway?
3. If my partner has dreams that are bigger than mine, can I support them completely?
4. Am I proud of my partner's decisions, or, if not, can I find a way to make peace with them?
5. Can I be vulnerable with my partner, and do I make it safe for them to be vulnerable with me?
6. Do we have the same vision for our lives, or do our lives intersect in beautiful ways that make each other's existence better?

Whether we are budgeting in the spreadsheets or playing in the bedsheets, we need to make sure both partners can show up in a safe environment, fully expressing with hearts wide open.

Chapter Eleven

NET WORTH

The budget's entire job is to increase net worth, so one of the other important financial fundamentals you'll need from here on out is an accounting of your net worth. Even those of us who are the absolute worst at math can figure this out. You take a list of all the things you own and a list of all the things you owe, and you subtract them. Boom. Net worth.

As a team, your game is to make this number go up with every paycheck. It won't always, because life. *But it becomes the goal. And the budget is the strategy.* The more you work at it, the easier it becomes.

The way we increase net worth is by increasing the amount of assets we own and decreasing the amount of liabilities we have or take on.

When you use the free financial resources on my website, you'll see that we have created a very basic color-coded spreadsheet. Red for liabilities, green for assets.

People often mistake assets as things you can sell for money. If that were true, it would mean that buying a pair of shoes for one hundred dollars and selling them for fifty dollars would be a wise investment. We don't want to count consumer purchases as assets. If you were buying shoes for fifty dollars and selling them for one hundred dollars with regularity, though—now we are talking assets!

If you've ever wondered to yourself, "Do I have enough to live on?" I'll teach you a little insider's secret: you must first know your actual net worth.

When you've added up all your assets and imagined selling them all to pay off your liabilities, put the number you're left with in a compound-interest calculator. If you aren't a huge nerd who keeps this app on your phone to bore people at parties—like I do—then you can simply Google it, and you'll find many to choose from. The number that is left over (after selling everything and paying off liabilities, including any fees or closing costs) is called the "principal."

Let's imagine that number is $1 million.

The interest rate you'll use needs to be fairly conservative—and even though you can certainly earn upwards of 15 percent on your $1 million if you are already a savvy investor, we'll use 5 percent to make all the grumpy people who say, "Where can you earn 15 percent on your money?" happy.

We'll compound it monthly at 5 percent.

And the duration will be one year. Because what we are trying to figure out, in a very rough way, is how much interest your $1 million can earn for you to live off, without depleting the $1 million.

As it turns out, if you don't invest any more money, and you simply live on the 5 percent interest per year on your $1 million, you'll have an annual income of about $51,152.

And now you have at least a basic idea of how all those fancy financial-planner people look at numbers.

If you cannot survive on $51,152, then you know you have to grow your net worth to more than $1 million, *or* you have to create additional passive income strategies to generate a higher income each year in retirement.

Again, this is all rough, and right about now the financial planners who are reading this are typing up angry emails to tell me that it is much more complicated than that, so to you I say this: Calm down, Chad. I believe in you. I believe in your industry. I just think we do a crap job of educating consumers on how to even begin *imagining* retirement, so cool your Tesla and stick with me.

If you are looking at your numbers and thinking, "Oh my gosh, I have a long way to go," then definitely call Chad. An amazing financial planner will help you forecast growth and buy investments, but, most importantly, an impeccable financial planner will create a strategy to reduce the amount of tax you pay when you start to use this money and withdraw it, in order to preserve the amount of capital you've worked for your whole life.

There are fees for this service. Sometimes these are up-front fees, and sometimes these are commissions or fees mashed in with the investments themselves, but you have a right to know, so please ask your planner if this information isn't disclosed or you don't fully understand the compensation structure. Make sure your financial planner isn't simply an investment adviser—you really want the full spectrum of planning, given that taxes are one of your greatest expenses. Most of us are distracted by thinking we pay too much for groceries, and we are not paying attention to how we will afford them in our old age.

Some couples choose to calculate their net worths separately, and some prefer to calculate them jointly. One thing to consider is the structure of your relationship. If you are dating and living separately, then you can calculate your own. If you are cohabitating, make sure you understand common-law rules in your area. Even if you are paying your partner rent, by living under their roof for a certain amount of time and conjugating, the courts may rule unfairly in your opinion in the event the relationship uncouples. When calculating your net worth, you want true and accurate numbers, not aspirational ones.

Brendan and Kim calculated their net worth after ten years of marriage. They had always been high-income earners, but Kim was working part-time while their kids were young, and suddenly Brendan lost his six-figure job during that same period. They had some savings to get by, but the real wake-up call happened when they added up their assets. For years, they'd spent the bulk of their income on toys—not just for the kids, but for themselves, too.

On paper, it looked like they had a decent net worth because they included all their cars and snowmobiles and motorcycles as assets.

Two snowmobiles: $20,000

Two motorcycles: $15,000

Two ATV/quads: $4,000

One pickup truck: $60,000

One Jeep: $40,000

This looks like a six-figure net worth. And Brendan started to feel as though it was going to be OK because he thought, "Worst-case scenario, I can sell these items and get cash."

The problem is that he had financed most of them, and they depreciate, meaning the value of them goes down with time, especially with wear and tear. The financing costs go up because of the interest on interest that we pay. Most of these items were "under water," meaning that he owed more than he could get if he sold them.

Brendan and Kim owed:

$23,211 for the snowmobiles

$15,802 for the motorcycles

$4,093 for the quads

$73,465 for that souped-up pickup truck

$37,566 for the Jeep

In total, even though they previously had no problem making the monthly payments on all their fun toys, the total they owed equaled $154,137.

If they were lucky enough to sell for what they believed the items were worth, they would get $139,000 in their pockets. This would leave them $15,137 in the hole.

Here's the worst news. When they did eventually put everything up for sale, they ended up owing closer to $30,000. Naturally, people wanted to negotiate on the resale market, and because some of the items were taking so long to sell, Brendan figured he better take what he could get.

He said all these realizations made him sick. But losing his job became the greatest money lesson of his life. While initially he had to drain some savings to finish paying off the loans, he needed to get rid of those liabilities because the monthly payments would have destroyed them without his income. When he eventually found another job, instead of allocating his paycheck to paying for his weekend toys, he started investing and buying assets. He laughed and said he eventually invested in some of the companies that build, make, and distribute those recreational vehicles, and he now "makes money from them" instead of giving it *to* them.

He and Kim and the children still spend their weekends outdoors. They will rent equipment when they need it, rather than pay for it to sit in their garage during the week. Brendan says taking a good honest look at his numbers and being truthful about what his lifestyle was costing him was the best eye-opening financial experience. He and Kim ended up having a *legitimate* six-figure net worth by their twelfth wedding anniversary.

Kim said, "He did most of this work on his own, and I was the reluctant spouse who wasn't as interested in talking about money. But once we were listing our toys for sale, it became obvious that we had done this together. I had also participated enthusiastically in purchasing these items by staying clueless about their actual cost. We have bigger dreams now. We are planning for the boys' education, our own retirement, and some epic summer adventures with our family."

Your net worth is your goal tracker. It's the neutral party between you and your spouse that acts as a loving agreement to help you build the life you actually dream of.

....

Chapter Twelve

....

BUILDING WEALTH AS A COUPLE

Y ou are about to understand why people who win the lottery are often soon completely broke.

In our online community we often ask a question, "What would you do if you won $1 million or $10 million?" (or whatever happens to be in the news that week), and inevitably people give us a list of what they would spend it on.

If they win $1 million dollars, they think that paying off debt is being really prudent, so they'll tell us that they'll pay off their house and car and buy a house for their mom, and the next thing you know they have zero dollars left over.

Understanding the future value of money is important to wealth building. If we compound your million-dollar lottery winnings, you start to realize, "Wow, if I actually had $73,000 in additional income from interest, *and* if I didn't touch the million dollars that I won, I would actually be able to pay off my mortgage in two or three years and still have $1.3 million in the bank."

(I played with my compound-interest calculator at a party to figure that out.)

If you can change the way you view assets and cash flow, you will change your life. Working with your partner to understand these concepts will also help you make decisions that are aligned with each other when it comes to your money.

There's an old analogy in financial circles that talks about the golden goose. (Not the fancy sneakers that are made to look like old ratty sneakers for hundreds of dollars.)

Let's imagine two things:

1. You have a goose that lays eggs that can feed your family.
2. You are not vegan.

The old story goes that this goose lays eggs over and over, and you are able to make omelets and breakfast burritos and Grand Slams for your family for a lifetime. Sometimes the goose even lays eggs that contain baby goslings, who then grow up and lay their own eggs. The more eggs each goose lays, the more valuable the geese become. When they are consistently producing eggs, we refer to them as "golden."

In financial terms, the original goose would be called an asset.

When people have accumulated lots of consumer debt, they are tempted to sell off assets to pay for the debt. But this is essentially killing your high-value geese for goose meat—and once that's gone, you have no goose and no eggs.

I absolutely want you to pay off your consumer debt. I just don't want you murdering any geese in the process.

If you listen to my podcast with Leanne, who had six figures of debt, or Jacqueline, who paid off her debt in six months during the pandemic with no income, you'll hear that both had golden geese they were tempted to cash in. Leanne had hefty retirement savings while Jacqueline had a severance. In both circumstances, I encouraged them not to strangle their geese. While they were using their active/employment (Leanne) or newly created income (Jacqueline) to aggressively pay down their debt, their geese were busy mating and laying eggs. By the time they were debt free, they were both extremely happy to take the money they had been putting into paying off the debt and focus on acquiring more geese.

When you are acquiring assets in a partnership, be clear from the time of purchase or acquisition what you plan to do with them. That way, you and your partner won't be tempted to sell the assets during challenging times and miss out on long-term financial wealth.

Managing your money is one thing. Figuring out how to budget those monthly expenses is critical to the well-being of your partnership. But once you have that figured out, what's next? I want you to consider the importance of building wealth. This isn't about being able to take a yacht or private jet to flex for your family or your high school friends on social media. This is about building a life and legacy for your children and your children's children.

There are lots of different movements out there encouraging you to die with nothing. That's probably a fantastic financial plan if you compare it to owing stuff when you die. But while I myself have never received an inheritance and will never get one, it is important to me that I'm living for something bigger than myself.

Even if you don't have children, you can leave this earth and still provide blessings to people, causes, charities, or communities that you believe in. This also ensures that you don't leave somebody to deal with your debt when you croak.

To reiterate, the budget's entire job is to increase the net worth. If your net worth is decreasing, you have a leak in the boat, and there is a hole in your financial strategy somewhere.

You want to work together with your partner (no matter how you decide to budget) to allocate cash each paycheck toward increasing wealth.

We want you to pay your fair share, of course, because it's such a privilege to live in a country with clean water and education and many other luxuries. But many people who manage their own investments miss out on this very critical step of understanding how taxes affect those dollars when they're going into and coming out of the marketplace, and if we are not careful you might lose hundreds of thousands of dollars of your retirement savings because of poor tax planning. Unless you're prepared to read through your state and federal budgets every year to stay on top of tax codes, I highly recommend working with someone whose full-time job it is to stay on top of them for you. Last I checked, the U.S. Internal Revenue Code has 9,834 sections. *Sections*. Not just pages. That does not sound like a fun way to spend a few weekends to me.

So, I'm going to want you to eventually find a great financial planner who will help you manage your money, but this comes at a cost, and you want to be in a stable financial position to access these services. We want to make sure that the planner you hire is a fiduciary, meaning they are actually looking out for your best interests.

In the meantime, there are many low-fee options to get you started, and it's important that you don't give most of your money away to commissions or fees when there are many things you can do yourself to build wealth.

To build a strong financial foundation, obviously you're going to have to budget your money and put a portion of it away. Some things you will have to do jointly, and some things you will want to do individually. If you are somebody who feels threatened at the idea of your partner having individual investments with full access to their own money, you need to take a really good look at your own issues. The reason you want them to have that freedom is not just so they have an escape plan in case you turn out to be a jerk. There are individual benefits that each individual taxpayer gets that make investing worthwhile.

This plan presumes you do not have any consumer debt. If one—or both—of you is carrying debt, then you need to first read *Get the Hell Out of Debt* and take all the steps mentioned in that book. But let's assume you've graduated from that program or that you've taken a solemn vow to not create consumer debt, and we'll work from the ground up.

EMERGENCY FUND

The first thing that you'll do is create an emergency fund. A joint emergency fund comes first because it's the thing that prevents us from getting into credit card debt if there is an actual emergency. So many lenders think that credit cards are the way to take care of an emergency, but they are not. The true emergency happens when you can't afford to pay for your emergency, and you end up in financial debt that allows the banking system to profit off you and your emergency.

You'll often hear people say, "Why would you have $5,000 or $10,000 in an emergency fund when that money could be doing something or earning interest?" But do you know who says these things? Broke people. Wealthy people know that having cash on hand saves money in the long run because you don't have to borrow in case of emergency.

This emergency fund is not locked in anywhere and does not need to earn interest, though many high-interest savings accounts allow you to withdraw without penalty, deposit without penalty, and come with no fees.

You want to make sure this account does not have fees. Some banks will tell you they will waive the fees if you keep a certain amount of money in the account, but this money is not for making money, so don't fall for that trap. This is simply money for an emergency you haven't yet had, and when you have that emergency you should not be dinged with fees.

This needs to be a true no-fee account such that if you have ten dollars it costs you zero dollars to put the money there, keep it there, or take it out. I believe bank fees are the most ridiculous expense. It is ridiculous not only that we are the only species that has to pay to live on this earth but also that we actually *pay* an institution money *to hold* our money. I hope I have a long life, but if I end up in an early grave it will surely say, "Here lies Erin Skye Kelly. She does not want you to pay bank fees.'"

(It's a bonus if you put this money in a high-interest savings account that both earns you interest and has *no fees*!)

In this emergency fund you will acquire a certain number of months' worth of your monthly expenses.

- If you have a job that is easy to come by, you'll have three months of expenses in here.
- If you have a more specialized job and it might take you extra time to find employment in the case that you are laid off, you'll want six months of expenses in the account.
- If you work a highly specialized job and it's really difficult for you to find work, or if you are a contractor or self-employed, you may even want nine months of expenses in the account when you are starting out.

Once you have acquired more assets, it will be less important for this bank account to be so full of cash. When you are starting out, though, and you are about to build wealth, you're going to experience a bit of a ride if you are even a little human, so it's going to be important for you to have the safety net.

You'll want to talk to your partner and figure out what number you are comfortable having in the emergency fund. Here is the sneaky part: if one partner is comfortable with $5,000 as an emergency fund and the other is comfortable with $12,000, the amount you'll need in the fund is $12,000. This isn't something on which you can split the difference or negotiate or compromise. Both partners have to feel completely financially safe in the relationship.

As you build wealth as a couple, grow your net worth, and begin to feel more secure in your finances and investing as a result, you can reduce the amount you have in savings. When you're starting out, it is absolutely critical that this emergency fund be a little bit larger than you actually need.

Your emergency fund lives in a high-interest savings account that you do not touch except in emergencies, but it's not meant to make you tons of money. So, the point of this money is not to accumulate wealth but to be a debt condom. It prevents you from getting debt.

THE EFF-OFF FUND

Then on top of this emergency fund, each partner needs a separate, tiny little baby emergency fund of a couple thousand dollars. If something tragic were to happen to your partner—or to the relationship in general—you would need a little bit of cash to manage while you wait for an insurance check. It's also for safety. In the early stages of every relationship, red flags have a barely yellow hue, and it can be difficult to know if the relationship will be safe long-term while you are working through the bumps. One of the best things that my friends have done is stashing a little bit of money away on their own in case they need to "f**k off" from the relationship and start over.

(As it turns out, the partners who were very bothered by this were the partners from whom my friends eventually fled, so it acts as a good barometer of human character, too.)

My friend Julie is adamant that every woman needs an "Eff-Off Fund." She's happily married and has been so for many years. But given she was in a previous relationship that started off beautifully and slowly turned abusive and toxic, she knows firsthand the importance of having access to money with which you can leave a relationship that is unsafe.

Her current partner knows how much this fund means to her. In his fund, he is happy with three months' worth of expenses, and he invests the rest of his personal money. Julie wanted a flat amount of $25,000. That's what her fund contains, and all her additional money also goes to investments. They have retirement planned out, and they take a few family trips each year, but she says her Eff-Off Fund doesn't exist for her financial health; it exists for her mental health. You could call it the "Vagus Nerve Fund" if you don't like the f-word.

INSURANCE

Once that's done, you'll make sure that you have budgeted for adequate insurance. You'll want life insurance, critical-illness insurance, and disability insurance.

Life insurance makes sure that your partner can function if you get killed by a bus; disability insurance ensures you have cash flow if you cannot work because you've been maimed by a bus; and critical illness covers you if end up with a serious disease that makes you feel as though you've been hit by a bus.

These are all important to keep the income flowing in the case of tragedy because, if you have health stress, it will not be made easier by financial stress.

INVESTMENTS—REGISTERED

Next, you'll start investing. You'll max out your 401(k). If you're Canadian, you'll max out your RRSP. Aussies, that's your Superannuation and my UK friends that's your pension. You're going to hear middle-class people often roll their eyes and scoff at the RRSP or 401(k) option, snarking that it's not a great tool to build wealth. This is a wonderful thing to believe if you are broke. The benefit to the RRSP or the 401(k) *today* has nothing to do with building wealth. It has everything to do with reducing the amount of tax you pay in the now. Why wouldn't you take advantage of an opportunity to pay less taxes to the government (which is your number-one expense, by the way—usually far more than your mortgage or any other budget item) and put more wealth in your own pocket for when you're old?

All the financial planning we do to prepare for when we are old and wrinkly like a raisin is imaginary. We never actually know what's going to happen in life. I was a teenager when I started investing in real estate, and I was absolutely 100 percent certain that I was going to marry Brian Littrell from the Backstreet Boys. He didn't want it that way. We're always gazing into a crystal ball and trying to make the best decisions we possibly can. But participating in your registered retirement plans can potentially allow you to save money on taxes, and if you are somebody who gets a tax refund as part of your tax planning, then you're going to take your refund and invest it in your Roth or your TFSA.

Boom.

That moves us to the next step of the plan, which is to max out that Roth or that tax-free savings account, in Canada, or that ISA in the UK. The whole time we're doing this, we are constantly checking in with the budget to make sure all these numbers work. And these things become primary necessities in the budget. I'm not going to tell you what to spend your money on, but *cough* these things might be more important than your streaming service *cough*.

Each partner is going to do what they can to max out this tax-free growth money. How this money works is that these after-tax dollars get invested, but the growth on that money does not get taxed. Normally, when you do any kind of investing and make a return on that money, you have to pay tax on the difference between the initial cost of the investment and how much it increased in value.

For most people, this means putting about five hundred dollars per month away in order to reach the max, depending on your country's existing rules, your age, and what you may have previously invested. You're going to have to look this up. Know that if this is all you ever did—from an investing standpoint—from the time you became an adult, you would live a really nice life and retire well and comfortably. It might not seem like a lot of money depending on your age, but it's the magic of compounding that makes this truly a money machine—especially if you start right now!

I'm not going to go into the different types of investments that you could potentially buy because this is a book, meaning that between the day I write them down and the day you read them, things could be drastically different. As an example, on the day I'm writing this, one of my riskier investments dropped 58 percent. Hopefully by the time your eyeballs are hitting the page I have recovered that amount, but if not, I'm not sweating, because it's not my only investment.

Once these things are done, you really get to look at how you're going to use any excess money in your budget. You've accounted for retirement, and now you have to decide as a couple what you're going to do as far as trips and travel and vehicles and all other kinds of spending are concerned. If you still have extra money left over (after the dollars you've already allocated first to build wealth), there are a number of options, including purchasing rental real estate or investing in alternative types of currencies, among other things.

PLANNING AHEAD

One of the questions most people have and one of the things most money books fail to answer is this: "How much money will I have in retirement, and how will I know if that will be enough?"

You really are going to have to consult your own personal financial planner to get a more accurate representation for your own life, but if you are just starting out and this whole concept seems completely foreign to you, I am going to walk you through what you could do to at least get a baseline understanding.

But first you need to know your net worth.

Now I know we *just* did this in the previous chapter, but let's make sure you've really got it. I work for a guy who always says, "Repetition is the mother of skill," and he has a few hundred million dollars more than you and I do, so let's review.

There are two tools you need to build wealth, and you'll use them your whole life. The first is your net worth, and the second is your budget. If you only mastered those two things, you would be set.

You're going to add up all your assets. Ideally, assets are "things that put money in your pocket," but for ease of calculations, the basic bank definition is "what you own." This can be homes, investments, or anything that can be sold.

The second thing you need to do is add up all your liabilities. These are the total balances on your loans, credit cards, student loans, mortgages, or any person or entity to whom you owe money.

The third part of the equation is the result when you subtract those two numbers.

What you end up with is what we call your net worth. If you completed this net-worth calculation, congratulations! You are more advanced than most of the world when it comes to financial literacy.

If you want the gold star, go over those calculations and make sure you are calculating the asset side as the "street value," which is what you could sell it for today if you had to, minus any fees or penalties. You'll also calculate the liabilities side, including any fees or penalties, because while you might think this is madness, some lenders ding you for paying things off early. It's in the fine print you didn't read. (I learned this the hard way, too.)

NEXT-LEVEL PLANNING FOR BEGINNERS

You'll need to pull out that compound-interest calculator.

There is actual math you can learn if you care about the calculations and boring people at parties, or you can save everyone you love and get one from your phone's app store, or you can find one online.

Now imagine you are having a life garage sale and are selling off all your assets, then paying off all your debt with that money.

Whatever is left over, after paying realtors, lawyers, lending fees, or penalties, is your net worth.

That's the number we are going to plug into the compound-interest calculator.

It's important to note here that if that number is negative—meaning you sold everything but wouldn't have enough money to pay off your debts—you should get your butt to the bookstore or use your free Audible credits to listen to *Get the Hell Out of Debt*.

But assuming this number is in the black, we consider that our principal, and it's the first number we plug into the calculator.

We then need to put it in an imaginary investment, and to be conservative we'll say that the investment pays 8 percent. Now, listen closely. This is not truly how investing works. Investments go up, and they go down, but your free online calculator isn't accounting for that, so we are just pretending that we are putting your principal amount in some kind of investment that will generate on average an 8 percent rate of return.

We are literally pulling that number out of our butt, so please don't go looking for "investments that pay 8 percent." You'll be missing the point.

As you build wealth, you'll have access to many more investments that will potentially pay 12 percent to 15 percent, or more. This depends on so many things, including your personal risk tolerance. Don't make any of this about the number or the rate of return—that means you're paying attention to the wrong thing right now. I can't say that enough.

The next thing the principal calculator is going to ask you to do is compound it, and this is such an important part of the calculation. People get so focused on the rate or the rate of return when it comes to assets and liabilities that they neglect to pay attention to the compounding period, which simply refers to the time between when interest was last compounded and when it will compound again.

Just for fun—because again, we aren't going to make this number mean anything—you're going to compound your principal at 8 percent monthly, and you'll do that for a number of years. If you are thirty-four years old and you think you might want to retire at sixty-five, you'll use thirty-one years as your number because you'll pretend you are putting your principal in an investment that pays 8 percent monthly for thirty-one years.

You are just *playing*. You're going to monkey with the numbers until you get an understanding of how they work. That's it. You'll hire your financial planner to dig deep into the plan and help you bring it to life.

Next, using your budget, you'll put in something called "additions." This is how much money you would be taking out of your existing budget each month to put into investing, in addition to everything you're using that you imaginarily cashed out.

And please do not actually cash out this money. I feel as though I have to say that many times because people just skim this part and think they have to cash everything out in order to start building wealth, and that is not what you're doing here! We're *just looking* into what life would look like in the future based on the decisions you've made so far.

So, if, for example, you put $1,500 per month from your budget into investments, and currently your net worth is $50,000, you can see that in twenty years you would have $3 million.

If you found a way to put $2,000 per month into your investments, you would have $3.8 million. You're going to just keep playing with the number to get a good understanding of how compounding works based on where you are at and the amount of money you want to invest.

Now, to figure out if you can survive on that compounded lump sum or not, you'll take that number (so, in this case, $3,866,873), and you'll put it back up in the principal section.

We are now going to change the duration to one year.

And we're going to only add one dollar monthly.

What we're trying to do here is figure out if we took that money, invested it, never touched it, and just lived off the interest each year, what would we have to live on?

It's really important here that we're conservative, so we're going to use 5 percent as our interest rate. That gives us a total interest each year of $197,836. If you look at that number and you think, "Yeah, I could live off that!" then you know you're going to have to be putting away $2,000 a month in order to have a life that pays $197,836 per year twenty years from now.

Now! Those of you that are more financially savvy are going to look at this and say, "What about inflation and what about all those other millions of factors that play into these numbers?" And I'm going to tell you to Netflix and chill because we are just giving our friends who have no idea and feel completely lost a way to start looking at these numbers, Chad.

We're not looking for perfection because we know a million things can change in twenty years. What we are looking for is a basic understanding of how it could be possible to make our financial dreams come true.

Lastly, depending on where in the world you live, those might seem like big numbers. They might seem like small numbers. That is not the point. The point is that you need to figure out *your* numbers for where you are in life, where you live, and what you could comfortably live on in *your* retirement.

If you can do that exercise with your spouse and not fight, then you are ready to go to IKEA and put furniture together.

YOUR CHILDREN'S EDUCATION

When I was expecting my first child, I started to research college-education funds because I was hoping to be in a position to prevent my children from starting out their adult lives with debt. When I was looking into all the available options, it didn't seem like a very good deal.

I started to run numbers and wondered if it made more sense to buy a rental property for each child. I would manage it, of course, because it's what I was doing anyway. My theory was that if I found high-quality tenants who would take care of a property, I could accomplish several things. I could provide the tenants with a beautiful, safe place to live for nearly twenty years. Then I could either give the property, mortgage free, to the child, allowing them to reduce their living expenses while attending school, or I could potentially sell the property and pay for their schooling.

Conversely, if I invested in a 529, or an RESP, or an education savings fund, I would be required to contribute monthly from my budget to an investment that would hopefully grow.

Over eighteen years, on average, Americans saved $28,953 in their 529 accounts, according to the Education Data Initiative as of this writing.

According to Statistics Canada as of this writing, the average RESP was $14,520.

At the time my kids were born, a typical one-bed, one-bath rental property was $225,000. Mortgage rates at the time were 3.95 percent, making payments on that property around $1,200 per month (including mortgage, taxes, condo fees, utilities, and repairs). Market rent was $1,400 per month, meaning I would gain a cash flow of some $200 per month.

If I took even some of that cash flow and put it toward an education savings plan of sorts, I could both contribute to the education plan *and* potentially leave my child with a windfall.

Of course, the question becomes: should a college-age child have a lump sum or an asset of six figures? The answer is almost resoundingly: "No, probably not!" but my point is this: you have so much more flexibility when you think outside of the typically available government box. Depending on your circumstances and where you live, there might be tax implications, but you would still come out ahead even after taxes.

I met Rachelle when we worked together, long before we had children, and she decided to do this same plan for her kids. She has three boys ages fourteen, twelve, and eleven, and she has purchased one home for each child. She didn't put any money down; she borrowed on a line of credit because the properties were able to "debt service." This means that the rent covers the line of credit payments. There have been months when the cash was flowing freely, and others when it was a little tighter. Currently, she has one property that is costing her about twenty-five dollars per month because she wanted to keep the tenants, as they were such good renters, incentivized to stay through the pandemic. I don't love that negative cash flow, but I understand why she's seeing it through, and she's more than made those twenty-five dollars back during the flush months.

Each property has over $100,000 in equity now.

Compare that to the average savings for education, and she's already tripled what she could've done the "traditional" way. She's not convinced her children are going to get these properties after all because she really did all the work and the management, and she's on the hook in terms of taxes.

These are technically her properties, but they do allow her so much freedom when it comes to financially assisting her children's education.

I think this is an important wealth-building strategy because we don't know when our little babies are born if they are going to be interested in higher education. We don't even know if they're going to be capable of it. And yet, we make financial decisions on their behalf from the time they are a zygote.

Here's why it's important to discuss this now.

When you bring your brand-new baby home, you aren't sleeping, you have a hormone storm brewing, and your breasts are leaking through your sweatshirt.

Our government gives your information to a *salesperson*, who calls you or shows up on your doorstep offering some sort of education plan for your tiny baby burrito. These are fixed plans that lock you in for a long period of time, based on a budget you don't even know if you have yet.

You don't know if your child is going to have medical expenses or elite-hockey-camp needs. You don't know anything, aside from the fact that this perfect little child in your arms is suddenly the most important thing in the entire world.

And the salespeople are amazing at making you think you are holding a baby genius who will go to Harvard, and you'll need to pay for it. You're making financial decisions in an emotionally vulnerably state, and you could be locking yourself into a long-term commitment of rigidity and strain.

I don't know why this is allowed to happen, but it's done under the guise of "taking care of the baby" when the only person who should be showing up on your doorstep in those first few weeks is someone willing to vacuum your floors while you nap near your infant.

Of course, past indicators of rental-property success have no bearing on the future value of a rental property, so it's always important to make real-estate decisions from a measured state. As you've learned in *Get the Hell Out of Debt*, rental property is not an asset unless it cash flows, so it's critical to buy wisely.

What if your kids are older and you've missed this opportunity?

So what?

I also missed the opportunity to see New Kids on the Block in concert in seventh grade, and I lived to see many other amazing concerts in my life. There's never only one way to do something.

You could start investing now and make your kids get student loans. I don't love that idea, and you don't love that idea, but hear me out. It's a little real-world tough love that teaches financial independence and money management. Then, after they graduate, or ten years later when they have been paying student loans for a decade (but only made a dent in the loan because student loans always seem like a good investment until you realize they are compounded by the friggin' second), you could pay off their student loans as a surprise or hand them the keys to a condo. I promise you that at no point in your child's life will they be disappointed that you invested.

The greatest financial gift you can give to them is taking care of your resources wisely so that when they are raising their own kids, they aren't worried about you as well.

Chapter Thirteen

GOALS

It used to be that women deferred financial decision-making to men. Property law in many parts of the world emphasized women's subordination to a man. Sometimes their father or brother, and often their husband, baron, or lord. When women married, their status as a separate legal entity ceased to exist, and anything they might have owned became their husband's property. Eventually, as human rights attempted to even out, women were allowed access to more education, jobs, votes, banking, and assets, without the permission of someone with a wiener. The challenge has been, even throughout all the time since, that we have not yet figured out how to properly communicate about money. Statistically, many women are working outside the home and still doing most of the labor inside it, too. And whether it is opposing attitudes about money, mismatched financial priorities, overextending our budgets, debt, surprise expenses, financial emergencies, or financial infidelity, what we know is that our relationships are breaking down because of financial resentments that might run generations deep.

Maybe you've decided that one partner will stay home and prioritize raising the children while the other partner works outside the home. Perhaps you are a couple of DINKs (Dual Income, No Kids.) and you have disposable income that you feel isn't being put to good use. Regardless, it's important that you learn to create financial harmony that sets your relationship up for success.

Most relationships designate one partner to carry the weight of paying bills and making the income work in all the ways it needs to. And sometimes it works out that the partner turns into some kind of money yogi who can make the dollars stretch and bend to cover all the necessary lifestyle choices and still have money left over for cute Alo Yoga unitards. But in most relationships, this causes more pain than an overstretched hamstring.

There isn't one right way to manage money as a couple, but I'll be so bold as to say that if you are feeling financial frustration in your relationship, then it's worth considering a different method. Many people will say they want to change their financial conflict, but then they'll keep managing money the same way they have been. What they really mean is: "I hope that my partner changes because I sure as hell am not going to."

If you have a partner who isn't interested in changing the way things are yet still hopes for a different outcome, you'll need your own financial goals.

Whether you get along beautifully like my friends Rebecca and Whitney with their big DINK energy, or argue like Piers Morgan with, well, everyone, you are still going to need your own financial goals.

If you read that sentence and freaked out because you thought, "There's no way I'm going to let my lady have her own financial goals," then put this book down and back away slowly to the year 1940 because I'm not going to be able to help you. If you do, however, want to get laid consistently with a consenting, ongoing, and enthusiastic yes, then we are onto something—because what I lay out in this book will create an incredible, intimate connection for you that will blow your…mind.

So. Back to those individual goals.

They are critical for the success of your relationship because they help you build individual financial confidence. They don't need to be big goals, and they certainly cannot detract from your major financial goals as a couple, but learning to manage your own money—especially when you are an income earner—is vital to your financial well-being.

If you've never set financial goals before, don't be intimidated. These can be about anything from an ongoing expense to a one-time purchase, to a net worth goal and beyond. Maybe you want to hire some help around the house, or you want to get an amazing e-bike, or you want to save up and pay cash for your master's degree. It doesn't matter what it is—though it might be helpful to start small and build up your money confidence if this is at all scaring you. Each partner needs to have their own goal and their own means to achieve it. So, if you are a one-income-but-two-grown-ups household, it's worth considering how much each partner gets to contribute to their individual needs.

In the case of Jennifer and Rebecca, they cover all their financial basics, and they each take $500 per month for their discretionary spending. Rebecca, who stays at home with their children, used to spend her $500 per month mostly on the children. Jennifer, who works outside the home, would use hers for coffee and lunch and spa treatments. When Rebecca started advocating for her own financial goals, she was able to cover more of the kids' expenses with a few tweaks in the budget, and she now uses part of her $500 per month to save up for a secret anniversary trip for Jennifer (which I might have blown if Jennifer is reading this). It gave Rebecca a renewed sense of purpose when it came to money. She has been paying close attention to high-interest savings accounts, along with travel savings, which she says have saved her from her past pattern of just putting things on the credit card and hoping for the best.

James and Lisa both work outside the home, but Lisa's job as a social worker pays far less than what James earns as a physiotherapist. They used to put aside an equal amount each month until Lisa bravely spoke up and suggested that her goals were just as important as his and that they needed to look at the numbers again. They eventually agreed on something that was equitable, and for the first time Lisa is putting money away to max out her IRA contributions, that she hadn't been able to do on her income alone. James felt great about this choice because he feels confident that if something happens to him, Lisa will be able to take care of herself and the children they hope to have in the future.

It doesn't matter what your financial goal is; it matters that you have one.

Financial confidence is built not in the amount you accumulate but in the act of doing what you promised yourself to do.

Here's the other important piece: you need to honor and celebrate your partner's financial goals.

If your partner decides they are going to put $300 of their own money each month into buying Beanie Babies, on the inside you might be screaming, "NOOOOOOOOOOO," because you, too, remember that photo of Frances Mountain and Harold Mountain from the 1990s dividing up their Beanie Baby collection in the courtroom while divorcing. But here's the thing: you don't get a say in how your partner spends their portion for their financial goals, unless it is something that is morally out of alignment for you as a couple or harmful to them in some way.

And just keeping your mouth shut isn't enough to honor their goals. We need to truly celebrate our partner. That might mean you send your partner Beanie Baby memes and defend them fiercely at parties when people mock tiny stuffies. That might mean you send your partner photos of Beanie Babies they might like. It means that you love and accept your partner wholly and completely and to the best of your ability, even if you yourself would not choose to have dust-mite-breeding, staph-carrying, adorable, mock-baby kittens with giant plastic eyeballs in your personal discretionary-spending category. All too often we put our hands in other people's wallets, but true financial freedom also means you are not emotionally tied to an outcome you can't control.

The most important thing I could add here is that you don't need to tell your partner that you are changing. And frankly, you don't need to make a big thing of it. You just need to make new, small choices repeatedly over time. And voila! Changed.

Talking about changing doesn't do much. There are probably a billion "Day One" gym photos on the internet because everyone gets excited at the idea of changing. The boring monotony of actual change is far less exciting. If you went to the gym every day for ten years and posted three thousand gym photos, eventually people would be like, "Yeah I get it—you went to the gym." What they care about is the before and after. It's the daily consistency in between that bores them. And that's also the thing that separates those who are successful from those who can't break the pattern.

CREATING SHARED GOALS

One other discussion piece you'll need to tackle is the importance of shared goals. A budget's entire job is (repeat it with me now!) to increase net worth and set you up for a life you love. If you don't have long-term shared goals, you're coasting through this financial opportunity.

When people with high incomes don't have a shared financial goal, they are at the mercy of consumerism. They'll typically spend (or overspend!) on items that don't add much to their quality of life. Many times after a boom in the economy, when things recede and money is tighter, people will look at all the cash they frittered away and feel a great sense of loss.

This is entirely preventable!

When we come up with a financial goal, we often feel a great sense of purpose. Even if you can't think of a personal financial goal, like "travel the world with my partner when we retire," consider coming up with something that benefits the people you love. Maybe you want to pay off your parents' mortgage or give large sums of money to charities that eradicate child trafficking. Connecting your finances to a purpose greater than yourself can be an integral part of a healthy financial plan.

If you have no idea where or how to start, I recommend what we do at Financial Transformation Weekend: start with your retirement in mind. We determine what you want your life to look like at age ninety-nine and work backward to figure out what we need to be consistently doing today in order to get us there.

Consider how you want to live, what you want to see, and whether you have any items that you haven't yet crossed off your bucket list. Be thorough, and try to paint yourself a picture of the things that will bring you true fulfilment. Maybe red-bottomed shoes don't do that for you, but taking your daughter on a hot-air balloon ride in Turkey might. Then make sure you are aligning your values—the things that matter to you and the philosophy by which you live—with your spending.

If you are struggling to think of these things, here's a list I work through with couples to help them find their alignment. If it is difficult for you or your partner to answer these things or to even imagine them, be patient. Some of us have given up dreaming in order to not disappoint ourselves, and we aren't used to thinking in terms of possibility.

My partner is a financial planner, and he talks about dividing the retirement years into the following:

The Go-Go Years
This is the decade of time when you might be newly retired, traveling a lot, and experiencing as much life and vitality as you can while you still have amazing health. This is about checking off the bucket-list items, enjoying freedom of time, and having adventures.

The Slow-Go Years
These are the years when you might not travel as often or have as much energy, but you still very much live with intention. You might be spending meaningful time with family and friends, and you are investing in quality relationships more than ever.

The No-Go Years
These are the years when you might require extra care. While your health probably isn't what it used to be, you still deserve the highest quality of life and care. These years are also about making sure your loved ones are independent and cared for, and you'll focus more on the legacy you'll leave.

Now hopefully you'll live an adventurous, loving life right up to the age of 120, and you'll pass while doing something you love, like surfing or sketching or having consensual, crazy, wild monkey sex. But if not, we have to ensure that we have dignity and independence, to the extent that both can be granted.

So here are some questions to which you will need to know the answers. You can do this for various stages of retirement, or simply start by picking an age and seeing what comes up.

What time do we wake up?

Who lives with us? How do we feel day to day?

What does our primary bedroom look like?

What do we eat for breakfast?

Who do we talk to throughout the day? What kinds of people do we interact with? Who do we care about, and who cares about us?

What is the first hour of our day like?

Do we leave the house regularly?

Where do we go? Why?

How much of your day is independent of me?

Do you involve physical activity in your day?

Is your day routine or full of adventures?

Do we have kids and grandkids? How old might they be?

What are some of our responsibilities?

What are we driving? (Or how do we get around?)

What does the rest of our home look like?

Describe our wardrobe. What are we wearing?

What is in our bank accounts?

Do you have other investments? Who manages those?

Who prepares the meals?

What do our evenings consist of?

With whom do we typically socialize?

What are your hobbies? What are mine? Do we have any shared hobbies?

Where do we like to travel? Where do we still want to go?

Describe our sex life. (I mean, that will matter!)

Once you've discussed these in detail, you can look at creating an imaginary budget.

The imaginary budget will use your best guess (in today's dollars) about what this whole scenario would cost month to month. From there, we can figure out how close you are to making it happen.

If you discover that you want to live in an adorable downtown studio condo in retirement, order takeout every night, and mostly travel the world, then we can put a rough estimate together based on what we know today.

If you discover that you want to live in a sprawling glass home on the ocean with an infinity pool and a chef, we can put a rough estimate together based on what we know today.

And then we simply have to figure out if your passive or retirement income could sustain that lifestyle, or if we have to spend a few years building that up.

Chapter Fourteen

FINANCIAL BOUNDARIES

One of the reasons why some people are reluctant to talk about their emotions is because their emotions have been weaponized against them in the past. You have to be absolutely committed to not doing this to the people in your life, even when you are upset. Even when you feel justified.

The minute you do this, the relationship is harmed. And it won't be easily fixed with an "I was just kidding" or "You made me upset."

The best relationships are made up of two people who can discuss difficult things without resorting to pushing the buttons of their partner, no matter how tempting that might be.

The weirdest part about human behavior is how we romanticize the sharing of money, and yet we argue relentlessly over it. If you ask people if they believe in prenuptial agreements, they will generally fall into two camps: those who believe it's unromantic to talk about and signifies that one person has a foot out the door before the relationship even starts, and those who think it absurd to enter into any financial agreement without it first being written down.

Both are right. Neither is wrong.

Every person is entitled to having financial boundaries, but it wasn't until recent times when we began acknowledging the importance of this.

An insecure partner might ask what the point is for each partner to manage their own separate bank account if it means they might leave. But then, why aren't we asking, "Why must they be held financially captive in order to stay in the relationship?"

What we've seen time and again is that when one partner doesn't have access to their own resources, they might not have access to safety. If one partner passes away, depending on where you live, assets might be frozen for months while the surviving partner is grieving and attempting to sort out all the duties that come with being an executor of a will or estate. Perhaps they're waiting for an executor to sort it all out for them, or even worse, perhaps no wishes have been expressed and a death creates a financial mess. If something happens to one of you, the other partner needs access to individual funds to be able to pay bills, get groceries, and make arrangements for the other's illness or death. It is an act of selfishness to require everything to be joint. It is an act of love to allow your partner the freedom to have an account of their own, even if the amount they are storing is modest.

Financial boundaries protect our dreams. When we have big financial goals, it's much easier to say no to distractions.

When we have unclear financial goals, wishy-washy hopes, or goals we can't articulate, it becomes so much easier to waste money.

Everyone has a financial agenda. Retailers have a financial agenda. They study psychology in order to get you to spend more. Your bank has a financial agenda. It wants a minimum of "five layers of penetration." (That means your checking account, your mortgage, your credit card, your investments, your car loan...all so they make money off you in multiple streams. It's just as horrible as it sounds.) And yet most people are walking around without a financial agenda of their own.

Do you know what this means? Unless you have financial goals, your bank account is a convenient holding tank for someone else's agenda.

Financial boundaries allow you to say no to something because you are saying yes to something more compelling. When your financial agenda is competing with Black Friday sales, it is so much easier to stay on track financially when you recognize that instead of saying no to yourself, you are actually saying yes to something even more amazing than two-for-one deals on dry shampoo.

In your relationship, you will need individual financial boundaries, as well as couple financial boundaries.

What financial boundaries do is protect our goals. Most of the time privileged adults struggle in retirement because they had bad financial boundaries.

Perhaps they didn't set any goals at all. But often what happens is adults will set a financial goal, but then something urgent-but-non-important will come along, and we'll undo our goals to take care of it. This can be poor boundary-setting.

Non-important urgency will always exist. We live in a time when we are marketed to from the time we wake until the time we sleep (or toss, in our cortisol-filled restlessness).

One of the most effective ways to market is by creating problems we didn't even know we had, then solving them with someone else's product or solution. The challenging part is that everything is made to feel urgent. What is actually urgent is the desire of the person or company, who desperately wants to sell to us to get that money in their pocket and deliberately work to create a sense of urgency. So we usually end up ignoring our own financial goals because the sale is about to end. The offer is only good until a certain time. The discount code will stop being in effect. The buy-one-get-one deal ends in a couple of days. All these things create a sense of urgency that makes us lose our financial boundaries, putting somebody else's needs ahead of our own.

So, when we create financial boundaries in a relationship, we need to build them both as a couple and as individuals. Financial boundaries as a couple means that you've set a common goal together and you're working toward it. The details of this boundary are outlined in your household budget.

Breaking a boundary without discussing it will feel like a violation, and it's supposed to. That feeling is what keeps us on track with our financial goals. Additionally, you will have a personal financial goal, and it, too, needs a boundary. So, with whatever part of the household income that becomes yours, how you choose to spend it is entirely your business, and nobody else gets a say. That is a boundary.

If you have a partner that is derailing themselves financially, remember that in this instance you wouldn't use a combined joint budget, and everything would need to be separate. This allows you to be responsible for you, and your spouse would be responsible for themselves—because the only person we can ever control is ourselves.

I hear you, friend. You want to buy a home together. You want to go on trips together. You want a partner who isn't going to spend money on things you don't want them to spend money on, and it's more romantic to have a partner read your mind than to budget. But you know what else is not romantic? Controlling a spouse like a puppet. If you feel the need to control your spouse's money or spending, then you are essentially saying, "It matters more to me how this relationship looks from the outside than what is actually happening inside it."

This is one of the hardest parts about being a couple: having very different money stories than your partner. We have to be really careful not to let other people into our circle. If you do not have proper money goals with proper budget boundaries, your money will be at the mercy of other people's agendas.

Let me give you an example to illustrate this.

Nasim and John are thirty-two and thirty-one years old, respectively, and have been married for five years. They overspent on their wedding, their honeymoon, and their home, all in their first year of marriage, so it's taken them a handful of years to get their finances back on track after splurging extravagantly in that first year.

They had paid off $40,000 in credit card debt, had a healthy emergency fund, and were regularly contributing to their retirement; however, they still felt that they were overspending and not really getting anywhere. I asked what their goals were, and they were like, "Huh?"

Like most grown-ups, they thought they were winning simply by being debt free, spending less than they earned, and putting a little away for retirement. But when I asked them about retirement, they had no idea how much they'd *have* in retirement, or how much income their investments would produce. They also had never talked about what they wanted retirement to look like or how they would like to spend their time. Most importantly, neither of them could even articulate *when* they'd be retired. Retirement simply lived in the far-off distance, and because it wasn't given a specific year, it was also never measured or tracked.

Chapter Fifteen

FINANCIAL IDENTITY

When we are in a relationship, our ability to create abundance is limited by the money blocks each of us have. This can often cause money friction—and enough financial friction, and you can start a full-on money-fight explosion. At the root of all these financial fights are two people, once children who experienced an emotional event they didn't know how to cope with. They associated some meaning to that event, and then they lived this out over and over again until it became part of who they are. And now, we are sharing a duvet cover with someone who is challenging that identity, and it messes us up.

If your partner is willing to look at their own money blocks and do the work to disarm and dissolve them, you will have an easier time; however, if you are dragging your partner into doing this work when they aren't ready, you are creating your own future agony. It will be very helpful for you to have an idea about your partner's money blocks, but it will also be extremely *un*helpful if you tell them what these are and how to fix them.

Only your partner can truly know what they experienced in their financial past that created this pattern. And only your partner can create a new financial identity should they choose.

If your partner is unwilling to change, you are not locked into a financial destiny of doom.

Here's the good news!

You and your partner together have created a financial identity. It's made up of your beliefs and their beliefs, and it has turned into a series of behaviors that when repeated created the pattern you now find yourselves in. It might have even created a couple identity for you two: "We collect credit card points, and we pay our cards off every month." "We buy a trip to Florida every year in the winter." "We don't budget together because I'm better at money, so I pay the bills." "We have rental properties." "We prefer to buy our groceries from Walmart."

Everything that follows that word *we* forms part of your identity as a couple. It comes with patterns of regularity, and if you recall, in order to create a new identity, you have to "create and condition" a new pattern. So, that's the good news! It only takes one person to break the pattern!

Who are you when it comes to money?

Your identity is your perspective on all your personality traits, beliefs, values, physical attributes, abilities, aspirations, and other identifiers that make you who you are based on who you believe yourself to be. Whether you are aware of this or not, you have a way of living and being that is directly related to your identity.

Your life will play this out, even when something happens that harms you. We get comfortable with what we know and who we believe we are.

Tony Robbins says, "The strongest force in the human personality is the need to stay consistent with how we define ourselves."

A few years ago, my partner and I went out for dinner with another couple, and as we left the restaurant I turned to my husband and said, "I am never doing that again."

Perhaps they are lovely people as individuals, but *as a couple* they had this hurtful dynamic: anytime he'd say anything, she'd roll her eyes in disgust or annoyance. She asked grilling and intrusive questions to everyone at the table, and he sat there staring blankly.

But here's where it got really weird: they were totally comfortable.

This is how they identify because "it's just who they are." They had created this relationship identity where he is constantly annoying and she constantly reminds him and others of how annoying he is. There is a power differential, and they live it out so regularly that it shows up unapologetically in social settings. It means the people they typically socialize with are people who would also be comfortable with this kind of behavior.

How they show up in the world is a reflection of what they accept and what they believe they deserve.

Let's compare two other examples:

My friend Emily believes that a financial system should be really simple. She has one checking account, one savings account, and one credit card. She also sincerely believes that every month you should take some money and put it toward savings. And she thinks anything outside of this is absolutely insane. She is entirely committed to this identity of financial simplicity, and the thought of having any sort of credit card debt makes her completely uncomfortable. This is an example of a positive identity when it comes to money. This identity has extended so much that she has a system where she and her partner live on only one paycheck and use the other paycheck for really great financial decisions that set them up for long-term success. It's not just a system; it's part of who she is and what she believes. She is so committed to this way of life and identity that she can spend freely, but never to the point that it would cause her to be in debt the next month. I asked Emily what drives her nuts, just to figure out what the opposite of her identity would look like, and she said she absolutely cannot stand when people take out a credit card just to get a $500 bonus. Emily does not play.

Contrast that with Amber. Amber's life is incredibly complicated. She is always borrowing from *this* account to pay *that* account. She is constantly taking out credit card loans and offers, and she is so focused on her credit score that she's stuck in the game where she consistently gets further into debt while her credit score gets higher. No matter who tries to talk to her or get her to simplify, she just continues to get entangled. She often meshes her finances with other people's, with joint partnerships and accounts everywhere, causing more financial stress. Because of the constant drama, Amber sometimes falls for get-rich-quick scams, as she's always in a financial crisis.

Even though this problem is an internal one—her identity is based in financial chaos—she keeps looking to external solutions. Amber is constantly grasping for financial relief, and it feels a lot like gasping for air.

Both women have similar backgrounds. Similar families. Similar social status. Similar education. The only difference is that Emily's money identity has been formed by a conscious choice, and it is one that she has rooted herself in. Amber has let the world tell her who she is and what she's worth, and unconsciously she is always reacting to life instead of creating her own compelling financial future.

Your financial identity:

> — will either cause you to rack up debt or
> be debt free your entire life
> — will either keep you from negotiating your worth
> or allow you to rise to the top of your field
> — will be the reason you either put other peo-
> ple's financial needs in front of your own or have
> incredible, badass financial boundaries
> — is the reason you have the exact amount of money
> you do in your bank account right now

Because many people are wishy washy about their identity, they have never really thought clearly or solidified who they are or what they believe about money. When you raise a young girl to believe she needs to marry rich, you teach her that she's not capable of handling money until a man comes along. That has disempowering financial consequences. When you raise a young person to believe in her own resourcefulness, she will find a way—even in hard times—to proactively problem-solve.

When we don't establish a clear financial identity from a young age, we tend to constantly give away our power. We might turn to a bank teller for financial advice—someone who is simply a salesperson for a bank product designed to profit from you.

When we are young, our identity becomes influenced by outside forces. Your peer group determines how you relate to money. If you spend time with people who are financial messes but start to strengthen your identity and relationship with money, you will likely begin to feel as though you can't identify with your old friends. This may also feel lonely, and if you are not paying attention, you could financially self-sabotage in order to stay socially comfortable.

Institutions also have an identity. We mostly call this a "brand," but it is usually a consciously created identity that gives the company or organization an unconscious operating guide; however, because brands are run by human beings, our own human identities will bleed into and potentially take over the brand identity.

If you are a parent, it is very important to start talking to your kids about money in a way that empowers them to determine their own financial identity. This is vastly different than trying to control your children's relationship with money. You want your kids to experience, manage their own, ask questions about, and enjoy money. We don't want to be too rigid, or too lax. For decades, I've been teaching an online financial parenting course called "How to Teach Your Kids about Money," and we've launched enough adults into the world to assert that if you are trying to teach your particular version of right and wrong when it comes to money, your children will have an unhealthy relationship with wealth. If you focus more on making the experience enjoyable and the discussions fun, your future adult children will have confidence with money, trust in themselves when it comes to it, and develop a healthy relationship with spending and saving and investing.

OK, let's think about you as a couple. Here are some questions you can ask your partner at your next naked money meeting:

> What is our identity as a couple?
> How do we show up for each other?
> In what ways do we encourage each other?
> What is our policy on forgiveness?
> What happens if one of us makes a mistake? Is it safe to do so?
> Do we have an expectation of perfectionism?

Are we constantly looking for what is wrong, or are we living in a beautiful state where we appreciate each other?

What do we believe financially?

Where are we going to be in twenty years?

What do we want for each other?

What if one of us needs money? How do we handle that situation?

Then you can get into the fine details if you'd like:

If you were a company, what would your money policies be?

Do you believe in lending money to family members?

Would you lend money to a friend?

Do you lend money to strangers?

What charities do you support?

How do you feel about giving money to people who are homeless?

How do you feel about taking disability?

What do you believe about car payments?

What are you doing together as a couple financially?

What are you doing separately?

Sidenote: I am not somebody who typically tells people what to do or think. I prefer to teach people how to think critically so that they can make their own clear decisions. But on the subject of homelessness, I do want to say this: please stop giving money with judgment. I cannot stand it when somebody who is in a position of generosity holds back that generosity because they are trying to control how somebody else spends money. When I hear people yell, "Get a job!" at a homeless person, I cringe at the piousness that is not at all heart centered.

If you were in desperate need of money, why do you need to give an accounting for it? Even if someone is an addict, and you chose not to give them money because you didn't want to contribute to their addiction, did you help them? Did you cure the addiction? Are they healed? Let's worry less about trying to control everyone else's relationship with money or lifestyle choices (or lack of choices, in most cases), and meet other human beings where they are at right now—with love and compassion.

Chapter Sixteen

FINANCIAL INTIMACY

You might be thinking that the term *financial intimacy* refers to gazing into the bank teller's eyes lovingly while you enter your PIN onto the keypad, but it's not nearly as creepy as that.

In regular emotional intimacy in a relationship, you will feel a greater connection to your partner when you can be wholly and completely open and loved unconditionally, and your partner has the freedom to do the same.

Psychologists have identified different forms of intimacy, such as physical, emotional, and spiritual, and all of these are important to a person's wellness. But we almost never hear about financial intimacy. When we talk about truly healing the financial fights in your relationship, we are also talking about building intimacy. Because most of us have not learned to properly communicate about money, we never develop deep financial intimacy with our partner.

There are five levels of emotional intimacy, and here's how they apply to your finances.

LEVEL ONE

The first level of financial intimacy takes the form of benign communication.

This is where you have very surface-level conversations that are not polarizing and require no emotional energy. You might talk about the stock or real-estate market in general terms, such as, "Wow, I heard that the stock market really took a nosedive today!" But you don't put your personal thoughts, opinions, or vulnerabilities on the line. There's no risk that your partner will say, "You're wrong!" or "You're stupid!" or otherwise hurt your feelings because you are only sharing common facts. You'd have this same conversation in passing with an Uber driver or a mom on the school council, as it isn't specific to your relationship or your needs. These conversations feel very safe.

It's important to note that if you and your partner are having Level One conversations, one or both of you are not comfortable sharing deeply. In order for your partner to feel safe, it's important to look inward and ask how you might be contributing to their need to hold back.

LEVEL TWO

This level of financial intimacy is like testing the waters. You're incorporating other people's opinions into the conversation to gauge a response. You might say, "My boss is convinced that now is the best time to invest in real estate," or, "Nancy next door says her wife, Jessie, is getting really good at options trading and that we should try it." This level of intimacy usually indicates you are trying to get to Level Three but are nervous that you will be rejected. You are trying to create enough distance so that if your partner thinks Jessie is an idiot, you won't have to say, "I've been curious about options trading," and therefore it won't feel like a direct rejection.

LEVEL THREE

This is where the good stuff starts to happen. It's also where a lot of pain is born if we aren't holding our partner's heart gingerly. This is where we start putting ourselves out there if our partner has demonstrated care in discussing other people's opinions in the previous levels. This is where we might start to express what *we* think about finances. We might carefully say, "I've been reading a lot about high-interest savings accounts and wondering if we should put our emergency fund in one of those?" Or we might even be more direct and say, "I need a new vehicle and have done my research and narrowed it down. I'm going to look at one tomorrow!"

This level has a knowing. It's where you feel your partner has your back, and you have theirs.

This is also the place where you or your partner might have been hurt previously. If they had a partner before you that hurt them when they were trying to be seen or heard, it might shoot them back to Level One intimacy with you.

When you have financial disagreements in a Level Three relationship, you can disagree without disappointment. You're still operating a little more on the logical than the emotional side of things—and being pragmatic—but you find hard money conversations easier to handle.

In order to get to this level, we often need to ask permission. You could try saying something like: "I have thoughts on our finances, but I'm worried it would trigger an old fight. Would it be OK if I just shared my thoughts so that we can both process them out loud?"

LEVEL FOUR

This is really where the feelings come into play. This is the land of vulnerability and risk-taking. This is the place where you can talk about money traumas that you might have experienced. If you've ever made dumb money decisions in your partnership, they aren't held against you, and you don't beat yourself up over them either. In this space, you can dream, talk, discuss, and dive deeper. You might have philosophical conversations about finances, or you might say, "Babe, I've been avoiding budgeting because I find the holiday season really triggering." And your partner might say, "I am so grateful you told me that. I hadn't considered how difficult this time of year might be for you. Do you want to work through this together tonight?" And you both might be annoyed because you call each other "babe" but you don't care because you are deeply loved.

Here, you can disagree without disappointment—but if you are disappointed, you and your partner can both handle that. You can cry about money. You can laugh about money. All emotions are welcome and held. You aren't trying to fix each other or correct each other; you feel truly all in it together.

You could try saying something like: "I'm feeling very vulnerable, but I'd be interested in trying to express how I feel about this, if you are open to just listening. Then I'd love if you shared, too."

LEVEL FIVE

This is the deepest, truest expression of intimacy. You are not only seen and heard; you are *known*. Your partner is known. You have an extreme amount of trust in each other. Your partner knows things about you that they could use to hurt you, and yet they never push that button. You could eviscerate your partner with one phrase, and yet you never would.

This level is all about your deep desires, emotions, thoughts—your personal expression as a human being—and you feel loved for it all. All of you is welcome here, and all of your spouse is welcome, even the parts each of you don't want the rest of the world to see.

This is where we can say, "I feel really scared about what is happening in my workplace right now," and have an ear, a shoulder, and an unconditional place to land. It's where you can say, "I am really disappointed that we didn't hit our investment target this year," and have your partner know it's not criticism. They will sit in the disappointment with you and later make a new plan with you. It's where you can say, "I had no idea what our financial planner was talking about!" and you aren't made to feel stupid. It's where you are loved, wholly and completely, for who you are today, and yet the person still sees unending potential and possibility for you both.

Hopefully, this gives you a bit of perspective on how any intimacy is built. It's also why some people can't connect. There are people who love to go deep really fast, but in doing so they invade a person's emotional consent.

When people on a first date hammer someone with many questions ("How much credit card debt do you have?" or "How much do you earn at your job?" or "Do you rent or do you own?"), they aren't creating intimacy; they are being invasive. If we were talking about physical intimacy, this would be the equivalent of surprising someone by waggling your weenie in their face on the first date. Intimacy is built slowly, with consent. You cannot force intimacy on your partner.

A relationship's intimacy can only grow as fast as the partner who is on the lowest intimacy level feels comfortable with. If you are craving more intimacy and connection with your partner, make sure they have a safe space to share and be themselves. Perhaps your partner has been hurt before, and while this isn't your fault, it is your responsibility to ensure the space between you is one in which they can comfortably grow.

Hopefully this chapter gave insight into where you are on the intimacy scale and where your partner might be. If you are a four and your partner is a two, you aren't actually a four. And you don't combine to make a three. Your relationship is actually at Level Two.

And now you also know your partner is really testing the waters when they say, "Hey, I just heard Nancy and Jessie are into butt stuff."

Chapter Seventeen

NAKED BUDGET MEETING AGENDAS

If you and your partner are already great at communication, you may find money conversations are easier now that you understand your blocks, your partner's blocks, and how they intersect.

If you and your beloved are new to money conversations, you might need to have a more formal sit-down in the beginning. If you have read this book in silence, hidden it in your purse, and been nervous to bring up the subject, you're going to broach the subject gently and vulnerably.

"Babe/Honeybuns/Schmoopy/LoveMuff/CaptainHottiePants, it would be meaningful to me if we could spend Saturday morning in bed with coffee, talking about money. I'm not looking to solve anything; I'm simply interested in getting better at talking about finances with you. Would you be open to that?"

"Sugarlips/Pickle/Viking/PeachDumpling, would you be open to talking finances with me this week? I want to get a handle on the things I can be doing to better contribute to our money goals and retirement, and I feel as though I've been avoiding hard conversations. Can we agree to talk about this on Sunday, and can we also agree to be gentle with each other as we navigate this new communication?"

"Poppet/Mopsy/Nugget/Hunk-a-Lunk, I would love it if we could focus some more attention on our finances so that we can reach our retirement goals and do some epic life stuff together. When will you have ten to fifteen minutes this week to look at our money with me?"

And if your partner likes it straight, you could simply say, "Yo. You and me. Wednesday. Wear nothing but a calculator."

For real, you don't actually have to be physically naked for a naked budget meeting. If it were a requirement, those community hall budget meetings would be awkward. (Though probably better attended.)

The whole point of the meeting is to make sure you are doing your part in the relationship in your daily activities to stay on track with the overall goals.

A few things need to happen when you are talking budgets with your bae:

AGENDA OF NAKED BUDGET MEETINGS

1. Celebrate your financial milestones together.

This is important, even though it might initially feel silly. This will allow you to focus on what is going well, and when do this, your mindset shifts to one of abundance. Many couples choose to make their favorite meals for their budget meetings, or to celebrate with a cappuccino run or a glass of bubbles. Whatever you do as a couple to mark a celebration will work; just be sure to acknowledge your positive shifts, no matter how small.

2. Check your goals and ensure you are still aligned.

Have a look at the big picture. Successful CEOs cast a vision and remind people of it often. It can be easy to forget where you are going when you are bogged down in details, receipts, deadlines, and more. You are the CEO of your life and a consistent reminder of what you are working toward can help you stay motivated. It can keep you on track when the online algorithms try to sell you things that derail you from your financial goals. It's easier to say no to something when you are happily choosing to say *yes* to something else.

3. *Airing of the grievances—you get* one.

If you are working through some hard times, you can pull a Frank Costanza and share one complaint or challenge that has come up. The aluminum pole is optional. This is not meant to be a dumping, so be sure that you are focused on the most important thing that needs to be changed. Ensure you are mostly focused on how *you* can take action on the item rather than on telling your partner what they need to do. We don't want to simply bring problems to our partner. We want to also bring solutions, and keeping the meeting short, simple, and solutions focused will help you both master your money faster.

4. *Divvy up any immediate action items.*

You each will be responsible for looking at the to-do list and picking the thing you will commit to. You do not need to hold your partner accountable to this. They are a grown-ass person who has the right to remember to do that thing, and they also have the right to forget. If they *do* remember, you get to high-five and woo-hoo and feel proud of each other. If they don't, they don't need you to nag them to do it. When we start "reminding" our partner to do things, they will soon rely on the reminders, and you will forever be the one who has to remember both things. You can make progress with an imperfect spouse.

5. *Set your next date and get it in the calendars.*

The agreement is that both people show up to the next money chat regardless of whether there has been progress. This is not a rigid meeting, and it's not meant to feel patronizing. Keep your budget meetings light and productive. If they get heavy, lean into that, and work to understand your partner and their needs. Every time you bring a problem to the budget meeting, bring a possible solution as well. Your budget meetings don't have to be at the same time every week or month, but they *can* be at the same time every week or month, if that is what works best for you both. The point of a meeting is not just to have a meeting. The point of a meeting is to reflect and progress.

You will have months when this is fun and easy and things are moving along, and then you'll have months when you forget and think, "We need to do that again; we were doing so well for a while." All of it is OK. You fall off when you fall off, and you get back on when you get back on. If you have a lapse for a while, that doesn't mean you suck or are a couple of failures, or that you need to start all over. It simply means you are human, and life got in the way. You draw back together as much as possible, and, over a lifetime, you won't have a collection of perfectly executed budget meetings, but you will have curated an abundant life.

If you are feeling as though you don't know where to start, here are some sample naked-budget-meeting agendas, based on the common things people need to discuss.

I almost never accept a meeting (naked or otherwise!) without an agenda, so it can help to consider the point of the meeting and your expected outcome so that you don't go round and round in circles.

SAMPLE AGENDAS:
Monthly—Regular
Monthly—Irregular or Crisis
Unspoken Expectations
Forgiveness and Self-Ownership
Celebration
Connection
Change
Future Planning
Estate Planning
Major Purchase
Investment

Kids, or General Planning (can also fall under Major Purchase, but the energy is different when you are thinking about medical expenses for a kid versus which jeep to buy)

MONTHLY—REGULAR

At least once a month, you'll sit down with your beloved and talk about money. This is where you both peer into the future to anticipate upcoming expenses and income and make decisions together. Even if one of you prefers to handle most of the finances, both parties come to the meeting willingly and are open to being heard and to hearing. No one is ever told, "This is how it's going to be."

WHAT YOU NEED:
— The last budget (some people budget weekly, while others budget monthly. It doesn't matter either way.)

— A list of upcoming expenses that are outside the typical expenses and could cause your budget to be out of whack for a bit

THE AGENDA:
You'll look at last month's budget and see what went askew, discuss how you handled it, and high-five if you are proud of the ways you mastered your money. If you feel money shame or disappointment, you'll talk about this openly and come to some sort of plan for what you would do differently if that same obstacle arises again.

EACH PARTNER:
1. What's one thing that needs work this coming month? (Most people associate budget meetings with "reining in the spending," but it doesn't always have to be restrictive! Sometimes the better thing is to be more generous.)

2. What's a decision I made or an action I took that I am proud of and want to celebrate?

MONTHLY—IRREGULAR OR CRISIS

WHAT YOU NEED:

— A copy of last month's budget and, most importantly, a list of expenses for what lies ahead (If this is a true financial crisis—maybe one of you has lost a job or source of income—or if someone has a health issue, or if there is any other challenge that you need to get through together, you want to be as proactive as possible.)

— A list of anticipated expenses, using your best guess

— A list of potential new or innovative income streams. (Listen, if there are women selling farts in a jar on the internet for $200,000, surely you can come up with something.)

THE AGENDA:

You'll focus together on the things you can control, not on the things that have happened to you. It's imperative that you consider creative new ideas without judgment. In a crisis, the strength of our need to survive might mean that we'll defensively shoot our partner's ideas down, but a good partner will always listen and consider and brainstorm in order to find a solution. Innovation is often born out from struggle or conflict, so if you can stay creative and flexible, this crisis could actually turn into a catalyst for growth.

EACH PARTNER:

1. Agrees to the next budget date/meeting before the crisis is over. You can meet daily to discuss what is happening, if necessary!

2. Agrees to be extra kind to each other. Because we are in crisis, we can be extra stretched, and sometimes the people we love most receive the brunt of our stress. Commit to giving the people closest to you your very best, because they need you, and they matter most.

UNSPOKEN EXPECTATIONS

This one is a doozy. Sometimes we have expectations that we never even communicate, and then we feel resentful of our partner. But we never even gave them a chance to show up for us and succeed—because, as it turns out, they weren't able to read our minds.

WHAT YOU NEED:

Honestly, this one can be a solo meeting. You can do this work without involving your partner, and, in fact, please don't involve them unless it will add to the relationship. If you are just clearing your guilt, then be careful to act out of love, not out of a selfishness disguised with justification and righteousness (as can often happen). Once you have acknowledged your unspoken expectations, be prepared with an apology and changed behavior, even if your partner didn't know about the expectations. You may also need to make more independent decisions instead of making them based on your hopes of eliciting a certain reaction from your partner. Make decisions based on your own happiness, the wellness of the relationship, and the well-being of your partner, but you don't get to be disappointed if they don't react the way you wish they would. You cannot control your partner.

THE AGENDA:

The purpose of this meeting is for you to apologize for the way you might have treated your partner in the past, even if they weren't aware of it. You might say, "I recently discovered that I had unspoken expectations of you that were completely unfair. I expected that when I got married, my partner would take care of the bills and I would be a stay-at-home parent. I realized I never communicated that to you or discovered if that is what you want. It's created a lot of turmoil within me, and I want to apologize to you for any snide remarks I might have made when I was operating from this place of assumption. I'm happy with our life/with you/with our decisions, and I promise to communicate my hopes and needs from now on and to be open to listening to yours as well."

We must get practiced at asking for what we need. It's important to do this from the outset. If we don't ask for what we need because we are too afraid of rejection, we are already rejecting ourselves.

If your partner rejects your needs, then you have learned so much more about that person and your compatibility than if you had molded yourself into something agreeable and later discovered you had needs they couldn't meet.

Here's how you ask for what you need:

— Be direct. (Do not hint, hoping they pick up on it.)

— Be kind.

— Be the kind of person who cares for and meets the needs of their partner.

— Do not ask for something that crosses your partner's boundary.

— Do not ask for something that harms the other person, financially or otherwise.

— There are no ultimatums with this need. Never say, "If you don't do this for me, then…"

EACH PARTNER:

1. This is the opportunity to clarify how you *are* showing up in the partnership and how you *want* to show up in the partnership. This is also the time to go over any financial roles you each have and how they are working.

2. This is also a great opportunity to *ask for what you need*. Do you want your partner to help figure out an aspect of the budget? Do you want your partner to help find money for the family vacation? What if your partner can't commit to those things? Can you find another way?

Erin here. I'm the author of this book.

I hope you are enjoying it so far and feeling inspired to build a beautiful financial relationship. I have a big favor to ask! Would you kindly give it a rating and review it in your own words on Amazon, or on whichever retailer's website you purchased it from?

One of the mistakes I made when I wrote my last book was that I didn't ask for reviews. I heard from thousands of people who loved it, but I already knew about the book. I wrote it!

I need you to tell *other people* about this book if you love it, and you can help solidify this book's status by sharing your thoughts.

(I would still love to hear from you!)

Sincerely grateful,
Erin Skye Kelly

See? That's an example of asking for what you need.

FORGIVENESS AND SELF-OWNERSHIP

I received this message from Nora, a podcast listener, and maybe you can relate:

> *I just had a moment of awareness. I'll do some sneaky spending on something "naughty" to me, yet totally benign. I was running errands and I was hungry, and I got a fast-food chicken sandwich meal through the drive-thru. It was eight dollars. And I did not tell my husband. Then, two days later he goes to the grocery store and gets fried chicken from the deli. And I flipped on him! I'm calling myself out. I'm frustrated with my own bullsh*t.*

This meeting is about taking ownership of your side of the street. In this meeting, you would apologize for berating your husband's chicken and talk about your own chicken.

You would make sure that you have *zero* expectations that your husband forgives you for hiding your chicken. When we lovingly apologize to someone, we have no expectation that they will apologize in return. I've heard people say they are "waiting for an apology," meaning they are sitting in a dirty diaper of resentment until they get it. If your happiness depends on receiving an apology from someone else, your happiness is cheap. Having an expectation that our partner "owes" us an apology puts us in a power differential. And I get it. Sometimes we hurt our partners badly, and they in turn hurt us. But you aren't actually looking for a partner who knows how to apologize. You are looking for a partner who owns their actions and consistently makes improved decisions. We also need to *be* that partner. That's far more valuable than an apology.

I say all that with this caveat: it is a dangerous personality trait if your partner never apologizes for anything.

But just like financial debt, we put our relationships in deep emotional debt when we make someone else owe us anything. Words or otherwise.

THE AGENDA

This meeting is for coming clean.

Even if there is no obvious harm (like your husband not knowing about the eight-dollar chicken sandwich), you are coming clean so that you can get practiced at brutal honesty. This is key to healing the part of you that felt the need to omit in the first place. One of the reasons why people lie or omit things is because they don't feel safe enough to tell the truth. When you can create a home or environment where it is safe to make mistakes and tell the truth, you create a space of trust.

I'd keep this budget meeting short and sweet. I would start with something like: "I need to let you know about something stupid I did and the awareness I had about it. I'm not telling you because I'm trying to alleviate my own guilt; I'm telling you because it matters to me that we have honest communication, and I haven't behaved in a way that honors that." Then I'd say, "I got mad at you about the fried chicken, and that was not how I want to show up in life. In my moment of frustration, I remembered that I had an eight-dollar chicken meal, and I failed to mention that to you when having my fit of righteousness over what you spent. I want to try this again and practice having a little more grace. I am very sorry that I behaved that way. Honestly, I think I have fears about running out of money, and those fears have manifested in petty ways, like losing my mind over fried chicken with the man I love most in the world. I am truly sorry."

EACH PARTNER

1. You mustn't have expectations of your partner. Simply own up to your own mistake. If it upsets them, let them work through their upset, and hold space for all the emotions that come up. They may also have something to share, or they may not.

2. After this, talk about how the budget will be managed this coming month, add a little room for personal discretionary spending, and discuss how mistakes will be handled. And maybe you two specifically need a line item for chicken.

CELEBRATION

Celebrating feels good, but it also significantly benefits your long-term well-being. We know that people who take time to celebrate are significantly less stressed, tend to take better care of themselves, and have a better handle on their mental health. Celebrating doesn't mean you need to throw an expensive-ass party for every small win, but it does mean you take a moment to *savor* it. In positive psychology, savoring an experience means focusing your attention on appreciation. You spend time noticing the sensations, emotions, perceptions, thoughts, and behaviors in which you are immersed. You wouldn't, for example, simply *go* to the beach. If you were to savor the experience, you would spend time noticing the breeze on your face, the way the sand feels between your toes, the warmth of the sunlight kissing your nose, the smell of the coconut sunblock on your skin, and the sound of the waves as they break on the shore. You would drink it all in and be grateful.

WHAT YOU NEED:

—The last budget so that you can compare where you were to where you are

—A list of all the things that went well

THE AGENDA:

When you reach a milestone, it's important to celebrate. It's also important that we acknowledge our partner's participation in and general awesomeness throughout this process. You can go out to dinner and celebrate if that is a budget-friendly decision for you. It's important here to have a ritual. Make this part of your identity as a couple: "When we _____, then we [have cake!]." It can be part of a tradition you form as you work toward your financial goals together. At this meeting, it's really important not to give "feedback" or "constructive criticism" to your partner. If you are super driven to achieve, you might be looking for ways to improve. I promise you: there is a time for that, and it's not now.

One of the environments in which I spend time working is a highly productive and world-class organization that is absolutely driven to improve. In almost every meeting we are looking for ways to get better, whether that be more efficiency, more profits, serving more people at the highest level, or just tiny tweaks. Sometimes we will achieve amazing things with incredible teamwork and resourcefulness, and, immediately, people will start looking for ways to improve. This means they've turned their focus to what went wrong or what they can fix. Nothing sucks the air out of the room faster.

There is absolutely a time to consider feedback. But let this celebration of you and your partner be just that—a celebration. Savor as much of it as you can. Drink it all in.

EACH PARTNER:

1. Talk about what obstacles you overcame and how you overcame them. Celebrate those moments.

2. Share what your partner did that you are proud of. Share what you did that you are proud of. Get used to speaking this way to each other. Your partner is meant to be your primary life cheerleader. While we wouldn't go around bragging to the general population, we want a relationship where it is safe to say, "Hey,

I did really awesome here," and have our partners chest-bump, fist-bump, and ugly-bump in celebration.

I think it's important to note here that you can also do this without your partner. If your partner is not big on celebrating the big things, you can absolutely do this for yourself. One of the best ways to call more things we want into our lives is to experience more of the things we want to call in. Not everyone finds celebrating easy. Ultimately, if you want to cultivate a winning life, you have to acknowledge and celebrate the wins. You can dream all you want about flying first-class, but it's not until you actually do it for the first time that you raise that standard for yourself.

CONNECTION

When we don't pay attention to our goals, they can get away from us. And money is very easy to avoid when you don't want to feel those feelings! Learning to connect (and reconnect) both to your partner and to your finances not only will help you stay on track financially but will allow you to build deeper intimacy and trust with your person.

One of the silliest but most profound things I learned early on in life was to ask for attention when I needed it. Sometimes when I feel life's busyness creeping in, I will text my partner, "PAY ATTENTION TO ME," and he will FaceTime or call at his next opportunity. I realize that when I put this in a book, it sounds all shouty and demanding. So, I asked him what happens when he is on the receiving end of a "PAY ATTENTION TO ME!" text.

He said, "The most unfair practice people do with their partner is when they make them guess. It's a losing game. When you text this, I usually laugh because it's kind of adorable and funny. It doesn't feel demanding, and it gives me the opportunity to be open about how I'm feeling too. I am quite happy and willing to recognize that when you say you want attention, you are actually making a bid for connection. This is an opportunity to respond to and strengthen that. I like feeling that I can succeed."

I know not everyone reading this is with a partner who is receptive to this method of communication. If you can find a way to work with your partner to find out how they prefer to communicate about disconnection, and to work to create your own couple-language, it will serve you so well in the long run.

WHAT YOU NEED:

— The last budget you ever made, even if it was many months ago and you've been procrastinating

— Your calendars so that you can schedule all the future dates when you want to reconnect

THE AGENDA:

The point of this meeting is to look into the relationship and finances, even if it's been a while. Reestablish regular connection points to ensure you are both working toward the same financial outcome.

It's important to share what you need to feel connected to each other and what you need to feel connected to the finances. Let's get real, the budget alone isn't sexy enough to connect over. But what the budget represents is. Are you planning an anniversary trip to Portugal? Knowing that the budget's job is to make that happen can be enough to reignite the financial discussions you need to have in order to get that done.

EACH PARTNER:

1. Will take ownership of how they are showing up. Will clearly and concisely ask for connection from their partner when they need it. Agrees to show up for their partner when their partner needs to connect.

2. Agrees to manage their own connection to money and to manage their parts of it well. Will communicate when it's not going well and agrees to be a safe place if their partner communicates that it's not going well for them.

3. Agrees to put the relationship above the finances and knows that the finances are there to support the relationship goals— not the other way around.

CHANGE

Whenever there is a major life change, it's time to gather. When there's been a death in the family or a job loss, or when one of you wants to go back to school or make a career shift, it's critical that you get together and proactively strategize about money.

Change is expensive. I hear about people making a move from an $1,800 apartment to one that's $1,600 to save money, but they don't account for the $800 in movers, the $300 in utility reconnection fees, the $500 in new furniture costs when the old stuff doesn't fit, the $80 in extra transportation costs, and the $250 huge grocery shopping trip in order to get settled. Not to mention the stress on the relationship caused by a move. And then, because there wasn't a plan for the $200 in rental savings each month, the money was simply frittered away. All this because they didn't have an honest-to-goodness naked money meeting when the discussion came up.

Leaning into discussions about expenses and challenges and stress radically diminishes the likelihood you'll experience much of them.

WHAT YOU NEED:

—Your current budget, plus a list of all known expenses and some wild guesses on the unknown expenses you could incur

—Your creative brains to come up with ideas and strategies you might not have previously considered, in order to make things happen with a positive outcome

THE AGENDA:

The desired outcome is to move toward the thing you would typically fear or avoid. Change is daunting, and most people find the route that quickly gets them back in their comfort zone. What you want to discover through this meeting is the most expansive way to grow into this change and the potential unintended consequences, along with some of the unimagined blessings. How do you want to feel? In what ways can your decision-making support the idea that this change will benefit your life or your growth?

EACH PARTNER:

1. Commits to an action list of items they can research or implement in order to support the team finances.

2. Commits to checking in with their partner frequently throughout the change, to see how they are doing and if they need any additional support.

3. Takes responsibility for their own feelings and their own experiences throughout this change.

4. Commits to taking care of their own mental, physical, emotional, financial, and spiritual health so that they are best prepared for the transition.

FUTURE PLANNING

Sometimes a big dreamer enters into a relationship with someone who likes things the way they are. Or sometimes someone who would describe themselves as "realistic" ends up with a partner who often gives them "dream whiplash" — changes the next thing they are chasing so quickly that the "realistic" partner struggles to adapt.

If you are the "realistic" partner, you must commit to taking your partner seriously no matter what. It can be extremely emotionally exhausting listening to plan after plan, with no real action or momentum toward the goal. But it is equally frustrating for the partner with big dreams to have those dreams diminished by the person they love the most. This type of naked budget meeting helps to sort out whether the big dream or future plan is viable, and whether you can take any immediate action steps toward it.

This can help the realistic partner figure out if they just need to listen and support their partner's ideas, or if they can actually get a plan in motion to support them. It also lets the dreamer on the team know what is possible.

I'm not a fan of SMART goals, just so you know. That's the standard goal-setting model they teach in school: goals need to be specific (agreed), measurable (agreed), attainable (yuck), relevant, and time bound. I love most of those things, except the bit about it being realistic, reasonable, and attainable. The very best goals worth going after always sound ridiculous. When it is easy or reasonable to do something, it is also very easy and reasonable not to do it. If you can reason your way into something, you can also very easily reason your way out of it. I believe goals need to be ridiculous, to be the kind of crazy that pulls you out of bed in the morning even when you don't feel like doing anything. So please know, if your partner comes up with a crazy plan that doesn't quite make sense yet on paper but isn't going to harm you in any way to go all in on, then I would be the first to encourage you to try it. The very best ideas and innovations have come about because of the most unrealistic or unreasonable circumstances, and there's nothing like going all-in together on a dream.

So definitely write all the things out at this naked budget meeting, but don't you dare for a minute talk yourself out of going after a big goal, financial or otherwise. If it's on your heart, it can probably be done, even if you don't quite know how to get there today.

WHAT YOU NEED:

— Your current numbers and some big ideas

THE AGENDA:

Here you'll create imaginary budgets. Let's say you want to buy a $2 million lake house, and currently, you have a combined household income of $100,000. Those numbers don't look as though they are going to work today. But what *would* make them work? The goal of this meeting is to figure out the budget for a $2 million lake house. What would the taxes on that be? What would utilities look like? Do some research and start getting those numbers down on paper. Then look at what kind of income and down payment you'd need to support this lake house. Then get creative again—how could you make that happen? Get playful and silly and fun. No ideas are off the table at this stage. You might be surprised at what you learn and how quickly you find new opportunities to make things happen when you get clarity.

EACH PARTNER:

1. Shows up with a positive attitude and looks for ways things can work, not the way they can't. ,

2. Finds ways for their partner's dreams to work, even if they aren't shared. The goal here is to be your partner's biggest fan. They will do the same for you.

3. If it turns out that there isn't a specific action item you can take at this meeting, then the goal is simply to do or find something in the next thirty days that reminds your partner of their dream. Maybe you can look for a photo that represents the trip they want to take. Maybe you can photoshop their face onto scrubs to represent what they will look like once they graduate the med school they want to attend.

ESTATE PLANNING

Thankfully, this is not a meeting you'll need to have regularly. This is one of those topics no one really enjoys talking about. It's like exercise. No one (except a few weirdos) likes doing it, but when it's over, everyone is glad they did it. This is one of the most loving acts you can do for the people in your life, for what good is a life well-lived if you then screw everyone over from beyond the grave, leaving a giant mess for them to clean up while already crying over your shirts hanging in the closet? Rude.

WHAT YOU NEED:

— Your net worth and a clear understanding of who owns what

— Your life insurance policies, your disability policies, and your critical-illness policies

— Tissues (trust me on this!)

THE AGENDA:

The goal of this meeting is to look for gaps in your coverage and unclear instructions when you pass. If you've never done a will before, then you want to put this in the calendar to make sure you handle it.

EACH PARTNER:

1. Will research professionals in their area who deal with all this morbid stuff. Make appointments, if necessary, with your insurance broker, your lawyer (wills and estates), and your funeral home/crematorium.

2. Writes each other a love letter. This is known as a legacy letter, and its purpose is to accompany the will so that while your lover is grieving and going through the boring legal work of settling your financial life, they can open this beautiful letter that outlines all the things you loved about them and how grateful you were to have shared a life together. You can read them aloud to each other if you are brave, but then you seal them up and put them with your will.

3. Consider how you want funeral instructions or other things outlined. Make these wishes known, clearly and concisely. The estate planning does take care of that from the macro sense, but in the micro sense, if you want to make sure your funeral has a slideshow of you in only the best lighting and angles set to Jeremy Camp songs, you will need to be very specific about that somewhere.

MAJOR PURCHASE

A major purchase will need to be defined by your relationship, but it is typically understood as something that would cost 5 percent, or more, of your annual income, if you are looking for a benchmark. Again, if that feels too steep or stringent, you can make your own rules. If you share money, these purchases will need to be planned and discussed. I know this because it only took one time of me coming home and seeing the look on my partner's face when I announced, "I bought a rental property today!" to realize that maybe he would have wanted to know about this ahead of time.

This approach can apply to trips, vehicles, electronics...or even what you might consider more prudent purchases, like investments. Your partner might have insight that you didn't think of. For example, if you want to invest $10,000 in a certain stock, they might know that you already have a mutual fund heavily invested in that company and suggest a more diverse choice for your portfolio.

Regardless, your first major-purchase meeting will involve discussing and defining what a major purchase is and how you plan to communicate about them.

THE AGENDA:

The outcome of this meeting is to determine how to best prepare and plan for major purchases and how to work out the details of the transaction to allow both parties to feel comfortable with the choice.

EACH PARTNER:

1. Needs to put their own biases aside and focus on what is in the best interest of the partnership if a conflict arises. In most partnerships, we would define one partner as the spender and one partner as the saver, but that is because spending and saving is a spectrum. We each land somewhere. The partner who is a saver in one relationship might be a spender with a different partner with tighter pockets. In this relationship, be very careful not to take on the identity of either a spender or saver, because ultimately you want to advance the financial well-being of the partnership while living a life you love. Deciding that you are "a spender or a saver" labels you in a way that creates unspoken rules instead of open opportunities.

2. If your partner desires a major purchase that you deem unnecessary, you need to give the partner options to potentially manage the purchase rather than a heavy-handed no. If your partner wants to buy the latest Cadillac and you think a Ford Focus would suffice, you'll hit frustration. Questions you could ask each other include: "What income level would we need for you to consider the Cadillac?" "What is it, financially speaking, that you are afraid of?" Or, if you are the Ford Focus fan, you could ask, "What is it about the Cadillac specifically that you

feel will improve our quality of life?" "What other vehicles are you considering that would give us that same feeling?" "Right now, are you looking to feel justified in this purchase, or do you want my honest feedback?" "What are you willing to give up in order to have it?"

3. Decide on a date/time for the purchase decision if you are torn about it. Sometimes taking a few days brings new perspective to each party, so you can consider reconvening when you've both had time to research the other person's position.

4. This is ultimately about respect. Make sure you aren't showing up to this meeting to be parented or do the parenting. You are a team, and unless you've each set aside money to do as you wish when it comes to major purchases, then this will be either a communication blessing or a learning opportunity.

INVESTMENT

This is a regular meeting you'll schedule if you have any investments separately or together, and it's also a necessary regular meeting once you are in the wealth-building phase of life. (Or, if you've read *Get the Hell Out of Debt*, you'll know we call this "Phase 3.")

WHAT YOU NEED:

— A list of all your assets and data on how they have performed. If you have a financial planner, you'll meet as a couple before your annual review with your planner, and once again as a couple after that meeting.

— An updated net-worth spreadsheet and your budget so that you can determine if you want to squeeze any more money out of the budget in order to invest during this season of your life.

THE AGENDA:

At this meeting, you will check in on the performance of your investments and review what they are and how they are structured. For example, if you have maxed out your registered investments (401(k), IRA, TFSA, RRSP, Super, ISA, and so on, depending on where you live), you will want to consider the tax implications of other investments (nonregistered investments typically don't contain the tax-sheltered advantages of registered investments). If you have not maxed out your registered investments (those investments that are registered with the federal government that might provide tax savings or tax deferrals), then you will want to compare these options with your current income situation or consider reallocating assets in order to maximize tax benefits. If none of this makes any sense to you, it's a great opportunity just to learn what you currently have and why you have it, and then to interview three financial planners to hear which strategies they would implement to maximize your investments and cash. All the while, you can be learning, and you can show up to your next Investment Meeting knowing that you and your partner will both teach each other something.

EACH PARTNER:

1. Agrees at each meeting to research one thing about their investments that they will bring to the meeting next time.

2. Will track the investments on their phone in an app and check in with those investments regularly, especially when the market is finicky or volatile. In those markets most people don't want to look, but you are a fearless couple, so you lean into knowledge when other people run in fear. You will research why and how volatile markets can be a potential opportunity, and why and how many people sabotage their long-term success due to short-term fear. As Warren Buffett famously said, "Be fearful when others are greedy, and greedy when others are fearful."

3. Agrees to set and work toward financial goals and looks for ways to squeeze their part of the budget or create income to meet the goals.

4. Actively invests. This is critical. If one partner is doing all the investing because they are "better at it," then a dangerous

power imbalance is created if something ever goes wrong. The most loving thing to do is to encourage both partners to learn all they can, even if for just minutes a day in the beginning. One partner will *always* be better at something. One partner in your relationship is better at doing the dishes, but that doesn't mean the other one will never have to wash a dish again in their lives. That is horribly irresponsible to humanity, never mind to the coworkers wondering who the goon is who keeps leaving their coffee cups beside the sink. Let's be fully functioning adults who take responsibility for our investments, our decisions, and, therefore, our retirement. By doing so, we can live out our days in the manner we choose, rather than leaving all our care up to chance. When you think about it, the person likely to be spoon-feeding you and wiping your dirty bottom during your most vulnerable time in palliative care won't even be born for another twenty years. Take care of your finances. The alternative is frightening.

KIDS

Because kids are such an emotional part of our lives, we can often overspend on the wrong things for our children and underspend in the areas they will most need us to prepare for in the long run.

WHAT YOU NEED:
— A list of all the upcoming anticipated expenses for your children. This is the most crystal ball-type thinking you can do financially because it is absolutely hard enough to predict what your *own* life is going to look like in twenty years, never mind what your beautiful, cooing, swaddled baby will do with their life.

— Depending on the age of your children, you might already know that number. Regardless, add 20 percent.

THE AGENDA:

Depending on what is happening in the lives of your children, you will do your best to look at both your own resources and the other available resources. For instance, if your brilliant son Aidan is going to play AAA ice hockey, and you know you only want to give him the best possible options, then the elite coaching and equipment you buy are going to be very different than the resources you devote to the son who picks his nose through his hockey mask and scores on his own team. One might be entitled to a hockey scholarship of some kind, and the other might be able to get a refund on their skates if you have the original receipt.

EACH PARTNER:

1. Shows up to the meeting having done self-care so they are less emotionally charged. Have sandwiches, just in case.

2. Outlines what they think are the priority spends and what they think are the "nice-to-haves."

3. In the case when the money doesn't quite cover what you need it to, a list of resources you are willing to sell or cut back on to make this happen for your sweet, innocent loin-fruit.

Chapter Eighteen

TURNING THE BLOCKS INTO STEPPING STONES

O ur money blocks are either obstacles to wealth or, when consciously
healed, stepping stones to wealth.

We are going to look at your blocks in detail as you continue to create
your custom plan for dissolving and diminishing your money blocks. Take
a glance back at the quiz you did earlier and look for the blocks you scored
the highest on—or the ways you typically block wealth from entering your
life—and search for the corresponding paragraph to begin to work on healing that blockage. Working on this healing as an individual, as you increase
your financial communication in naked money meetings with your partner,
will bring financial abundance and greater intimacy in your relationship to
money, and each other.

THE LACK BLOCK

I am scared that I am going to run out of money.

There is a human phenomenon that essentially proves that what we
focus on and think about is most likely to be true. This is because
our beliefs and our subsequent focuses tend to become self-fulfill-

ing. One of the reasons you feel this money lack is because you are focused on lack as an outcome. It's one of the reasons why gratitude is the antidote to lack—focusing on abundance brings more of it into your life. Intentionally focusing on all the abundance you have will be extremely beneficial to healing this block. From a practical standpoint, this means you need to buffer your emergency-fund account and keep more cash in your checking account. If funds are tight right now, consider looking at your abundance and finding things to sell, or create an income source that will allow you to pad up your life.

I tend to react to financial stress instead of anticipating and dissipating it.

When we fear something, or when we are stuck in a lack mentality, we often go into avoidance mode. This creates more stress. Most of the time, we are financially reacting to something we could have anticipated had we been diligent in confronting it in the first place. This can be as simple as looking ahead to upcoming financial challenges, deciding to do all you can to deal with it today, and repeating that approach tomorrow. For example, sometimes people start worrying about running out of money by the end of the month. But they start worrying about it on the third of the month. They technically have twenty-seven-ish days to work on this to dissipate their financial stress! You have the opportunity to look at the patterns of financial stress in your life and change how you have been handling it, along with deciding that financial stress is no longer welcome in your life.

I don't like to be around people who are "bigger thinkers" than I am.

Let's be serious: some people are just big cocky talkers. But it's highly likely that when you are around people who talk about money in a different way than you are used to, you will be uncomfortable simply because it is unfamiliar. Here's a fun tip: most people want to talk about themselves anyway. If you feel as though you can't keep up in a big-think conversation, take all the pressure off yourself—you don't have to! Simply ask a lot of questions. This does a couple of things: it activates your curiosity, which is a great wealth-building tool, and it makes the other person in the conversation the expert, which everyone loves being anyway! If this brings out the lack thinking in you, challenge yourself to get around *more* people who are bigger thinkers, or wealthier than you, and ask lots of questions *more often*. You'll condition your comfort zone this way, and you'll become a bigger thinker in the process!

Even though I fear I will run out of money, I still spend all my money or resources.

When we get used to not having money, *having* money will be a challenge. It will feel uncomfortable. You might be thinking, "How can I worry about not having enough and yet suddenly put myself in a position where I actually don't have enough?" Welcome to upper limiting. Since you are nearly done with this book, this is a great time to order a new one by Gay Hendricks, *The Big Leap*. Most forms of self-sabotage are experienced this way, because you have an unconscious limit on how much abundance, success, and love you think you deserve. When we aren't aware of these limits, we self-sabotage, or limit ourselves, so that we can get back to the level of wealth we think we deserve. To start shifting this, I recommend you "spend" all your money—but, rather than wasting it, you "spend" it on assets so that it's out of your account while you work on the psychology behind your patterns. When we can get comfortable with getting uncomfortable, we can transform any area of our life.

I tend to feel resentful of other people's success.

Because resentment is unexpressed emotion, usually brought on by envy or self-anger, we can often point it back to ourselves. We're actually upset we aren't living up to our own potential. It's easier to be mad at other people's success than at our own shortcomings, especially when we are in denial about having them. The undertone of this lack block implies that you can't be successful because someone else already is. Isn't that absurd? To heal this block, you must become practiced at celebrating, admiring, and respecting other people's successes. Additionally, you must allow them to celebrate yours. Comment on their social media posts. Text them high-five emojis. Show up and bring them a gift or write them a letter of admiration. I was backstage at an event and heard Alex Hormozi say, "No one ahead of you is sh*t-talking you. In fact, they're not even thinking about you. If someone talks sh*t about you, take that as an admission of the fact that you are further ahead than they are." As soon as you sh*t-talk or sh*t-think someone else, you are playing small.

If I don't know something, I feel stupid.

You'd think this is obvious, but it isn't. Of course, you don't know when you don't know something. You haven't learned it yet. I don't know when we decided that once you've grown up you ought to know everything, but it's categorically untrue. It was decades before I realized that animals who hibernate don't sleep for the entire winter. I discovered this by reading a news article. My whole life I believed that hibernation meant that bears slept for months on end. Initially, I felt stupid. But then I realized, "Wait. I am not a forest ranger. I am also not a bear. I would have only known this if I had ever asked the question before, and I didn't ask the question because I didn't know to ask it." If you don't know something, it doesn't make you stupid. It just means you don't know something. You know lots of other things though, like how to calculate your net worth and your budget, and now you're in the know that bears don't sleep for an entire winter. So you and I, as medium-smart people, just need to promise each other that we will keep asking questions, even when we think we *do* know things.

I tend to focus on what is not working financially.

Often we are doing better than we think we are; however, we expect that our results ought to be bigger than they are. So, we focus on what we are doing wrong as a form of self-flagellation, as a weird way to relieve ourselves of the guilt we feel for not being "as good as" someone else. By focusing on what isn't working financially we can stay small, where we are comfortable. Instead, change the focus to what *is* small. Achieving small wins that might not be impressive to the world—but that did shift your typical decision-making—will be the easiest way to move into abundance. You might be celebrating that you remembered to put the cap back on the toothpaste tube this morning, saving you a couple of bucks per month (or much more, if leaving it off one more time will spark a divorce). That might not seem significant, but even minor shifts are massive when they are repeated consistently over time.

I compare myself to other people who have more financial resources.

Because we are wired to be in relationships with other people, there will always be a part of our brain that considers how we measure up. When it becomes one of the primary ways in which you measure success, you are setting yourself up for misery. One of the keys to wealth building is mastering your personal integrity, and one of the ways to master your personal integrity is to keep in competition with *yourself*. When we become our only comparison, and the measure is simply: "How often did I keep my word to myself this month?" we build our own integrity. We will also find that we have less of a desire to compare ourselves to others. We have no control over what other people do or accomplish, but we do have some measure of control over the actions we take in our own lives. Focusing on you and your promises to yourself will be a radical shift out of the lack-brained life.

I am often afraid of change.

Some of the cornerstones of wealth are flexibility and innovation. While there are a lot of solid, stable financial investments that have stood the test of time, the ability to read the market, pay attention to your finances, stay on top of technology, and act with precision in a moment of decision are key to growing and maintaining your wealth. I was in the "blue" bank in my hometown recently, after they underwent some radical renovation where they removed the big teller desk and replaced it with these little floating tables. The vibe is not business casual; it's "a bunch of boomers decided to host cocktail hour at some hipster bar in the midafternoon." The even-worse news is you can hear everything everyone is doing, and it has eliminated privacy.

A gentleman was ahead of me, both in line and in years, and he needed help with a transaction. The bank teller was explaining that he could do it instantly if he did it online, and he said he didn't like online banking. She told him it was easy and said, "I'll show you," and he repeated that he didn't want to learn; he just wanted help with the transaction. She started to get condescending with him, and it made me think she either doesn't have grandparents or doesn't miss hers the way I miss mine. She was doing more talking than listening, and the man left in tears. It was the most heartbreaking thing to watch. Now, I know deep in my soul that the bank teller was in the wrong as she needed to meet this man where he was at—she too was not the best at navigating change. But this man was experiencing deep suffering because, for whatever reason, he was not able to change how he handled his finances. You might not want or be able to change but the world is not going to stop progressing for you, as heartbreaking as that is to say.

I often feel financially helpless or hopeless.

I have been here, so I want to say that you might be feeling this way if you've recently had some financial trauma. It could also be a result of chronic stress. Be mindful not to rely on the notion that someone should come rescue you from this state, that things would become easier if only you could receive some support. This work is entirely yours to do. This is where it will be critical for you to focus on what you can control and what *is* going well, and, again, find some moments of gratitude, no matter how small. It's important to know that feeling helpless doesn't mean that you *are* helpless. Our thoughts are not always accurate. Cognitive distortions are defined in part as irregular or irrational patterns of thinking, and they are very good at contributing to the idea of helplessness or hopelessness. Byron Katie has developed a process of self-inquiry that asking yourself four liberation questions: Is it true?

Can I absolutely know that it is true? How do I react when I believe that thought? Who would I be without that thought? If this is resonating, pick up any of her books. I've referenced them in the back.

I compare myself to others frequently, and not just financially.

This is where we know you are at home in Lack Land. This thinking keeps you in lack indefinitely because you will always find people who do things differently than you. What's interesting is that some people compare themselves to you, too. One of the ways to help heal this is to imagine that you are someone with terrible self-esteem who is looking at your life (from afar or though the death lens of social media) and listing all the things you have or do that are better than what that person might experience day to day. It's a twisted way to practice gratitude, but it will allow you to focus on what is going well. Another solution is to take a break from social media for a while, both so that you aren't comparing yourself to others and so that you aren't posting things to impress others. You don't want to participate in comparison on either side—comparing to or being compared to—if you want to live in abundance. The other solution is to create a goal big enough that it holds your focus daily. This way, you won't have time for distraction and can accomplish your goal.

I have a mental list of things I wish I could afford to buy.

This focus on lack is the stuff retailers dream of! And, in fact, I'm not convinced retailers didn't plant those seeds of lack in you to begin with. Having a mental list of things you wish you could afford versus having a financial plan to purchase what you want are two different things, divided only by lack and worry. The first abundance shift we have to make involves looking at all the things you *have* been able to purchase, and celebrating those. Maybe you didn't have proper living room furniture for a long time, and now everyone in your family has a place to gather, and you are able to think of all the most wonderful memories you've had while sitting on the furniture you already own.

Boom. Abundant shift. Do a precise mental inventory of everything you own in this way. Next, you'll move from spending time wishing you could afford things to figuring out on how you can afford them. What would you have to change in your life in order to afford what you desire? If money weren't an issue, would you still want that thing in three years? In ten years? Sometimes, shifting your thinking will also shift your desires, and when we move from wondering whether we can afford something to planning how we can make it happen (using what is in our control), abundance begins to move in our favor.

I often wonder how other people seem to have so much because I just don't get it.

We can only see things through the perspectives we have been given and have developed, and sometimes our lenses are a little foggy. It may be true that other people don't have as much as they appear to, and/or they might be up to their eyeballs in consumer debt, so what looks like freedom might actually be financial hell. When we think everyone should live how we live, we push our judgment on others—lack thinking. This is a great opportunity to begin to embrace curiosity. We don't know what we don't know. When I was younger, I thought grown-ups had to save cash to own homes, and I didn't think I'd ever be able to save up enough money to buy a home. Then I learned some people have multiple properties, and I thought they must be extremely rich! Where did they get all that money to buy all those houses? It wasn't until someone talked to me about mortgages and cash flow that I started to shift my thinking. Maybe there is a way for you to have what you want, but you have an assumption about how you are going to get there, and that dang assumption is keeping you stuck. Focus instead on what you *can* do, and ask lots of questions of the people who are doing the things you dream of. I've noticed that people who are doing better than I am in life seem to have the best advice and are usually willing to help.

When I dream about my future, I have no idea how I will get there.

I don't know why we place this pressure on ourselves to know how things will happen. Sometimes, when we don't know *how* they will happen, we assume that means they *can't* happen, and then we stay put in our lack thinking. Obviously, I want you to find ways to do the things your heart desires. But you don't have to know the way today. I was once on this incredible five-peak hike that many people had raved about doing, but we couldn't see the route from the ground. We could only see part of the first summit. When we arrived, my group kept asking, "But *how* do we get to the top of the fifth peak?" Someone just finishing the hike passed us and said, "Don't worry about the fifth peak right now. You have to get to the first one. And at the top of the first peak, you'll see the trail to the second. The fifth will be revealed in time." We didn't know it at the time, but that Yoda-in-human-form was right. We couldn't even fathom how beautiful that hike was until we reached the first summit, when a whole new beautiful vista was revealed, something we would not have been able to imagine from our starting point on the ground. Lack will keep you from moving forward, so when you dream about your future today, focus not on how you will get to your goal but on how you will get to the first leg of that entire journey. And then worry about the next part later.

The idea of having wealth seems so hard that I don't even try to achieve it.

Scarcity thinking legitimately limits the functioning of your brain. Living in lack affects your ability to solve problems, hold information, plan, and make decisions. Your brain is so full of thinking about the things you don't have that, of course, the idea of achieving wealth seems hard and exhausting. That's why, before you even start to learn about wealth, which I promise you is easier than you ever imagined, you've got to shift to a mindset of gratitude and abundance. If this block feels heavy for you, I want you to also carefully consider the company you keep. It's highly likely you are also surrounded by people who do not have the motivation to learn and grow. Sometimes the simple act of being around people who are positive, proactive learners is contagious and can ignite the spark for learning—and the desire to multiply your money—within you. Frankly, if you are this far into the book, you've already made some shifts in lack thinking, and those shifts have already started your personal transformation. Keep up these habits by engaging with a group of peers who require more from you than you've been requiring of yourself.

I often feel that "positive thinking" is a waste of time and not for me.

A scarcity mindset will obviously tell you that an abundance mindset is a waste of time, otherwise it wouldn't be doing its job. If you really struggle to focus on thinking positively, try recalling a memory of someone or something you love. One of my favorite memories with my oldest son is that of when we were going through the Starbucks drive-through and he, at five years old, wanted a "Naked Juice," the brand name for a prepackaged smoothie in a bottle. For whatever reason the barista could not hear us, and she kept saying, "Bacon juice?" And I would say, "Naked Juice!" And she finally said, "We don't sell bacon juice." So I started yelling, "Naked! Naked! Not pigs! People with no clothes!" into the speaker, confusing her more. Eventually, one of her coworkers figured it out and got him the juice smoothie. My son was laughing so hard he could barely breathe. Lack says, "How stupid that she didn't know what I was talking about!" and is annoyed. Abundance says, "Thank goodness she had no idea what I was talking about because his laughter made my day and created one of my most favorite memories." To this day, we call it "Bacon Juice." No matter how you feel about positive thinking, I am certain you can recall a memory of a situation that could have or ought to have been frustrating, but that makes you laugh or smile. Stack enough of those together, and you start moving away from the lack mindset quite quickly.

It is easy for me to focus on what I don't have.

This is easy for you because you've been training for it for a long time. Sit down with one leg crossed over the other—likely the same leg will cross over the other every time you cross your legs. If you try to switch legs, you feel less comfortable. This is simply because you've trained your body repeatedly. You can, however, train your body to sit a different way if you commit to it. It's the same with this mindset. Just because it's easy for you to focus on what you don't have doesn't mean that this is how you are meant to live forever. You are going to shift your focus to what you do have. When you catch yourself thinking about what you lack, you'll celebrate this new awareness—if you weren't aware, you wouldn't be able to shift, and look at you go! You are aware! Now shift! Now repeat. And honestly, that's how it's done. It will get easier in time, but only if you condition yourself.

I am used to having very little money.

Here, we have to work at getting used to a new normal. Maybe you want to color your hair red, but you aren't sure how it will look because you are used to having it dark. If you've ever made a dramatic hair color change, you know it takes a few days to get used to. Sometimes we don't like things at first simply because they are different. Some people will fry their hair by immediately turning it back to what they had before. But if we are committed to a new result or outcome, we only need to spend a bit of time adjusting before we can focus on the benefits. If you are used to having $500 in your bank account, then of course $5,000 will feel uncomfortable because that is a huge leap, so you are likely to self-sabotage. Start by keeping $600 in your account until that amount feels normal. When you are comfortable, add another $200. Work your way up to $5,000 so that you can make it your new normal. If you do too much too fast, you'll "fry" your bank account because you've gotten comfortable with very little money.

When I do have more money than I'm used to having, I usually feel stressed about it.

If something is outside your comfort zone, it will be stressful for you. Be mindful of how you name this stress, however. Stress can feel an awful lot like excitement if we decide it is so, and it might be helpful to tell yourself, "Wow! I'm excited to grow my wealth by buying an asset with the extra money I have this month!" If you are stressed about it, you will likely waste it or give it away. If you are excited about it, you can make a decision about how to use it in a way that will feel exciting, helping you to attract more money. Staying on top of that budget—so that you can decide where that money goes *before* it hits your bank account—will ensure your emotions don't dictate your financial behaviors.

I have been described as "cheap."

The question I have for you is this: "Does being called 'cheap' bother you?" Because, for some people, this is a compliment. It entirely depends on how you see yourself or what you've decided is your financial identity. Lack can sometimes culminate in cheapness, and it can sometimes culminate in extravagance. Doing the intentional identity work of defining who you actually are—versus who you've been told you are throughout your whole life—will start this shift to abundance. When you can get to that place where you know who you are, and where what other people say about you doesn't affect you, you know you've shifted into an abundance mindset. We want to consider other people's feedback, but we don't want to take it on as an identity unless it aligns with how we choose to see ourselves.

THE SPEND BLOCK

I can't control my spending easily.

It's important to note that not being able to control your spending could be a serious condition, but this really depends on *why* you spend. A typical consumer will be motivated to spend based on value and usefulness, whereas if you are spending to improve your mood, deal with stress, increase your social standing, or improve your self-image, you might have a compulsive buying behavior. If spending feels persistent, excessive, impulsive, and uncontrollable despite financial consequences, it could be time for you to consult a mental-health professional. If it seems as though you simply don't know how to say no to yourself, the key may be for you to put a few healthy boundaries between you and advertisements, influencers, and stores (physical or online) where you might slip up. It is vitally important for you to incorporate exercise into your life. Regular exercise remodels the part of the brain that helps anticipate pleasure and is linked with so many other psychological benefits that often something as simple as regularly moving your body can reduce the urge to spend unnecessarily. Anything you can do to regulate your nervous system and provide self-care will be good for you, no matter what!

Money doesn't stay in my bank account for very long.

This spend block is tricky to navigate, but with a few shifts in thinking, this can actually be turned into a wealth strategy. If the reason you are spending is that you unconsciously feel uncomfortable with money in your account, we can maintain your comfort level by shifting the spending toward buying more assets. If you find that you spend the money in your account quickly, make sure you allocate it before it hits the account and implement a strategy called "zero-based budgeting." Essentially, you plan every dollar down to zero, and as soon as they hit your account you take out the portions designated for investing and savings and move them into accounts that are more difficult to access. Then you buy those investments as soon as you can so that money is "spent," and your spending money becomes whatever is left. As your net worth increases, you will be less concerned with trying to keep money in that account because your habits are already setting you up for success.

I often feel the urge to cash out my investments to pay off debt or buy things.

Feeling uncomfortable doing deep inner work can cause us to crave a quick fix to get rid of the discomfort. Instead, if we can get comfortable feeling uncomfortable, we will usually find that leaving the investments, and "building our money muscles" by using our income to pay off debt, teaches us how to handle money properly while not losing out on the value of compounding. Killing the golden goose is a temporary cash strategy that destroys future wealth building. Charlie Munger, vice chairman of Berkshire Hathaway and Warren Buffett's right-hand dude, has said, "The first rule of compounding is to never interrupt it unnecessarily." And those two billionaires know a thing or two about money. If this is you, promise yourself that for the next five years you will not cash out any savings or investments, and you will focus on increasing your net worth (by paying down liabilities and increasing assets). Set some solid financial goals that you can actively work toward. Pay attention to how your investments are performing, and maximize them if you can. Most people who cash out have deep regret later, so shift your focus to growing your net worth.

I make good money, but I am still living paycheck to paycheck.

When we aren't in tune with our expenses, they can easily creep up and multiply. Most people who live paycheck to paycheck throughout their early twenties still live that way today, even though their income may have doubled or increased exponentially. We call this "lifestyle creep," which sounds as though a pervert might be waiting in your bushes, but that pervert is likely to be a retailer, and they are waiting in your phone. It refers to the fact that increased income leads to increased discretionary spending. If you can maintain your lifestyle and expenses when you have an increase in income and properly allocate that new income to increase your net worth, you are highly likely to escape paycheck-to-paycheck living. You also need to ensure your budget has factored in irregular expenses so that any progress you make doesn't come undone by forgotten bills. If you have been creeped, go back to a basic budget and look at what you were spending before. See what you can cut so that you can start putting money away in order to get ahead. The more ruthless you are now, the easier it will be later.

I spend money to look as though I have money or status.

You might be spending money as a protection mechanism in order to fit in, or as the result of a lifetime of people-pleasing. This probably shows up in more ways than your finances, and getting yourself to that place where you aren't looking for other people's approval will serve you well in all areas of your life. It's a losing game to try to be what other people want. Being aware of who you are trying to impress, and why, is the first step to freedom. Then, you must figure out your real priorities. Committing to those priorities—and communicating them, if necessary—is the next brave step. You may need to be prepared for some relationships to change, especially if you hang out with a group of friends who only wear Cartier and make you feel "less than" for wearing a knockoff Fartier. I think we can all agree these friendships aren't authentic. Make sure you are unapologetic about your decisions to realign your financial goals. In my experience with clients who undergo this type of transformation, most of their friends eventually follow. Sometimes having a friend who takes the lead on clearly articulating their financial goals is an inspiration to those who can't, but who desperately want out of the fickle rat race anyway.

Even if I go into a store to purchase one thing, I will leave with more.

While good prices or deals are often blamed for this, leaving with more than you originally intended is a personal-integrity issue. I don't mean to say that you have deep moral failings as a human being; I mean that you need some work on keeping your word to yourself. We can't ever achieve our goals if we don't keep our word, so doing some basic integrity exercises with yourself will be hugely beneficial here. These might consist of something as simple as practicing saying no to things you don't want to do, instead of overcommitting and bailing later. You might simply bring the exact amount of money you need with you or transfer only that amount to the account from which you do your shopping. Maybe follow through on your promise to yourself to go to the gym tomorrow in spite of how you feel when the alarm clock buzzes in the morning. As you flex that personal-integrity muscle, you will become the type of person who can completely trust that when you say you are going into the store to extra purchases one thing, you will come out with one thing. Even if a half-naked Jason Momoa were the salesclerk, offering to carry both you and your extra purchases to your car.

I can look through my bank statements and still be unsure of what I spent money on.

We can create financial chaos in an odd attempt to avoid pain, or to avoid shame, if we have made decisions we aren't proud of. In some seasons of our lives, we know we aren't making financial choices that line up with our goals, but our more urgent needs outshine our future ones. When this happens, and we are finally brave enough to face what we've been avoiding, we will notice that we might have had temporary spending blackout moments. To resolve it, you have a few choices. You can reevaluate the spending and make returns, you can adjust spending in other areas, you can increase income by getting creative, or you can come up with a solution of your own. The important piece is that you are looking at the problem and then making decisions in advance on how to handle it next time. We will never be perfect when it comes to money, but we can be more prepared. And next time you screw up, you'll have a system to catch yourself. Making sure you are doing what you can to stay emotionally regulated will help you avoid blind spending sprees, but giving yourself grace and forgiveness to recover from them is a loving response, too.

I spend money to meet an emotional need.

When we don't acknowledge or respect our needs (or assume we shouldn't have them!), we run an emotional deficit. Retail or consumer psychologists know this and are paid to help companies market products to you that meet the needs you aren't meeting for yourself. This makes it sound as though consumer psychologists originally went to psychology school to do good things in the world, but then they had some messed-up shopping experience that led to their villain origin story and now are out here messing with algorithms to get you to buy overpriced laundry detergent. Most consumer psychologists study human patterns and work for organizations they believe make people's lives better or easier. When I talk to consumers, most of them hadn't even realized that consumer psychologists were a thing, and simply having awareness of the part they play in the consumer cycle helps interrupt this pattern. Being aware of the deep, true need you are trying to meet, and strategizing ways to actively meet your own needs, will help heal this block.

When money comes into my life, I instantly think of things to spend it on.

This spend block might show up as compulsive spending or chrematophobia, which is a fancy word for the fear of spending money. Both conditions are what we would consider irrational fixations on money. In the first case, you mentally get rid of money the moment it enters your life, and in the second case, you are fearful of spending anything, so the overwhelming lists of things you may need but are afraid to buy pop up in your brain, bringing a dose of anxiety along for the ride. Having a great sense of distrust in how we manage money might cause us to unconsciously create scenarios in our life that prove we can't be trusted and so justify those negative feelings about ourselves. If you feel obsessive about spending, whether you act on that feeling or not, it would be appropriate to contact a therapist. If you struggle with the thoughts but they aren't obsessive, you want to ensure you are creating a budget and working out on paper what makes sense for your life. Otherwise, the thoughts will just keep swirling around, and you'll go through this same dance every paycheck.

I often feel as though I have to justify or explain purchases to other people.

Your need to justify your purchases can sometimes be a people-pleasing tactic or can happen because you don't feel you deserve to have something simply because you want it. In response to this belief, you feel the need to justify an expenditure before someone else can question it. This may show up in really minor ways, like when someone pays you a compliment on your outfit and you immediately blurt out that you got it on sale. Or it can show up in more severe ways, where you are hiding purchases from a spouse and committing forms of financial infidelity until you can find the right time or the right excuse to explain the purchase. It's OK for you to want the things that you want simply because you want them. If they are in your budget, they won't cause harm to your finances, and they aren't destructive in other ways (to your health, your relationship, or other people), then the work you need to focus on is that of receiving. It's OK to simply say, "Thank you," when you receive a compliment. And it's OK to treat yourself without receiving permission from someone else.

I have a hard time saying no to myself.

Having difficulty saying no to yourself often comes from having been told no so many times—or even once at a crucial time—that you made a silent vow to allow yourself freedom with your finances (in other words, to not restrict yourself), instead of to seek financial freedom. If the person who told you no was a parent or authority figure, to heal this block we have to look at this wound through the eyes of an adult, not a child. Maybe there wasn't enough money, or maybe everyone was doing the best they could, even if it was a painful experience for you. Perhaps you can come to some understanding as to why the no was necessary, then offer silent forgiveness both to the authority figure and for your younger self, who took it personally. Then, create a large, compelling financial goal so that you can say no to yourself comfortably today knowing that you are working toward a bigger yes in the future. There's an old business saying that goes something like: "The person who is the most certain in a negotiation will always win." If you aren't absolutely certain what you are choosing to say yes to, a compelling argument to spend money will win you over. Knowing you are working toward something massive, like paying off your mortgage or taking your ailing relative on a trip around the world, makes it so much easier to say no to your favorite retailer's supposedly deeply discounted products.

I will spend recklessly but then underestimate what I've done, and I'm surprised when I add it up.

This used to happen to me with tequila, too, so no judgment here. What is true, though, is that eventually we have to pay attention to our spending, or our life will become a trainwreck caused by the consequences of our own actions. Avoidance is one of those things that feels good in the moment but isn't good for us long-term. To truly live a financially healthy life, we need to spend time doing things that might not feel good (paying attention to our spending and reconciling our budgets) but that are good for us. We can't manage money unless we are "in" the money, so one way to work through this block is to commit to spending three to five minutes every day checking your money. And if you tell me you don't have time, I will remind you that your banking app is on your phone, and I know you check your phone on the toilet anyway. Spending a few minutes per day focusing on where your money is going, and following up to make sure it got to where it was supposed to go, will help you feel more connected to it. You can't avoid your money when you are connecting with it daily.

I will buy more items than I intend to because they are on sale or a good deal.

This one is both a lack block and a spend block because the origin is scarcity, and the action is spending. When we spend to overcome lack, we put ourselves into a state of more lack. We get tricked into bulk spending, but most of the time when we bulk spend, we bulk consume, so the savings aren't really there anyway. Here's how we know: if you buy a giant bottle of shampoo from a warehouse, you use a full pump of shampoo each time you shower. But as you start to run out, one pump of shampoo will last you two weeks. The minute you get a new shampoo bottle, you'll start making it rain shampoo in the shower. Sometimes bulk buying even reinforces scarcity in your life. It will use up your available cash flow but give you four tubes of toothpaste under the sink. Instead, it might be better to have the cash flow and rely on your own resourcefulness if the toothpaste starts to become scarce. This is abundant thinking. Remember that you don't save money when you get a discount; you simply spend less than full retail price. But you *do* still part with money.

If you were to ask me randomly what was in my bank account, I'd have no idea.

If you don't know what's in your bank account, it's never because you are bad at math; it's usually because you are good at letting your emotions drive your spending. Often when we really want to spend, we will use confirmation bias, meaning we'll justify the expense by looking for reasons that support the purchase. This allows us to ignore the cost. We've already decided to spend the money; all we need to do is justify spending it. It amazes me that our bank accounts live in our pockets, purses, and hands all day long, and yet most of us need to check our accounts to see what's left in it. If you feel lost when it comes to your spending, it can be beneficial to set up alerts with your bank that send you notifications every time you run a transaction. This way the actual amount of money pops up on your device and reduces the risk of overspending, since you know the available balance in your account. The strategy you use doesn't matter; you simply need to come up with a system that requires you to pay attention, like grandma did with her checkbook.

I feel a tiny little high when I buy things.

It is wonderful to feel a high if you are buying assets! If you are simply spending as a consumer, this could be dangerous for your net worth. Sometimes this wealth shift simply requires turning your consumer-purchase spending into asset spending. I once worked with a woman who took what she used to spend on clothing every year and instead bought stock in the companies that she used to buy clothing from. She said she got the same "high" from spending but also loved the way her net worth increased. She also started to pay more attention to how the companies were run, how they treated their people, and how they were performing, instead of merely what products they were producing. We humans love our little highs, so we need to make sure that the way we indulge this dose of dopamine gets us closer to our goals. It may be meaningful for you to make a list of things you do or value that give you those good yummy feelings, and when you are tempted to spend, you can choose a directional activity (an action that moves us closer to our goals) from that list.

I probably have things in my closet with the tags still attached.

We had a participant in the *Get the Hell Out of Debt* online course once who added up the price of all her still-tagged clothing, and she nearly had a coronary. She ended up returning as much as she could, and while she was still emotional from the impact of seeing that in-the-thousands number, she read what she could about minimalism and quickly changed her life. She had previously mistaken minimalism to mean a life free of possessions. What she eventually discovered is that minimalism is the practice of aligning ourselves with the things we value most in life and removing all other distractions. When she decided what she valued most was people, she could no longer overspend "just in case" because it distracted her from what mattered—her children and her partner. And if she had excess spending money, she chose to spend it on and with her family, creating memories. Interestingly, she eventually did end up with fewer possessions because for the most part time with her family is free, and now, with so much extra cash flow, she says, "Simple life, cluttered bank account." If you have unused items that you purchased, make a list of what really, truly matters to you. When you go to spend, if the purchase doesn't align with the list, don't follow through with it.

When I can't find something, I'll just buy a new one.

This may be a sign of ADHD, or maybe you are simply disorganized! If this is happening because it's easier to purchase something than to look for the one you have, you might find it helpful to reorganize your home. It doesn't matter to me if you channel your inner Marie Kondo or Joanna and Clea, but I want you to funnel that energy into creating a home you love, where you can find everything and only have what you need. If this is overwhelming for you—and it's in your budget—hire someone for this, as it's emotionally exhaustive work even when you have help. The trick is that our home is often an expression of what is going on inside us, so it's not as though you will organize it once and be good for life. It will likely slowly become disorganized again, so setting up systems to make sure things are easy to find and put away will be key to keeping you from wasting money on things you already have.

I purchase things I don't need "just in case" I might need them one day.

If you purchase things "just in case," you have the same mindset as people who don't recycle or dispose of items, just in case they need them one day. This spending habit is blocking you from obtaining wealth because you are preparing for the future with worry at top of mind. When we overspend on just-in-cases, we are telling our current selves that we don't trust our future selves to take care of things. You can imagine that wealth will not come in abundance to the version of you that doesn't yet exist but already can't be trusted!

These behaviors have been trained into us by some retailers who purposely create scarcity so that we will buy more. As it happens, you have survived every time Costco has run out of kayaks, so I have a sneaking suspicion you are going to be OK.

I want you to be prepared for the future, but it doesn't serve your wealth to be overprepared but not contributing to your wealth today. Be clear in your budget about what is absolutely needed today, and what can be put into a different month's budget. When wealth building gets pushed out of the way in the name of spending, you are definitely building wealth—just for the retailer, not for you.

I often won't bother returning something if it's not suitable.

There are two ways you can tackle this one. At the time of purchase, you can look ahead at your calendar and decide when you'll return it within the return-policy guidelines if it doesn't work out, or you can make only purchases that are certain. Some people get lax with spending because they use the return policy as an excuse to purchase something they feel uncertain about. But it's almost as though they know they are lying to themselves; they will use the return-policy excuse to buy, all the while knowing the money will be wasted because they don't intend to return it. Make sure your personal integrity—your word to yourself—stays intact. If you feel uncertain about your decisions, you can promise yourself to increase the quality and decrease the frequency of your purchases. It may be that you are purchasing within a financial threshold that doesn't feel meaningful to you, and often increasing the quality means you'll make a better purchase in the first place. If not, you'll definitely want that money back.

Sometimes I feel as though I'm drunk or not thinking clearly when I spend.

In you feel this way when spending, you want to ascertain whether this could be an addiction that requires a twelve-step program. We certainly know that addictions have a negative impact on money, but if you feel that you are a bit out of it when spending, you might not have to take control of your spending. You may need to surrender some control and get professional and spiritual help. If you feel unable to self-regulate, as though you always are obsessing or wanting more, acting secretive, lying, not taking responsibility, or sensation-seeking (looking for a rush when you spend), you might have traits of an addictive personality. This means that money is likely just one way in which you are experiencing out-of-control behaviors. Talking this out with a mental-health professional is never a bad idea! Even if it's not serious, and you are simply "numbing out" with spending, the cost of the time with a therapist will still be well spent.

THE WORTHINESS BLOCK

I'm not good enough to be wealthy.

We need to remember that unworthiness isn't a feeling; it's a thought. And we do have more control over our thoughts than we allow ourselves to believe. This idea that you are not good enough to be wealthy comes from some lie you picked up along the way, a form of comparison that tells you wealthy people are "better than." The fix for most comparison issues is to connect. Lean into relationships where people know more about finances than you, get curious, and ask questions! Perhaps you don't yet know any wealthy people to connect with. In that case, read their books, listen to their podcasts, and familiarize yourself with the language they use. I promise there are wealthy people who are normal, kind, funny, and all the things you value. If you keep your distance, you will live in the land of "them." If you move into proximity and relationship, you will live in the land of "us." Connection is always the key.

I treat other people better than I treat myself.

When we treat others better than ourselves, we externalize our own happiness. We need to equalize this. Treating yourself badly doesn't mean you also need to treat other people poorly. It means you need to treat yourself better. Maybe you believe that being hard on yourself is the way to better yourself. Research out of Stanford University's Center for Compassion and Altruism Research and Education has determined this is not true. In fact, "self-criticism makes us weaker in the face of failure." It makes us "more emotional" and "less likely to assimilate lessons from our failures." Transitioning away from this block will be a slow process, but the results will be so meaningful. Here's an old trick that works: imagine how you'd treat your best friend or most loved person on earth, and treat yourself that way. Don't put up with treatment from anyone else that diminishes this. Keep this up, and over time you'll see a drastic improvement not only in the way you treat and feel about yourself, but also in the way the world treats you, too.

People like me never succeed financially.

The belief that you won't succeed is likely something you picked up from someone else's opinion or treatment of you. And I'm sorry that you went through whatever happened to you because this imprint has likely cost you a lot of wealth in the past. If this is your block, your primary focus for the next four months needs to be on identity work, which we looked at in previous chapters. It's critical that you undo all the labels in your life that have formed your image of who you are, and that you begin to decide this for yourself. It will be uncomfortable, so you'll need to condition yourself to step into uncomfortable situations; make new, empowering choices; and repeat until this new way of being is comfortable. Four months will start your training, but the empowering self-identity will continue for the rest of your life.

I struggle to say no.

You might struggle to say no because you were raised to be polite, and this may have manifested by you putting other people's needs ahead of your own. You might also struggle because, deep down, you believe you don't deserve to say no. There are always ways you can practice this over and over. You don't need to give a reason for the no. You can simply say, "No, thank you." If for any reason a yes makes you uncomfortable, you will choose to say no. This does not mean you won't take risks or challenge your own fears, but you mustn't ignore that deep-down inner-belly knowing. If someone tries to manipulate you into saying yes, you say no. When you are overwhelmed or exhausted, you say no. Anytime you've said yes in any of these circumstances, you have reinforced your perceived lack of worth. When you say, "No, thank you," you are teaching the world how to treat you while exercising your own sense of self-respect, which in turn will make the world respect you more. (Some people will not like it, but, if so, then they weren't in the relationship to respect you in the first place.) This work could very well be your most challenging, but it certainly will be rewarding in more areas of your life than just your finances.

I haven't done enough to deserve financial freedom.

If you don't feel deserving of financial freedom, you will unconsciously not allow yourself to have something. And it might be wealth, but it also might be relationships, career progress, optimal physical health, or really anything at all! Remember that these feelings begin as thoughts, and in order to change this mindset we need to pay attention to when these thoughts arise, then consciously shift the deeply engrained patterns. When you allow yourself to continue with the belief that you have to "deserve" financial freedom, you will always be operating from a place that expects you to *do* instead of *be*. Challenge these thoughts with new ones that empower you. While shifting that thinking, become aware of all the people who have the things you want—not because they are special, but because they wanted them. Thinking we need to deserve something means judging our lives by an external, imaginary measure. But this is another time when it's really one of those inside jobs.

I put a lot of pressure on myself to do things perfectly.

We've been acting as though perfectionism is an admirable trait when it truly is an obsession with all things that need fixing. When we impose these unrealistic standards on ourselves, we consistently set ourselves up to fail. Remember when Lucy would put the football on the field, then pull it away every time Charlie Brown kicked? That is your life. You are constantly setting yourself up to fail. In order to heal this block, you need to shift your thinking toward taking small actions that, when finished, immediately move you closer to your goal. So, if your financial goal is putting $500 this month into your IRA, but you don't have a lump sum of $500, with this block you might never deposit into the IRA. If you shift that goal to be "goodish or even baddish," as Karissa Kouchis would say, you could deposit $200, then $150, then $25, then another $125—and you'll hit your goal. Is the goal to do it perfectly or to get it done? I want you to have high standards for life; don't misunderstand me! But I want you to make progress toward a life of high standards. I don't want you stuck at the first obstacle that you can't perfectly overcome!

I struggle to ask for help.

Struggling to ask for help can be a form of self-sabotage, but it's also possible that it is a trauma response, in addition to being a fear of rejection. When people are successful in any area of their life, they often say that they could not have done it on their own, so this block not only affects you in the present but will also impact your future wealth. It's critical that you ask for help from the right source—the person or entity needs to be trustworthy. But most people *want* to help. I've seen people give up their own goals in order to help someone else with theirs, and maybe you've even done this yourself. To get comfortable asking for help, start small, and with something that is inconsequential. You could ask someone to help you with a door if your arms are full. You could ask someone for a recommendation for a good financial planner. And when you are comfortable, you can ask for help on the things you really need help with. We all need help. We are all designed to be able to give help. Finding the right teammates for your wealth journey will make it all the more awesome.

If I am with a financial professional or someone who I think knows more than me, even if I disagree with them, I will not speak up.

This block may be partially a skill/intelligence block, but it stems from a place where you might believe that what you have to say has little value. It can be difficult to advocate for yourself if you are unpracticed at it, so experts will often suggest you create a "trigger phrase" for yourself. This is a comfortable sentence starter that allows you to do the hard work of using your voice to express yourself. This might be as simple as saying, "That reminds me," or "I have a question about that, if you don't mind my asking," These sentence starters are used to train your brain to bridge conversation in order to support you expressing your ideas, instead of sitting in silence. As someone whose best comebacks in confrontations often come to mind days after they would have been useful, I have found these to also be helpful in conversations with difficult people.

I struggle to keep promises I've made to myself.

This worthiness block is a great opportunity to strengthen your personal integrity. We do this by keeping promises made to ourselves, and those promises kept build confidence. Confidence is the antidote to unworthiness. On the *Get the Hell Out of Debt* podcast, you've likely heard me talk about how confidence only comes from keeping your word to yourself. Often people who have made progress with a goal such as "lose weight" aren't actually more confident as a result of losing a few pounds. What built that confidence was the fact that they promised themselves they'd go to the gym, or eat salad, or drink less, and honored themselves by doing what they said they were going to do. That, not the lost weight, is what is making them walk with swagger. If you struggle with big promises, start small. Make your bed. Floss your teeth. Drink a glass of water when you wake up. Even the tiniest of things, when done after you promise yourself you'll do them, will start to shift this block.

There are people in my life who often criticize me.

Well, obviously, the answer to solving the problem of people in your life criticizing you is to spend less time with those arseholes, but I know from experience that this is easier said than done. There are two things at play here: the first is that you are surrounded by criticism, and the second is that you let yourself be with people who are critical. Sometimes people think they are doing us a favor by pointing out our flaws. But criticism is never an act of love. Because you can't control what comes out of other people's mouths, there are just a few things that need to be done here. First, model kindness and honesty through your own words. You mustn't have an expectation that people will follow your example because that's unlikely. Second, limit your time with people who are critical and look to surround yourself with people who love you for you. This is easier to do if you are not critical of yourself and others because, if you are critical, you will attract what you already have present in your life—people who criticize. Lastly, you must watch very carefully the way you speak to yourself in your own head. If you are used to calling yourself names when you mess up, you are more likely to accept that treatment from others. Be very discerning when it comes to how you treat yourself, even if you are the only one listening.

I buy from discount shops and rarely treat myself to luxury items.

You are welcome to spend your money on whatever you want, but be sure that you don't choose discount shops because you believe that it is all you deserve. If you want to be able to treat yourself, then you must find a way, whether that be by buying from Ross Dress for Less, Nordstrom, or Louis Vuitton. If you value luxury goods, but you spend at the dollar store, something deeply unconscious is happening there. In this case, it is often manifested as people buying a *lot* of things on discount, but if they simply adjusted their spending, they could purchase one higher-quality item instead of a bunch of future landfill waste. I'm not saying higher-priced items are higher-quality—you will decide what your philosophy is here. Have a look at how much money is going out the door, and why, and see if you can realign that amount and spend it on products you believe hold value or are of better quality.

I often have feelings of inferiority.

We live in a culture that normalizes and encourages competition, and when our brains use competition to keep us aware of perceived threats, we can experience massive feelings of unworthiness. One of the ways to overcome this is to take small risks daily. This doesn't mean you take unhealthy risks; instead, doing little things that make you nervous can help, like pushing yourself during a workout, or raising your hand in a meeting, or telling your partner all the things you love about them. The trick is to set yourself up to succeed. We do this by removing expectations of how it will go. You could tell yourself, "Today I'm going to touch the top of the climbing wall," even if you are embarrassed by how that harness makes it look as though you are hiding a chalk bag in your shorts. You could tell yourself, "Bring up the solution for the big project at work," even though someone else might shoot it down or, worse, use it as their own solution later. You'd do this because it's in the best interests of the project. Or you could decide to tell your partner all the things you love about them, even if they say nothing in return, because this isn't about your feelings. It's about taking risks and being brave, something the majority of people won't do. When you start competing with yourself, you will always win.

I lack confidence when it comes to money and other areas of my life.

You likely lack this confidence due to the combination of putting other people first and not always keeping your word to yourself. Taking a personal inventory of the areas in your life where you want to improve your confidence can help…and then look at tiny little ways you can make and keep promises to yourself in those areas. Start small. Rather than saying, "I'm going to clean my car every week on Saturdays at 3 p.m."—a surefire way to set yourself up for failure—you would say, "I'm the type of person who drives a clean car." Then, when you notice it's getting a little icky, you would say, "This Friday I'm going to detail my car," (or you'll make an appointment to have it detailed, if that is in the budget!) and follow through. This builds confidence quickly, especially when that type of action is repeated.

I can be a people pleaser.

If you are a people pleaser, we want to honor the part of you that is kind because nice people make the world a better place. We can, however, be nice and still have boundaries. What we want to shift here is any concern about whether you are making other people happy, and instead move the focus to how *you* feel about the other person. Are they kind? Do they treat you and others well? Do they go out of their way for you or others? Often as a people pleaser, we tie our worth to how many people like us. Instead, we can ask, "Who am I in service to?" If you are going out of your way for true friends, you might decide it is worth it. But if you are constantly over-functioning for people in order to be liked, you are attracting people who need you to do things for them. You are not in true relationship with them; you are in unpaid employment.

I often look for external validation.

When we have thoughts or feelings of unworthiness, we will often look to other people in order to feel better about ourselves. The trouble is that if you outsource your self-worth, you might also outsource your decision-making to people who are not qualified to be you. Soon, you will be living someone else's life and agenda.

We see this in unhappy grown-ups who don't consciously realize that they are living out their parent's dream until they are middle age and marginally unhappy. It's important to recognize that benefited you until now. You weren't doing it to be miserable. But now, in order to grow, you have to learn how to self-validate. Ask yourself what is motivating you. Are you looking to feel better about a decision you already made? Instead of asking what someone thinks, call a trusted friend, be honest, and ask for what you really need. Saying, "I need you to celebrate this decision with me!" sets you both up for success. Taking ownership of your decisions is important, even if you don't make the best ones in the beginning. Learning to trust yourself will be far more valuable than letting someone else's opinion determine your life's course.

There have been times in my life when I've had or wondered if I had depression or anxiety, or when I've struggled with mental wellness.

I'm hoping that if you did ever wonder if you had a mental illness, you had proper mental health support. Mental illness can be a financial block in and of itself. A physical ailment can be a financial block, too, say, for example, if you are unable to work for a period of time because of an illness or injury. If you have ever wondered this, the absolute best thing you can do is get checked out—physically, mentally, emotionally, spiritually. Even if the feelings have passed, it can be worthwhile sitting down with a properly trained professional to talk about your experience. This will give you the tools and resources you can use to help yourself if it happens again, and it will give you the language and compassion to help others, because odds are someone in your sphere is struggling right now. That's all. I'm leaving this one to the pros.

I'm known for putting other people's needs ahead of my own.

In financial terms, the wealthiest people employ a strategy called "pay yourself first," ensuring you take action on net-worth-growing strategies *before* you rack up other expenses. You'll need to do the same with every area of your life. Before you take care of the kids, you'll need to make sure you've done self-care so you can show up as your best. I have only ever lost my mind with my kids when I am tired, hungry, and stressed. My best parenting always comes after a sandwich. You have got to start prioritizing what you need. To do that, you'll first have to figure out what that is. Your form of self-care will be unique to you, and it must reflect what you need to do to feel emotionally regulated and capable of handling challenges. Financially speaking, this means figuring out what you have to do to meet your financial goals so that you can better take care of others. What usually happens is the reverse: we take care of other people financially, and we have less to give to charities. We sometimes look at wealthy people as though they are greedy, but they can drop a seven-figure check at a charity gala while we hide from the Girl Scouts at the door selling cookies. To make a generous impact, you have to put yourself first.

I have used money or resources to get people to like me.

I really wanted a Beaver Canoe sweatshirt in junior high because all the cool kids wore one, but it turned out that not even a popular fleece crewneck could save me from being the bucktoothed trumpet player from band class. Whether you use your resources to buy votes in an election or look cool to fit in, the outcome you hope to achieve will always be fickle. If your love language (or your partner's love language!) is receiving gifts, know that this need can be met without spending money. But using money or resources to get people to like you or to fit in is a sign of a major wealth block. When you use spending to get people to like you, you give off "chasing" energy, which has a desperate aftertaste to it. When we chase things…they run! When you can be your magnetic, awesome, and beautiful self, you will radiate attraction energy; this won't require you to bleed your resources dry in order to be in relationship with people. Give from a place of generosity, but make sure you have no motives and expect nothing in return.

My credit score can dictate how I feel about myself.

The credit score is an imaginary system that the credit card industry made up in order to determine the absolute maximum amount of profit they can make from you.

Don't fall for their birdsh*t. At ninety-nine years old, you likely won't look back and think, "These grandchildren are OK, but if only I could have increased my FICO Score…"

You determine how you feel about yourself by looking at how you show up to your life every day. Let that be the measure.

I have a hard time speaking up in the moment.

I once had an imaginary conversation with Ricky Gervais's character in *After Life* because I did not like one of the lines in the show, but I couldn't process it until later. I noticed myself having this conversation in my vehicle by myself, when someone else at a red light also noticed I was doing it.

This is all to say that I understand this completely. But what I've learned is that most conversations don't have an expiry date. We can actually go back to people later and say, "I was thinking about what you said earlier, and it occurred to me…"

You can also say, "I'd like some time to process my thoughts. Can we reconvene later this afternoon?" Especially if a topic makes you emotionally charged.

Maybe it doesn't feel safe to speak up in the moment. Maybe you are feeling too emotional to properly articulate what you want. Or maybe you just need a break to gain some perspective. No matter the reason, it's acceptable for you to not have all the answers all the time. Those people who do are so obnoxious anyway.

THE INTELLIGENCE/SKILL BLOCK

I'm not smart enough to be wealthy.

The education system has convinced us that we will be rewarded if we are smart and get good grades. This is only partially true. We all have a friend from school who used to eat his boogers and now is somehow crushing it at life. Deciding we aren't smart enough to do something means we are choosing to avoid pain. We fear making a mistake because somehow we've connected pain to not getting things exactly right. Wealth building involves risk-taking, and while you can mitigate these risks, you still need to take some in order to invest in yourself. As you work to overcome this block, you'll ask yourself, "What can go right?" By training your brain to focus on the upside, you'll start to notice possibility, and that will assist you in transitioning from avoiding pain to embracing pleasure.

I often think that when I hit my financial goals, my life will be easier.

It might be true that when you hit your financial goals your life will be easier, but as long as you are always pushing your financial happiness into the future, it will never arrive. In order to shift this mindset, you'll need to look at all the abundance you have today and make sure you are taking some direct steps every day toward your goals.

When working toward a financial goal, there are two actions you can take. One involves a directional activity—an action that moves you immediately toward your goal and that, when done repeatedly, guarantees your success. The second, a supporting activity, is an action that supports your goal but doesn't move you directly there. If you did some supporting action repeatedly, you wouldn't move closer to your goals, but it's still necessary. For example, budgeting is a supporting activity. It's necessary that you know your cash flow and stay on top of incoming and outgoing money. But the money you budget must be used in order to increase your net worth. You actually have to pay down debt and buy assets (the directional activities). And those things don't happen in the future; they happen today.

I am scared of looking foolish around people.

The wonderful news is that being nervous about looking foolish means you are absolutely on the right track! It's important to know that the only people who will judge you are the people who are too afraid to take action. Those who have already gone where you want to go will have overcome the same things you are currently struggling with in order to get there, so be mindful that you aren't trying to impress people, and instead focus on going after what you want, what serves your family or your life's calling. Shift your awareness to offering grace to people who have done brave things, even if they failed in doing them. Sometimes our fears of looking foolish come from the same place from which we judge others. When we start to have grace for others, we change the expectations we have for our own performance.

I secretly feel resentful of wealthy people.

When we've experienced the pain of financial struggle in our lives, it can be easy to feel angry or hurt that other people had resources when it feels as though we didn't. The trouble is that this is not an empowering stance, and harboring this resentment only serves to further divide you. One of two things may be hiding beneath the surface here: you are upset that you were not given something you felt you deserved, or you feel that the other person should have been more generous; or you are mad at yourself for not having been resourceful enough to avoid struggle. Only one of these things is in your control. To heal this block, we first have to express all of that resentment. It can be helpful to journal all those feelings on flammable paper (you don't want to keep those pages!). Once you've done this, take a look at the parts you're able to shift within yourself. The best part about healing this block is that you often become one of the most generous and compassionate humans around because you know struggle, and when you see it, you help others.

I would be embarrassed if other people knew my financial situation.

Being embarrassed about your financial situation usually means we have to remove the masks we wear that keep us performing for other people instead of engaging with them. It might not be safe for you to do so, as you might be with people who would judge those in your circumstances, so it's OK if you decide it's not safe after doing a gut check. But that doesn't mean you continue to wear a mask around them; it means that you need to surround yourself with people who are truly supportive. Every human being needs a safe group of people around whom they can be fully themselves, fully expressed. This will prompt you to consider whether you are someone whom people can be fully themselves around, too. If you don't have these types of relationships today, they can be built in time. Look for communities that are safe and help you grow, and if you don't know of any, you can always join mine!

I avoid situations where money or finances will be discussed.

The interesting part about avoiding situations where money will be discussed is the level of self-sabotage it requires. One of the ways we learn is through engaging with other people in community or in relationship. When we avoid money conversations, we restrict our own success. This is another block where getting curious and asking questions will benefit you. Avoiding these conversations will keep you stuck because if you believe you don't know enough to discuss money, and, consequently, you never discuss money, you will never know enough to discuss money. The solution is often to start reading or listening to podcasts, gather information, and then ask others what they think. Get in the game. Be willing to look stupid. I promise you that unless you are hanging around hurtful people, you will have a better and more positive experience than your fear currently allows you to believe.

I am afraid that if I make a lot of money, I will lose it.

This fear of losing money comes from somewhere deep down and a long way back, doesn't it? You either experienced some kind of loss or watched someone else experience financial hardship, then unconsciously decided that in order to avoid that pain you needed to avoid having money. Here's the truth: you've already lost money. By not growing financial opportunities, you've lost out on wealth. And it is true that most people, when handed a large sum of money they didn't earn, will struggle to keep it; so, the best way to actually keep money is to earn it and manage it well. We know that if you are consistent with wealth-building habits, you will build those "money muscles," and that greatly increases your chances of keeping what you earn. Start small, and stay consistent with fulfilling small money goals. Expand your comfort zone a little at a time.

I behave immaturely with money, or I act rebelliously with it.

Behaving immaturely or rebelliously with money is often a default response to stress or anxiety. In the past when you struggled, did someone rescue or take care of you? Immature behavior is usually a cry for help, though not always an obvious or effective one. It is critical for you to realize that achieving your results in life is almost always within your control. Yes, lots of things can happen to you, but how you respond to them and the actions you take contain the opportunity to grow your maturity.

This block may also be a response to how you truly see yourself, and it may be time to do some identity work. You might be unconsciously living out the expectations of people in your life who see you as immature or as a rebel. When you are become aware, next time, that you are about to act immaturely with money, make a new choice. Celebrate that choice. And repeat. Small steps taken over time will help you grow your maturity and eventually shift how you and others see yourself.

Because I have delayed taking care of myself financially, I often look for opportunities to build wealth quickly.

Anthony Trucks is a former NFL athlete and an incredible speaker, a great podcaster, and the creator of the Shift Method. Once, on his podcast, we chatted about identity and the importance of stretching yourself, and how in football this is called "outkicking your coverage." This is when the kicker launches the ball super far down the field in hopes of getting yardage. Sometimes outkicking your coverage is *necessary* to grow and stretch yourself. It is possible to build wealth quickly. It's also possible to be scammed if you are feeling desperate and not being financially wise. One of the best ways to heal this inner panic is to consistently stretch just outside of where you are comfortable. If you know you have $1,000 this month to invest, what would happen if you committed $1,100? For most people, they would simply find a way to make it work. Then, eventually, $1,100 becomes your new normal. And you keep outkicking your coverage until your entire life has leveled up!

I feel shame around money and finances.

Shame cannot exist in the light. This doesn't mean you shine a flashlight in your mouth and instantly feel better. (Though send me a photo of that if you do because I think it's hilarious when you light up like a jack-o'-lantern.) Shame leads us to believe that unless we do something perfectly, we are not lovable, and that's one of the major reasons we don't talk about it. Who wants to reveal that they aren't lovable? Sometimes even confessing to yourself, "I feel shame when it comes to money and finances," can start to lift it. If it really feels heavy, it's important to talk to a licensed therapist, who will work with you to alleviate the burden. Sometimes making the call to book that appointment feels like the hardest task, but it could very well be the catalyst to ending a lot of struggle.

I'm often looking in the rearview mirror at my life and wishing I'd started learning earlier.

There is a popular proverb that starts:

"When is the best time to plant a tree?"

Answer: "Twenty years ago."

"And when is the next best time?"

"Today."

This money block has the potential to become a massive regret if you don't begin to implement what you've learned now. Everything that has happened up until now has led you to this moment of clarity, and what you've lost in time you can make up for in action. Make a list of what you wish you had done earlier in life. Then, make a plan to do those things, with dates on the calendar to ensure they will get done. Then, look at your life today through the lens of your ninety-nine-year-old self. If you see your future self as happy with the changes you made today, you are on the right track.

I start reading money books, but I rarely finish them.

Well, let's be serious. Most money books are boring. My gosh. I am fascinated by economics and money, and even I have unfinished books in my TBR pile. In all seriousness, here's what sometimes happens when we take a course or listen to a podcast or read a great book: you get overwhelmed or overloaded, and you pause. Often what's happening mean is that your brain is saying, "Whoa, stop. Let's take action on this. Let me integrate this. Then, let's continue." Here's what I recommend: mix up the nonfiction with some fiction, or some learning and some pleasure. And when you find a great money book you enjoy, read it again and again. Sometimes it doesn't help to "go wide" with financial literacy, but it can help to "go deep." Really master and know the content in front of you before you expand.

It would be easier if someone just took over my finances or told me what to do.

Having someone take over your finances is a really fun way to get taken advantage of! I'm teasing you, but you do put yourself in a disempowered position often because you are afraid of failing. Sometimes we want other people to make decisions so that if something goes wrong, we have someone to blame. But the way to heal this is by taking radical responsibility. You start by taking responsibility for achieving your own results. Look at what is going on in your life, and then consider what thoughts and patterns got you here. What would life be like if you had started thinking differently five or ten years ago? What stands in the way of your results right now? And then answer this question: if you had to give life advice to someone like you who was in similar circumstances, what would you tell them to do first? Whatever your answer is, do that thing!

I won't ask questions of wealthy people because I don't want to look dumb.

I don't think I've ever been asked a question and thought, "That person is dumb." I have, however, had people talk as though they knew about something they clearly did not and thought, "Wow, this person is dumb." I once wrote a real-estate contract with a man who didn't ask me a single question about my real-estate experience, and he mansplained the whole contract to me. I decided not to bother telling him that I had been investing for decades and was a licensed mortgage broker. I just sat there, amused by his dumb arrogance. Rather than be a jerk about it, I simply asked him questions (as he *was* very successful), and he was very happy to be braggadocious about it all. People love to talk about themselves, and they love to hear themselves talk. Trust me, the dumbest person in the room isn't the one asking questions. Ask away. Learn all you can.

I have exaggerated my financial circumstances before so that I look smarter to others.

There's a part of me that feels sad knowing that you didn't feel safe just being you. Dishonesty might be a quick fix in a moment of insecurity, but it doesn't solve the problem: you don't feel proud of where you are today. We've talked a lot in this book about how keeping your word to yourself is the most important thing that brings you confidence, so it stands to reason that exaggerating or lying destroys confidence, even when it seems harmless. For this one, you will simply have to practice telling the truth. I fully understand that sometimes it isn't safe to tell the truth, and that not everyone loves unconditionally. In my experience, there are people who will twist the truth and manipulate you no matter what you say, so those people are best kept at a distance, especially while you heal your relationship with exaggeration. The nice thing about having people who don't love and accept you for who you are is that they provide an efficient filtering system for who you let into your life by conveniently filtering themselves out.

I don't trust myself to make smart decisions, so I often outsource my decision-making.

Outsourcing your decision-making is a learned pattern that—good news!—you can break. This is a covert self-criticism that says, "I am not competent or capable of doing this," but much like the other skill/intelligence blocks, you might simply be looking for someone to blame when things go poorly. Other people are great to learn from, but at the end of the day, you need to become a critical thinker and make your own decisions. Consider why people give the advice they do. And always consider whether you would want to live the life of the person from whom you're receiving advice. The quality of life of the person giving advice, in relation to what they are trying to get you to do or to not do, is relevant. Next time you have a little decision to make, consider asking no one for their opinion. Often when you ask other people for advice, you end up following the advice that most closely reflects what your heart was telling you to do, anyway.

I worry that I am managing my money "wrong."

The day we make a decision is not the day we see results, in most cases, so this money block requires a bit of trust in order to heal. This feeling of doing something "wrong" could be the result of receiving contradictory advice from someone whom you love and don't want to disappoint, or of you continually doing things that aren't achieving the outcomes you desire. It can be important for your healing and growth that you focus on your net worth. This is an activity that allows you to truly see what is happening in the big picture. And when you make little money mistakes along the way, you're less likely to derail your progress because you've connected the day-to-day with bigger results.

When I do invest money, I ignore it because I don't know what to do from there.

Congratulations! Look at you! You are an investor! This is incredible progress, so make sure to celebrate. Most people stall out before the actual investing, and you have overcome that obstacle. Next, you simply have to pay attention to what you've invested. You're not going to obsess over it the way middle-aged women obsess over Harry Styles. You're going to make sure you check in on it regularly, sometime between once a week and once a month, and spend a few minutes learning how it is performing. There are websites where you can input your investment (if it's publicly traded), and they will email you articles, news alerts, and other information directly related to your holdings.

Consider creating a separate account for this, like RosemarySmith Investments@gmail.com, if in fact your name is Rosemary, or you want to be incognito. Your confidence as an investor will come from investing. Learning any new language is best done by immersion, and you can read every book out there, but unless you actually invest, you haven't learned much at all.

I assume rich people must be smarter than me.

There are rich people who are smarter than you, sure. There are rich people who are less intelligent than you, too. There are people who are less wealthy than you who are smarter than you. And there are some people who are broke who are dumb as bricks.

Healing this block requires acceptance. Economist James Heckman once did a study and, as it turns out, discovered that smarts have very little bearing on wealth. This is such good news for people like me, who sometimes squirt the windshield with washer fluid and then realize it's just their eyeglasses that are dirty.

You're going to sherlock your life and look for evidence that people like you can be wealthy. If you need some proof, check out Thomas J. Stanley's incredibly insightful book called *The Millionaire Next Door*.

I'm just not good at math.

Given we all walk around with little pocket computers that have a handy calculator function, I'm not sure what the math is that you can't grasp. Money is so much more about patterns and behaviors than it is about adding and subtracting. We all know what we need to be doing financially—it's the *doing it* part that we fumble.

Instead of focusing on whether you're good at something, you'll stack celebrations of your positive behaviors. Just like how your third-grade math teacher might have given you a gold star when you aced that multiplication quiz, you will give yourself gold stars when you don't blow your budget. Shifting your focus to what you are good at will go miles toward advancing your wealth and healing this block, that tells you the lie that you are not good enough.

THE HARD WORK BLOCK

In order to make money, I must work really hard.

When we are encouraged to please the authority figures in our lives, we can develop this block because it makes us focus on a result without regard for its efficiency. Be mindful that I am not saying the "quickest" or "fastest'" way because that can trap us into a "get-rich-quick scheme," and this is about building the skills you need to free yourself, not becoming entrapped. Don't make hard work an ethical issue. It's possible to have characteristics of a hard worker—attentiveness, determination, self-discipline—and not burn yourself out. You'll heal this block by studying compound interest and how to make your money work for you. There are many great books and resources on this, but taking action will be critical so that you aren't simply overthinking. Start by making an appointment with a financial planner, and make this happen within the next seven days.

If it comes easily, it's not worth it.

Thinking that something's only worth it if it's difficult to achieve often means that you overlook incredible opportunities because they feel too good to be true. You might instinctively mistrust people who make massive shifts in a short amount of time and dismiss their success by assuming there must be a catch. If money does come easily, you might then quickly give it away—if you haven't worked hard, it will feel meaningless to you. Two questions that will radically assist your healing are: "Is there a simpler way?" "Is there a kinder way?" By staying open to new possibilities, you can heal the way you view hard work as a necessary step to achieving the results you don't yet have, anyway.

If I need more money, I must work more hours.

Thinking you need to work more hours to gain more money is a very easy trap to fall into. And, naturally, this blocks money and wealth from flowing into your life because at a certain point the hours in the day will run out. Your income will be capped. If you spend at a rate faster than you earn, you will burn out, and you will likely experience many other health issues, mental and physical, as a result. In addition, you might find you are missing out on a lot in life.

In order to heal this block, you must learn to leverage your time. Depending on your expertise and field, you might be able to build a team to support you. This might mean having help at home, or it might mean using your income to hire people who are less skilled and can help with basic tasks so that you can focus on income-producing activities.

I judge people who appear to be rich and lazy.

That you judge people who appear to be rich and lazy is great insight into what is happening within you, because it means you judge yourself harshly when you rest—if, in fact, you are even able to rest. In addition, maybe you were judged harshly for resting when you were younger, or perhaps the influential figures in your life at the time spoke poorly of people who didn't work hard. As a survival mechanism, formed to avoid being unliked, you figured out that working hard was a way to earn love. While judgment is a normal, natural response that we can work to eliminate through awareness and conditioning, the bigger thing at play is your lack of self-compassion. When we treat ourselves with kindness are happy with where we are in life, we aren't focused on other people or our perceived shortcomings. You aren't going to change how other people live or make money, but you can change the way you view them.

I feel constantly distracted by work, even when I'm not working.

Are you experiencing persistent or chronic stress? Sometimes that can keep you in this weird, semi-emergency-readiness state, which your brain activates in order to keep you alive and ready. Your healing process will really involve presence and learning to stay attuned to where you are while you are there. If you work from home, this might mean creating a separation or ritual to signal the start and end of a workday. It might also mean keeping a notepad for things you randomly remember so that you can jot them down and act on them later when you turn your work phone back on again. I have a "batphone," a personal phone with a separate number that is only accessible to my kids. That's the phone I read my books on, and the one I take family photos with. There's no social media on it, and I can keep the ringer and notifications on because it only receives messages when my kids need something—and I prioritize them over work anyway. (They also don't use it unnecessarily.) Make sure you are not blaming work for being distracted. Watching where you put your attention is *your* work to do. Sometimes having a large personal goal can help—and it will make you more successful at work.

I am scared to slow down in case money dries up.

Understanding how cash flow *and* net worth come together will be important for healing this block. If you rely on a regular income source to bring you stability, you and your financial health are on unstable ground. Learning to build wealth so that you can eventually rely on your own cash flow generated by the profits from your investments will be critical to removing this fear. When we operate from a position of scarcity (worrying that the money will dry up), we focus on what is not going well, and you are likely missing out on opportunities right in front of your nose that could help you increase your wealth.

I may be using work to avoid other areas of my life (including finances).

We glorify workaholism in our culture, but the truth is that like any other ism, it will destroy your life. If you receive your identity from something external, like your title, your role, or your income, and this thing changes (and it *will* change, because everything changes), you will be in a state of suffering while you try to find new meaning in life. You first need to uncover the real issue. Are you craving approval? Connection? Do you have a fear of rejection? What is going on in your personal life that needs your attention? If you feel unable to look into this seriously, reaching out to a professional for help can not only expedite your ability to be present in your life but also increase your overall life satisfaction.

If money comes into my life easily, I assume there must be a catch.

There's a phrase that allegedly came from New Yorkers in the last century as a result of apartments that were built with bedrooms on top of one another. It was common to hear your upstairs neighbor take off a shoe and then drop it on the floor. "Waiting for the other shoe to drop" then apparently evolved to became a phrase to describe the feeling of waiting for something annoying, negative, or awful to happen. When we look for things to go wrong, we will find them. But if you weren't listening for the shoe and instead were focused on the birds singing outside your window in Central Park, then that's what you would hear. We can choose to stack the negative things that happen to us, or we can choose to stack the positive things. You are probably looking for something more intense than "count your blessings," but frankly, the universe wants to bless you. So why are you intent on blocking those lessons? What if you received every blessing?

Wealthy people probably did something unethical to get their money.

Maybe. There are also people doing unethical things who don't have money. The idea that money is tied to ethics is simply a story you are telling yourself. It's not an empowering story, however, because if you believe that in order to have money you need to do unethical things, and you see yourself as an ethical person, then you will never have wealth because you won't want to be viewed as unethical. It can be helpful to read biographies of people who are wealthy in order to learn about their lives and choices and see if you can find commonalities.

When I have free time, I can feel guilty that I'm being unproductive or feel that I "should" be working.

It's been said that the lack of productivity is the intersection of burnout, fear, and anxiety. This seems like an intersection you should want to pass through, not park at! We often make the mistake of assuming that growth must happen 24-7, but growth happens in rest, too. In nature, there are seasons when living things lay dormant for a time in order to conserve energy for more growth later. Working all the time doesn't increase productivity. Using free time to rest, restore, and regenerate has been proven to increase efficiency and results while lowering stress. If you struggle to rest, try putting it on your to-do list and being intentional about it, instead of letting it be something you do accidentally when you aren't busy working.

I am working or have worked multiple jobs at the same time to get by.

Working multiple jobs at the same time can be a temporary fix to a transitory financial emergency, but it is a block to long-term wealth. This is the fast track to burnout, and as we've discovered with similar blocks, there are only so many hours in a day. We must be careful not to merely live to work, but to work to build and enjoy a life we are passionate about. If you are currently in financial distress, simply quitting may not serve you at this time, but ensuring you have a plan to follow will be instrumental in helping you get ahead. In the meantime, try to find an opportunity to listen to podcasts or audiobooks during your commute to help you train your mindset. Little bits add up over time.

When I need more money, I instantly think of ways to work.

Being solutions oriented when struggle arises is a brilliant thing, but we want to make sure we aren't applying a temporary solution to a problem that might be much deeper. While not everyone may be cut out for the entrepreneurial life, thinking of ways to create income could be a solution that allows you a little more freedom of time. When most entrepreneurs start out, they end up unintentionally creating a job for themselves that they can't escape. If you can find a way to generate income without it requiring a lot of extra hours, or if you leverage your time efficiently, you will not only solve your temporary cash problem; you might also create a new form of sustainable, long-term cash flow. What other ways can you contribute or add value to the world or your communities that would reward you financially? What problems do other people have that you can solve easily and without much effort?

Burnout is a very real concern of mine.

I hate saying this, because it seems so ridiculous to say to someone who is tired, but your most precious healing tool will be sleep. If you are under stress, this is easier said than done, as there may be nervous-system repercussions from the burnout life that are making rest difficult. Take the opportunity to see a nurse practitioner, naturopath, or doctor to help monitor your health if you can, as this is a critical time to get clear markers to see how this is affecting your adrenal system, gut, organs, and all the amazing chemistry systems that make up your physical body. Your healing will come from being still; this might seem like an impossible task at the moment, but when we can make time to just "be," our creativity can flow, allowing abundance to flow. Sometimes even staring at the shower wall can be a start.

I often feel as though I am the hardest-working person I know.

We all have different ideas about what constitutes hard work. A laborer might see a CEO as lazy because they don't get their hands dirty, but the laborer might miss that the CEO is constantly playing a game of mental chess to make all the systems of the company work together. And the CEO might think the laborer is lazy because "all they do is stand around outside," but what they don't see is the backbreaking long hours and the toll on the body. You might be the hardest-working person you know at the thing you work hardest at. But this perception only reinforces your identity, where you believe working hard is a virtue. Healing this block will come by truly seeing the contributions of others, even if they look different than yours. Acknowledging other people's contributions will increase your personal abundance. Especially your partner's contributions.

I have a hard time relaxing if work or chores are not finished.

While it can be helpful to feel as though you have a clean, organized space and fewer things on your to-do list, quite often regular chore doing is an exhaustive practice. To heal this block, pay close attention to whether your "relaxing" is actually restorative or whether it is zoning out. If you find you are doing work or chores until you drop and then numbing out with television or other zombie-like activities, you are likely not resting or relaxing at all. If rest feels restorative and inspires creativity, you are more likely to attract abundance. The shift for you might require that you build stillness, creativity, or relaxing into your day and week with the same importance as work, leaving chores to come after. Try it as a shift, and see if you notice an increase in abundance and true relaxation.

People have told me, "You work too much" or "You work too hard."

It's likely that you've been told you work too much as a response to their own needs or even their own insecurities. The phrase "too much" is a signal that they believe, for example, that you are working too much *in relation* to how much *they* work. You have a beautiful opportunity to take a look inside when people make comments like that, to see if anything they say resonates or feels true. If so, you can make a shift. But if people make that comment and it doesn't feel true, then you are given the most wonderful gift—learning how to better love the people you care about. If they are making a bid for your attention or time, you can still work to heal this block, but scheduling more personal time and putting your phone away will heal the relationship, which is frankly more important than the block. The abundance will flow from there.

I often overcomplicate things.

When we believe that things have to be hard, or that we don't deserve ease, we often create our own suffering. To heal this complexity bias, we need to focus instead on simplifying things in order to get them done. Sometimes just making a simple list can help. If you need to open a high-interest savings account in which to keep some emergency-fund money, but the task never happens, you might write down the following:

— Call the bank; make an appointment
— Gather required documentation
— Put date in calendar
— On day of appointment, stop at coffee shop and get a latte
— Go to appointment

Try to calculate the simplest steps of the task. Then ask, "Is there a simpler way?" Does the banking website have an online, automated option to open the account? Does it offer video instead of in-person appointments? Whatever it is, ask yourself how you can make the task easier to accomplish and, therefore, offer yourself a chance to succeed.

It feels as though I have worked hard all my life and don't have much to show for it.

This block requires filling the gap between where you are today and where you think you should be. If we close that gap, we can squeeze out the block. The block won't be healed by chasing after where you think you should be, though. The block will be healed when we make peace with where we are. Where you are right now, in this very moment with your eyeballs hitting this page, is exactly where you are supposed to be. And this change will bring so much more abundance if you work toward your goals while being completely grateful for every small incremental lesson along the way.

I seem to be surrounded by a lot of drama.

To heal this block, we have to recognize how we participate in the drama we are surrounded by. A lot of drama might indicate that you are the common denominator, meaning that one small shift from you will change the pattern. Sometimes this happens simply after shifting your reaction to other people's actions. This is also a beautiful opportunity to reevaluate the relationships around you, or the amount of time and attention you are giving to them. Also, consider labeling it not as drama and instead as leaning in with love. Sometimes people create drama because they want attention or have a need that isn't being met, and maybe if you can help them meet it (by serving them lovingly, or by pointing them to the habit/hobby/thing that can), you'll notice the drama is reduced.

When I work more hours to make more money, it seems as though my expenses go up too.

Oh my goodness, this is a very real thing! It's called lifestyle inflation, and you are not imagining it, though the bad news is that you are creating it. This happens when we don't stay in touch with our expenses. Now, it's absolutely acceptable to increase your expenses if you are still meeting your financial goals, and your budget is increasing your net worth. But if you have financial goals that you consistently miss or move away from because your expenses are out of control, it's time to refocus, reprioritize, and realign. To heal this wealth block, you'll employ the "pay yourself first" strategy, then go ahead and increase your lifestyle after you've met your financial goals.

THE STRESS BLOCK

Money is stressful.

Everyone experiences stress to some degree, and our responses to stress will vary. When people say, "I'm stressed," and the person they are talking to says, "I'm stressed too," they are likely undergoing very different responses. Stress is usually experienced after an event or specific incident, but if you feel that money in general is stressful, it's likely you are experiencing more of a chronic stress. Consistently feeling overwhelmed by money is definitely a block to building wealth. The healing comes from leaning into the stress and changing the language you use to talk about it. Rather than saying, "I feel stressed about money," you might say, "There's still a few things I have left to learn about money." That simple change in vocabulary will instantly change your relationship with wealth. Setting smaller, daily money goals and accomplishing those goals will build your comfort level and reduce that block. Avoiding stress does not make it go away.

Dealing with finances overwhelms me.

It's likely that only the parts you don't know or understand are what overwhelm you! The more practiced you are at something, the more competent you are. If it is your first day babysitting eight-year-old octuplets, you will be exhausted. But after a few months, you might be making four PB and J sammies at a time while shouting multiplication tables from the kitchen and ignoring recorder practice in the living room. Worry is a very close cousin of fear, and feeling as though we will fail can stop us from leaning in to take care of what we need to do. This ironically creates the very feelings and failures we fear. Healing this block is all about doing as much as you can today and leaving tomorrow's worries for tomorrow. If you do all you can today to get closer to where you want to be, you'll stay in the present, and it's hard to feel overwhelmed when you are right where you are.

I can lose sleep over my finances.

Ahhh, good ol' impending doom. I've experienced these nights many times. The key to healing this block is to stop the swirl—the part of your brain that thinks of everything late at night. It is also key not to distract yourself by avoiding the worry. Staying in the stillness can be really helpful. Obviously, coming up with a sleep hygiene routine will be key for you (shutting screens off well before bed, limiting caffeine, staying hydrated, and finding calming rituals), but even keeping a list of some kind beside the bed for when you wake up and your brain starts thinking about the things you have to knock off your to-do list—that can be useful for stopping the brain swirl. It would also be beneficial to look into healing frequencies to listen to before bed. There are great options on Spotify and YouTube, or you can sign up for my (nonspammy) emails, as I share cool playlists often.

Thinking about money takes up a huge amount of the real estate in my brain.

How you are thinking about money will determine the way we heal this potential block. If you notice you are obsessing or stressing, this could be interfering with typical daily living, and we want to make sure you have implemented the strategies you need so you can live the life you want while being supported by your finances. One of the best things to do is to simply check your bank account(s) every morning. You want to simply get familiar with what is happening. Eventually, you'll expand this into net worth–building activities, but one of the reasons why money is always on your mind is because you lack certainty about it. Checking in every day for forty-five seconds will begin to create that certainty.

I find it hard to dream about things if I don't have the money to achieve them.

When we are in survival mode, it is extremely difficult to dream. Who wants to make a vision board when all you can think about is whether you can feed your family or whether the lights will be cut off? Maslow's hierarchy of needs shows us how difficult it is to dream when you are concerned about basic safety and security. If you are in this place right now, you don't need a dream; you need a plan. When you get to the place where basics are covered, I promise that you will have an easier time dreaming. I was once asked to speak at a shelter for women and to help them do a vision-board exercise. I nearly lost my mind. The women did not need magazines to cut images out of—they needed *resources*. Instead, I came and talked about basic money management and how to handle money during a financial crisis. Since then, many of them have attended my Financial Transformation Weekend, where we begin to dream and vision-plan—but first, they had to know and feel it was safe to do so. If you are in this space right now, you need to activate your resourcefulness and gain some clarity about what you need in order to function month to month.

I constantly think about money or the lack thereof.

Staying focused on what we don't have doesn't bring us more, yet it is absolutely in human nature to focus on the lack. We have to *train ourselves* to focus on abundance when it is appropriate to do so. It's OK if you initially think, "I don't have enough." You'll simply train yourself to create a second, more healthy thought. It's been said that we don't really have much control over the first thought that pops into our heads, but the second thought is where we find mindfulness. It's the thought we can consciously choose. Noticing these thoughts is what will help build your mental strength because you can condition yourself to change the way you see the world, and, therefore, how the world sees you—once you start being intentional with your thoughts.

I am unclear on how I will retire.

This is simply a lack of knowing—but not knowing is certainly a block to wealth building because you can't take action or make supporting decisions to get you there. Becoming as clear as you absolutely can by hiring a financial planner will be critically important. Then, when you know what your gaps are, you can start to make strategic decisions. Sometimes people think, "I can't hire a financial planner if I don't have any money to manage," but that is why they are called planners—they help you come up with the missing parts of your plan. You don't even need to know exactly all the steps you'll have to take; you just need to know the next few, and then you can update the plan. Just think: if you'd been actively planning for the last ten years, where would you be today? Great! Now do that for the version of you that will exist ten years from now.

I feel financially disorganized.

To heal this block, we need to keep your financial life as simple as possible. When people feel disorganized, they have a natural tendency to create a lot of organizational systems that are too complex and not sustainable. Try lumping your financial life into seven to ten categories. So, rather than "mortgage, property taxes, insurance, HOA fees, utilities," you could have one category called "housing." Call all the companies involved, and arrange for the payments to come out of a specific no-fee bank account each month—and have *only* those things come out of that account. Do this for other categories in your life. Consider your lifestyle, and come up with a system that works for your life. Rather than trying to teach yourself a new way to manage money, consider creating a way that goes with what you are already doing. Make your life simpler, not more "organized."

I tend to get into black-and-white or all-or-nothing thinking when it comes to my money.

Dichotomous thinking will definitely hold you back financially and block your wealth because if something doesn't go the way it should, you will have created a specific set of internal rules that are not being met, and subsequently you'll create your own internal suffering. But trying to control the economy—or aspects of it—is a surefire way to fail financially.

We want to avoid acting on extreme thoughts because they will be emotionally driven, and we want to be measured when making money decisions. Ask yourself if there is evidence to support your thoughts and whether there is evidence to support the opposing thought. Ask yourself if there is a less extreme way. Ask yourself if you are considering all angles, or if you are leaving out important information because you are trying to "be right." Carefully questioning your thinking will lead to expanded options and more opportunity.

I have created financial chaos by missing payments, hitting overdraft, or making little mistakes that have big consequences.

This might be really frustrating for you, but is there a part of you that likes it? I'm asking because some people like having problems as it gives them something to solve. This is not always a conscious thought, but if it feels in any way true for you, you are going to have to start anticipating the ways you self-sabotage and decide ahead of time how to handle your money, instead of going by how you feel in the moment. Getting you out of financial-crisis mode will help you not only with your money but also with all aspects of your life.

I avoid conversations about finances because they stress me out.

I suspect you're avoiding financial conversations might just be a conditioned pattern that was created because, at some point, something stressful happened when you tried to talk about money. It might be really helpful to decide ahead of time that a conversation about money is not going to be stressful. If you do the work laid out in this book, come at conversations from a level of compassion and curiosity, and stay present in the moment, the stress will dissipate, and this block will heal. The stress is coming *from* you in anticipation of the conversation—your mind senses a need for it to go a different way than it actually is. Now if, of course, you are in a situation where conversations about money are abusive, that's a whole different situation that's indisputably going to be stressful, but there is much bigger work to be done in that situation than healing a block.

I find it hard to trust others when it comes to money.

I learned something profound from something Sage Robbins once said: "This is not that." If something happened in the past that broke your trust or hurt you financially, it stands to reason that you might naturally feel a little nervous about trusting people when it comes to money; however, if this a new situation with a new set of circumstances and/or a new person who has not given you a reason to distrust them, then you need to do the work to heal the block. Understanding that "this is not that" has helped me even in my relationships. Just because I was once with a partner who wasn't trustworthy doesn't make my current partner untrustworthy. This is not that. And this mindset allows me to stay focused on what actually is, to stay present to what's actually happening, instead of bringing my old challenges into a new situation.

I have physical stress symptoms when I deal with money (headaches, stomach troubles, anxiety, sweatiness, loss of focus, moodiness, short emotional fuse, insomnia, clenched jaw, poor judgement, and so on).

If you're struggling with physical stress symptoms, it's important to discover the pattern, if one exists. Often when a person thinks, "Oh, I have a headache," they will just take a pain reliever and not actually deal with the underlying issue. I live in a city with a lot of chinooks, a type of weather pattern that changes the barometric pressure and causes some people, including many people in my town, to live with migraines. They can go to a doctor and get all the different medications, but nothing really alleviates it until they move. It is absolutely ridiculous to me that people would continue to live in a city that gives them debilitating, splitting headaches for much of the year. Yet because we are human beings, conditioned to stay in familiar circumstances, these folks never take the step that would give them a life of freedom. It's the same with your finances. If you don't change the environment or trigger (or your response to the trigger), these symptoms will continue. If you have a one-off situation, of course you're going to deal with that health challenge in the moment, but if you notice that it's chronic…you have an obligation to yourself to see both a mental health professional and a medical doctor. Just as importantly, you'll seek to discover the underlying cause (instead of merely treating the overt symptoms) and do whatever is in your capacity to change this.

When I am stressed financially, I notice an increase in my use of alcohol, drugs, cigarettes, or food to cope.

A word of caution here: if this is a full-blown addiction or becoming one, it's easy to justify it by blaming your overuse of some good on financial stress. Here's an important question: if I didn't have the financial stress, on what would I blame my consumption of alcohol, drug, cigarettes, or food? If this is a problem for you, I encourage you to get proper help. What you may find is that the addiction is the reason for the financial stress, not the other way around. If it's not, and if it more closely resembles numbing out once in a while, then the way to heal this money block is to stop using the coping mechanism as you've been using it. When you take care of yourself first and deal with the things you have been avoiding, the numbing out typically subsides.

I often feel caught between the feeling of losing control and the need to take control.

What you are trying to do is take the *illusion* of control. There's not much in life that we can truly control. We can control our own inputs and outputs, meaning we can control what we allow into our lives, as well as the actions we take. Anything else is imaginary. Trying to control things external to ourselves is never going to work. This is the block you'll need to heal. You can do this by making a little list of the stresses in your life, and then making two columns. In one column you'll list all the things you can control, and in the other column you'll list everything beyond your control. You're going to work on accepting the list of things that you can't control and only taking responsibility for acting daily and consistently on the things you can control.

I have had sudden angry outbursts because of money.

These angry outbursts you've had are not because of money, I promise! You've had them because you've been pushed to your emotional limits. You need some amazing self-care and some amazing boundaries. Everything will be easier to deal with when you can manage your own emotions. If you have a chronic history of anger, I highly recommend a book by my amazing friend Julie Christiansen, *the Rise of Rage*. Learning how to deal with all the intensity you feel inside will help you not only when it comes to finances, but in all areas of your life. If you are having sudden, angry outbursts because of money, you are likely also having sudden angry outbursts about other things. Money isn't the reason for the outburst. It might be the trigger, but the reason is your own emotional deregulation. You have the ability to heal this!

Dealing with money has caused me to cry at least once in the past year.

I hope you've cried because you won the lottery and have a flock of golden geese, but given the lottery odds, I suspect this is absolutely because of stress. Healing this block will require you to become extra proactive when it comes to your finances. Sometimes we cry as a reaction to a financial obstacle, but if we are able to proactively anticipate what could arise, our finances can become a source of joy. We know that there will be some financial disasters because you're a living, breathing human being. Being proactive means having a fantastic emergency fund stashed away in a high-interest savings account and having proper insurance for all of life's challenges. Taking this kind of action will really help you when things veer out of control.

I have had relationship problems because of finances.

Finances are a beautiful magnifier for all the things that are going wrong already. We have to remember that money does not have a moral compass. It is not what that is causing problems in your relationships, but it will magnify existing problems. It's never about the money. If you and your partner are not getting along, and the reason appears to be money, or if you are struggling to understand one another, the secret here is to heal the deeper problems in the relationship and work on becoming better with openly communicating about money. Healing this money block is what this book is all about, and as you've learned by now, taking care of your own block before trying to get your partner to change (which we know won't work anyway) will be key. Personal responsibility will be what sets you free.

I often think, "If only I had more money, then these problems would go away."

One of my favorite quotes from Tony Robbins is: "Your biggest problem is you think you shouldn't have them." This is critical because when we can recognize that our job isn't to avoid trouble or to create a perfectly curated life where no problems exist, we can realize instead that our job is to be exceptional problem anticipators and overcomers. Having more money is a great solution to not having enough money, but only if that solution is ongoing and truly stops the problem. If this is your block, your healing will come not from trying to perfectly react to financial stress every time it happens, but from anticipating and preparing for future cash-flow problems so that "not having enough" isn't the problem anymore. (Don't worry. When you solve that one, a new problem will appear! But it will be a higher-quality problem, like: "What is the best investment for my surplus?")

I sometimes wish I could start all over financially.

Oh gosh, I love a good makeover, don't you? A comeback story. A fresh start. It's why I used to buy a new planner every six months, even though it's a twelve-month planner. I'd already messed up half my plans by the time the year was underway. But eventually I embraced those messes because there are so many learning opportunities there. Here's an exercise to help you heal this block: you're going to make a list of all the things you would do *if* you were starting over. Think back to when you were eighteen years old. Knowing what you know now, what advice would you give yourself? What would you spend? What would you save? What would you prioritize? Do this for yourself through all the years until you reach your current age. Now, looking at that list, what can you implement? Imagine you are ninety-nine years old. What advice would old-person-you give current-age-you? What can you implement today?

THE PROCRASTINATION BLOCK

I am afraid of financial success.

When we are afraid of success, we are actually afraid of what we might have to lose in order to gain that success. What is that for you? Sometimes it can be things like: I'm afraid my current friends won't like me; I'm afraid I'll have to give up unsupportive but comforting habits; I'm afraid I will miss important social events. It can be anything, but it is usually something that relates to the unknown. Here are the facts: you are going to have to give up something in order to get something. You can't get to the other side of the swimming pool unless you let go of the ledge. But what do you want more? The comfort of the ledge, or the success of getting to the other side? Healing this block will require you to leap a little. Come up with a list of a few things you are afraid to start, and start one of them right away.

I am afraid of financial failure.

If you are afraid of financial failure, it's possible that you are both afraid to fail *and* afraid to succeed, and both fears are associated with levels of self-sabotage. You're afraid of loss. The uncertainty of money can make us avoid challenges, but here is the truth: you will lose money. If you have investments that you hold for a long time, there will be points in your life when those investments drop in value, and points when they gain. What most millionaires have discovered is that being an investor for decades of their life allows the gains to far outweigh the losses. Inaction, according to them, is never the right call. Understanding your own risk tolerance when it comes to money can help you, and ensuring you are adequately hedged against risk will also help create enough financial certainty that you can take calculated, educated risks—after doing your investment homework. This block will dissipate as you adequately allocate money both for riskier investments and for emergencies.

I delay taking action on things that would bring me more income.

I was an amateur for a long time, but when I went Pro at crastinating my life became worse. I was so exhausted by the thought that bringing in more income meant doing more work that I started to choose short-term relief over long-term happiness. I ended up in a downward lack spiral where things weren't getting better, yet I still wasn't taking action. Eventually, this self-defeating pattern had long-term costs, and I had no choice. I soon learned that I work extremely well under deadlines, so I began to create imaginary urgent deadlines to get things done. This worked especially if I linked a reward to the end. For example, if I get this manuscript submitted early, I can use those extra three days to binge-watch *The Righteous Gemstones* on HBOMax. Or, if I make those business-development calls I've been putting off, I can treat myself to a honey citrus mint tea. This strategy only works for a small time, though, so make it punchy and act fast to build momentum and, thus, build results. Soon you'll be back in the abundant cycle.

I avoid hard or important conversations about money.

I have never heard a single person say, "I wish I hadn't had that hard conversation." Have you? There are only two end results to a hard conversation. The first is that it goes much better than you expected or imagined, and you're glad that you finally took action—and sometimes you even wish you had done it sooner. The second is that it doesn't go well, but the fact that the conversation is off your chest and you've taken action on something long overdue often brings such a sense of relief that you're happy you had it. The only way to heal this block is to decide that for the next twelve months, you'll have every hard conversation that needs to be had as soon as you realize it needs having. There's no other way around healing this block. If you remember to approach all conversations with loving kindness, there's no way you can go wrong.

I can feel paralyzed by indecision.

Procrastination has a way of inducing so much fear that worrying about making the wrong choice stops us from making any choice at all. What wealthy people will tell you is that making decisions quickly is one of the reasons they succeed. It allows space to make the wrong decision, and then to correct that decision if necessary. The key here is to never ask yourself, "What is the right decision?" The key is to instead ask yourself, "What is the *next best* decision, or the *next right* decision?" Here's another truth: the only way to know if the decision is right is to make it. So, there's no way to even guess if something is the right decision. You actually have to *act* to know that for sure.

I am continually saying, "I'll do it tomorrow."

A good decision leads to an increase in self-worth, and a bad decision leads to an increase in negative self-talk (in most cases). But you do have control over continually saying to yourself, "I'll do it tomorrow."

What we need to do is shift the way you talk to yourself when you make a mistake. To heal this block, you'll want to develop a philosophy that allows you to do all the things that can be done today and save tomorrow's challenges for tomorrow. And then when you do make a mistake, which you will because you're human, you get to say things like, "Whoopsie doodle!" or "Oh I was knacker-cream-crackered and made a boo-boo." Speak in a silly way that reduces the emotional sting you feel when you mess up, and work at looking at "how much of this can I get done today?" instead of "should I get this done today?"

I will often file my taxes or hand in forms just under a deadline or late.

I am certainly not going to judge you for always filing your taxes almost late or late because I know that the government does a good enough job of that, and obviously as taxpayers we want our fellow taxpayers to do their part, so there's enough pressure in the world. The reason we procrastinate on taxes or forms is because they can feel overwhelming, and often there's penalties or challenges if we make a mistake. Or it's because these things can require a lot of bandwidth depending on how your brain works. If you are in a period of busyness, you may decide that you need to sit down and take some time to digest the information in the forms. Unless we actually schedule this time in the calendar, it will never arrive. The key to healing this block is to give your future self a huge gift—block off time every year to do your taxes rather than waiting to find the time. Setting yourself up for success is one simple way you can radically transform your relationship with procrastination.

I often find excuses for not dealing with my finances.

Most of us don't have to look too far to find excuses to not deal with our finances because, although there are lots of really fun things to do with finances, actually dealing with them is very much unfun. When we concern ourselves more with short-term pleasure than long-term happiness, we can easily procrastinate. It can be helpful when healing this block to make it fun. I know people often think that the activity determines whether something is fun or isn't fun, but it's never actually the activity that makes it fun. This is why kids cry at Disneyland. You can be completely happy doing nothing when doing it from a place of joy, and you can be completely miserable at The Happiest Place on Earth. It's not that the bank is fun. It's not that finances are fun. It's what you make of it. So, if I'm in your shoes and I'm really struggling, I'm going to figure out what I think is fun and bring that attitude to my money. I have a friend who, when she does her banking, pretends she's the CEO of the bank and that she's just going undercover to check on the tellers to see if they're doing a good job. She's a gym teacher. But when she goes to the bank, she wears a suit and bright-red lipstick and says, "I'm going to ask them a lot of questions to see if they know what they're talking about!" when really she actually needs to find out the answers to those questions. It makes it fun for her, and then she'll leave and text me, "I think I'll keep that teller around for another year," as if she even has a say!

I will needlessly delay doing things even if they are important to me.

If you needlessly delay doing things, you'll want to remember that procrastination still does meet a need that you have. It is doing something for you. We have to figure out what that need is. Do you delay things because you're fearful of the unknown? Are you comfortable? Do you not have a lot going on right now? There is a saying that goes, "If you want something done, give it to a busy person." When people are busy, they are often more decisive. One strategy that helps with procrastination is to allow yourself all week to do nothing. Live your life, enjoy time with your family, watch your streaming service, and chill. But then designate a time of the week as your Super Bowl. Maybe on Saturday mornings for three hours, you bang out all the things you've been accumulating on your to-do list. And you have to get it all done before the kids need to be shuttled to gymnastics and swimming. Parkinson's Law states that the amount of time something takes is the amount of time you give it. So set short deadlines and put the important stuff before the urgent stuff, and your whole life will change for the better.

I can sometimes overcommit or overbook myself and set myself up to fail.

My friend Danita recently worked her way through the issue of over-committing—she is notorious for booking herself back-to-back and then having to cancel at the last minute. She said, "I can't figure it out!" and then I reminded her that she is human and has to pee. And that she can't teleport places, so she has traffic to consider, and that means different things at different parts of the day. And she has children who don't care how tightly scheduled she is, and she made a commitment to stop telling them, "Just a minute," and promised herself she'd be more present with them. Often when we are busy *doing* life, we forget we are *living* it. When looking ahead at your next year, consider what you want it to look and feel like, and schedule *that* stuff in first. Family. Friends. Exercise. Painting lessons. Travel. And then book in everything else around that. Leave space for life and laundry. Or hire help. Danita decided to start saying no to things, even if she wanted to do them, if they didn't fit into this vision for her life.

I often feel as though I am in "financial crisis."

There is no denying that being in financial crisis is an actual reality for so many people on our planet. If you picked up this book, it is highly likely that you live a privileged life, even though you might experience financial stress. I do personally understand what it is like to live in a catastrophic financial situation that is self-created, so I do carry a lot of empathy for you if that is where you are. What I can tell you is this: when you get tired enough of it, you will make a change. When it's not systemic, a crisis can be a gift, a turning point, and a launching pad.

When I can't do something perfectly, I will often avoid doing it.

If you're avoiding doing something due to perfectionism, what you're doing here that is *actually* perfect is putting yourself into something known as the "crazy eights." It's not nearly as fun as the card game. Essentially, what happens is that because you will never actually attain perfection—there is no such thing—you'll loop back to avoiding it, and that allows you refuse to do it, because you won't have done it perfectly, so you can't do it, and it never gets done. *Phew.* That is exhausting mental work for no results! The healing here comes by making tiny little shifts more often than pressurized, larger, perfect shifts.

I often can't figure out how to break down big goals into smaller pieces, so I get lost not knowing what to do next.

We don't know what we don't know, so when struggling with breaking down big goals into smaller pieces, it might be very helpful for you to hire a financial coach who can help you see what tiny daily actions you could be taking in order to have massive long-term results. Taking no action at all is more harmful to your progress than making an educated decision and then possibly correcting a decision once you've learned even more. Another way to work through this block is to stop focusing on the next big goal to want to hit. Instead, ask yourself, "What is the next tiny goal that I would be pleased with?" That shift in thinking will allow your next step to appear. Then you take action and repeat. After enough time, you'll hit your big goal.

I think finances are boring therefore, I don't like to spend time on them.

Fully understood. They also think you are boring AF, so you and finances are even-steven. In all seriousness, have you ever sat down and talked with someone who is passionate about finances? It might change your perspective. I can tell you that I never once thought of trains until I met my friend Paul O'Neil. We worked in the radio industry together, but when we weren't talking about radio, we were talking about trains. The dude knows so much about trains, and he speaks about them with such passion, that he made trains so much more interesting to me. When my boys were toddlers and obsessed with Thomas the Tank Engine, I had so many cool train facts to share with them. To this day, I can't see a train without thinking about Paul. What I would tell you is that it's up to you to make finances interesting. If there are products or companies you appreciate or support, you can start investing in them to increase your interest.

When I don't have clear deadlines or dire consequences for not doing something, I just keep putting it off.

Deadlines are a powerful force of productivity, and if you don't have them, you must create them. You've already identified both your problem and your solution. What's really happening is it is difficult to figure out the deadline if there are no consequences for missing it. We get stuck in Languish Land. It's a very blah place with no excitement or energy, and nothing gets done—but nothing needs to get done. It's got a great coastline, though, with a potentially dire money consequence. Think about the future: if you delay taking action, what happens to your retirement? To heal this block, you'll want to download a compound-interest calculator or play with the ones online. Understanding the future consequences of today's delayed action can help motivate you to take action when it feels as though nothing bad will happen today if you don't.

I underestimate how long things will take.

Underestimating how long something will take is easy to do if you haven't done it before. When our assistant is booking time for Keri and me to record the *Get the Hell Out of Debt* podcast, which is typically between twenty and forty minutes, she books us for at least seventy-five minutes because she knows that "you two will start gabbing about random useless stuff before you get to the point." As much as Keri and I can convince ourselves we'll get right to it, I cannot help but be interested in the random useless stuff because she's been my BFF for three decades, and her little nothings are everything to me. When you have a procrastination block, allow time for the things you know you will do, like surf social media, Google random things on the internet, stop and get a coffee…whatever you do, make sure that it is built into the time block so that you are working *with* your psychology rather than trying to control it.

A lot of financial tasks feel like a waste of my time.

As I am typing this, I Just got off the phone with a financial institution because I wanted to update my "investor profile," something you have to do every twelve months in my country. I had to verify my identity with some robot, enter the number of checking accounts and savings accounts I have with them, and then enter the last few digits on the back of my debit card. Then I got transferred twice, and twelve minutes later a recording came on and said, "Thank you so much for calling. Our department is open Monday to Friday from 8:30 p.m. to 4:30 p.m. Please call again during those hours." Holy heck, there are so many things that feel like a waste of your financial time. There are so many checks and balances when it comes to investing and building wealth, and yet they will give unemployed students a credit card. The system is not designed to make good use of your time. It's up to you to decide that in spite of these obstacles, your wealth is worth the time it takes. Look at it from a wealth perspective—compounded over time versus a time-waster today.

I take on too many things and then get overwhelmed and do none of those things.

If you tend to take on too many things, use this little rule of thumb: when you are operating at 80 percent capacity, it's time to delegate or hire help. Most people wait until they are maxed out at 120 percent before they look for help, but then they don't have the time to train people or teach them how to do things properly, or the person doesn't it do it to your standard, so you trick yourself into thinking it's easier to just do it yourself anyway. You've got to delegate, or you've got to say no. If this is your block, you are a high achiever—there's no doubt. But you must delegate to people who want to help if you want to actually move the needle. You are the bottleneck of progress in your own life if you are trying to do everything alone. Practice saying no without excuses or apologies, or delegate and encourage others to help you on your mission.

There are small financial to-do items that I've been meaning to do for a long time that I still haven't done (enroll in my 401(k) at work, buy life insurance, start an emergency fund, and so on).

Jim Rohn was a brilliant philosopher who would say, "What is easy to do is also easy not to do." What's interesting about the small financial items on your to-do list is that doing them will build massive confidence even though they are very simple tasks. Whenever we keep our word to ourselves, we build our confidence. It is crucial for you to set a time when you block out any other distractions, and you just knock a bunch of these off your list. Make sure you celebrate afterward! These tiny little items are things that most people don't do, and why most people struggle financially. This procrastination block comes not from a fear of failure but from a strong belief that not doing them won't negatively impact you, as they're not terribly difficult things to do. But cognitively you know that not doing them has big consequences because regret is one of the biggest life consequences we can experience, and if twenty years from now you still have not gotten around to doing these things, you will be kicking yourself. So, rather than kick yourself in twenty years, why not kick yourself in the butt right now? Stay connected to *why* you are doing things, and it will become easier to lose the procrastination.

If I were not a procrastinator, I would be much wealthier by now. I've wasted a lot of time by not taking action.

Be careful not to identify yourself as a procrastinator. Make sure that you say, "I used to procrastinate," because the language we use is very powerful. You don't want procrastination to become part of your identity. The truth is that you will become wealthy because you stop procrastinating. Making that belief shift and reinforcing it often will ensure that when something comes up that you need to handle, you handle it quickly because you don't identify as a procrastinator. That would be absurd. You are a badass money genius who doesn't eff around and find out. Shift your identity, and you'll make a powerful stride toward healing this wealth block.

THE MONEY GUILT BLOCK

I feel guilty when I have money and other people are struggling.

Caring so deeply about other people's well-being that you harm your own is an act of ego, even though it's disguised as an act of good. I'm sure that's an ugly sentence to read because it sure pains me to even write it. I'm not saying that you are egotistical; I'm suggesting that you might be attempting to feel better about your own privilege by allowing yourself to feel poorly about your circumstances. It's not an effective use of emotion, however, because taking action to help others serves to actually change things, whereas feeling that things need to change is ineffective unless that feeling leads to action. You have a radical responsibility to help people whenever you can, but your guilt is coming from your inner knowing that you aren't doing enough, not that you aren't feeling enough.

It feels greedy or unfair if I have money while other people are hurting financially.

Feeling greedy for having money while others struggle financially is a block full of "should" because you are comparing how you *think* things should be to how they *are*. Even though your heart's intention may be love and caring, your ego is likely taking over. In other words, you are sitting in a place of judgment, criticizing how unfair everything is and labeling it in such a way that allows you to make excuses for not growing your own wealth. We heal this block by rejecting the excuses and growing our wealth so that we can do more, be more, give more. Simply stewing in our negative feelings allows us to protect our egos from our fears of failure. We remain trapped, unable to help people who are hurting. When you begin to take action by building wealth and including giving in your financial plan, you know that you are doing all you can every day to help others, and this block will dissolve.

I didn't earn money the way I had anticipated, so I feel bad having it.

Feeling guilty about not earning money the way you had anticipated is very closely related to the hard work block because it indicates that you have a deeply rooted belief regarding who deserves money and who does not. To heal this block, we must work at removing any assumptions about other people, to help us with our own inner critic. A book to read and revisit that may help you is *The Four Agreements* by don Miguel Ruiz. Your ability to receive has been cut off, meaning that the givers in your life may be frustrated by your conditions or expectations. To reopen this loop, you'll also need to work on receiving everything that comes your way—even those things you might not yet be able to see as gifts.

I often worry about things that aren't in my control.

There's this saying I came up with that changed my life when I personally was working through this block: "Nothing is permanent and everything is a miracle." It arose when someone asked me how I managed to stay so calm during a challenging time, and I just blurted it out. I wrote it down and told myself to see what would happen if I looked at life through that lens for ninety days. And guess what? My level of stress and worry was dramatically reduced. We'd like to think we are in control of our lives, but the truth is that there is so much more at play. If we do all we can every day to move toward our goals and leave the rest up to God (or your creator), you'll be partners in the act of miracle making for life, but you won't have to do the heavy lifting. A great book for you is *The Alchemist* by Paulo Coelho.

I often find that I'm trying to "pour from an empty cup," or give what I don't have.

If you find you often try to give what you don't have, this will seem completely out of left field, but I promise you that it will help you give from a place of abundance: you must put yourself first. Not selfishly—I'm not suggesting you abandon feeding your children to go for margs with the ladies—but in an act of deep self-care. There is a cool internet urban legend called the "rock philosophy," which says that if you try to fill a jar with rocks, pebbles, and sand but pour the sand in first, there will be no room left for the pebbles or rocks. Here, the rocks represent the important things in life, whatever you deem those to be: health, family, wealth/abundance. If you prioritize putting those rocks in the jar first, then you'll have room for first the pebbles and then the sand, and you'll have a very full life-jar. To heal this block, you need to adjust your priorities by having them align with your time and your wallet and your attention. The result will be a massive shift in available abundance, but the work will always be ongoing, as you'll constantly need to realign your priorities with your baseline.

I often spend time thinking about what life would be like if my circumstances were different.

Most people never consider what life would be like if their circumstances were different, so it's very admirable that you understand how where you were born, who you were born to, and how you were raised has played a major role in your life. But simply feeling bad about these immutable circumstances blocks wealth building. Being aware of privilege, whether it's in your favor or not, is the first step toward change. Then you must act. Begin to heal this block by journaling about what you would do if you were in the shoes of another person. How would you treat people? How would you educate yourself? Who would you surround yourself with? What would safety be to you? And then when you get a clear picture of how life would look under your control, decide what you can do today in your current situation to make a difference to even one person. And repeat.

I will make decisions today based on things that happened in my childhood, sometimes unconsciously.

Hello, humanity. It's amazing that you notice you make decisions based on what happened in your childhood because most people are blind to it and go their whole lives without any awareness of their deep wounds. This is a block that can be healed beautifully in partnership with a great therapist or mental-health professional. It is amazing how closely your mental health and your financial health are related. Understanding that you are not the things that happened to you, and that maybe you started responding to money the way you do because of something you were led to believe when you were little, will help you interrupt these patterns in adulthood and create new financial habits and results.

I am comfortable feeling negative about money.

Oh, that stinky comfort zone. The yucky belief in being comfortable feeling negative about money has been reinforced so many times that you have accepted it, and now wealth makes you uncomfortable. Shifting this mentality will require you to look for reasons to feel positive about money. To start to heal this block, start a list of all the reasons why wealth will benefit you, your loved ones, and the causes and communities that matter to you. Add to it for the next twelve weeks. Focus on all the ways eliminating financial stress will alleviate other stress. In time you'll find that feeling negative about money is actually very uncomfortable.

I will give money to other people, charities, or causes before I spend on myself.

Giving money to others before spending on yourself is often a result of how you see yourself in relation to others and sometimes a result of people-pleasing, but it is always a result of your awesome generosity. So, while we do need to heal this block, we also need to acknowledge the good you have done. When you are properly budgeting, you want to make this kind of giving come from your paycheck or out of your account right off the top. The challenge arises when you are struggling financially and need to buy groceries, yet you are also giving money to your sister for her groceries because she is struggling. This doesn't solve the problem in the long run. When you budget, decide ahead of time what organizations and charities get your support so that you are clear on who gets your yes. You can then more comfortably say no to others. Your healing will require establishing healthy boundaries, and it's usually true that when we have flimsy financial boundaries, we have boundaries in other areas that need work too.

I often feel upset that other people don't care as much about the world as I do.

To create a movement, whether it be pushing massive global outreach or simply inspiring the people in your home, you need clear, compelling goals, a constant and relentless purpose, and ongoing communication, and all that needs to be channeled into three things:

- Systems
- Relationships
- Follow-through

And repeat! It's not enough to tell people what is wrong in the world. You must paint a picture for them of how it could be. What is the next step? What is the outcome? And the biggest challenge with sharing your compelling vision with the people you love is that sometimes, in our passion for the cause, we can make them feel as though we care more about the cause than about them. The truth? Not everyone will feel as passionate about certain causes as you do. I have friends who are enraged that people eat meat, and I personally get upset easily about child trafficking. You will have a cause that you are called to champion, and it's important to recognize that for you to heal this block, you need to work at letting go of trying to get everyone to believe what you believe. All the while, keep educating others while linking arms with those people who can help you make an impact.

I am uncomfortable when people I know talk about their possessions.

It might be uncomfortable for you to hear others talk about their possessions, but think carefully about why it bothers you. Are you embarrassed or uncomfortable that you don't have the possessions, or do you feel awkward about the conversation because it feels like bragging? Some people are simply looking to connect, while others may be using this as an opportunity to feel significant.

If you can spend time thinking about what specifically makes you uncomfortable and make a list of those things, you can start to heal this block. Then look at that list and try to imagine what need that person is trying to meet. If you can meet that need in a loving way, you might find that the behavior will slowly shift. For instance, if your partner is showing off his new watch, and you feel uncomfortable about the amount of money that was spent, consider working at making your partner feel significant and loved. If they feel insecure around the people they are talking about possessions to, it might be that they have a deep insecurity or just don't feel safe enough (look back at the five levels of intimacy described in Chapter Sixteen). Acknowledging this may allow you to have greater compassion for people who struggle to connect at a deeper level.

I have a hard time enjoying life and luxuries.

There is a healthy extent to which we can acknowledge the unfairness of life and the existence of suffering, but if we live in a space where we constantly focus on these realities, we will create our own difficulties. I want you to do the things that you are called to do. But even superheroes like social workers need to relax and watch a sitcom now and then. You will decide what a luxury is to you, and you will decide which ones matter. But work at being grateful for them all because the rejection of luxury items in your life could be an indicator of acceptance of lower standards for you and the people you meet.

Sometimes I mentally punish myself to ward off feelings of guilt.

Mentally punishing yourself to ward off guilt creates quite the double whammy. You create the guilt, and you create the punishment! You usually punish yourself to alleviate the guilt, but you can see how this might create a negative spiral quite quickly. When this is practiced with regularity, you might find that your overall self-talk is becoming more negative and that you might be getting comfortable with it. Your healing will have to come from self-compassion. This block not only will keep you from wealth but will lock you in this cycle until you begin to forgive yourself. Understanding that you are human and a beautiful, messy, flawed, breathing meat sack of emotions will help you begin the process. Work through something called the Four Rs: responsibility, or taking ownership of what happened and accepting that it did; remorse, or recognizing what you feel guilty about and deciding what you would do differently knowing what you know now; restoration, or making amends with yourself and treating yourself with kindness and respect; and renewal, or changing the behaviors that lead to feelings of guilt and taking a proactive stance instead of a reactive one.

I feel very sensitive to financial injustice.

I believe that you feel sensitive to financial injustice by design, because can you imagine the world we would live in if people didn't care? Caring is important, as it is the first step toward mobilizing change. You simply need to make sure your priorities are aligned in such a way that allows to receive so that you might give. Many people who are sensitive to the fact that the world is not fair are caught in lack mentality, meaning that they pour out more than they bring in, and that is not sustainable. Make sure you regularly give to an organization that is aligned with your beliefs, and that you are doing what you can with what you have to help. Using this as a motivator to increase your own wealth might be helpful, too, because when you have more, you can do more.

Sometimes I feel all consumed by guilt, and this cuts me off from experiencing a full range of emotions.

Feeling all consumed by guilt is what is known as your emotional home or comfort zone—the emotion you are most used to feeling. This emotion is not who you are but who you have become by training yourself to live in it. Most of us let our emotions run the show, and we make our decisions and experience our lives through this lens. But when you understand that you actually have some management over your emotions, you can train yourself to choose to feel a new way if you want to. The trouble is that most of us get really comfortable in and have given significance to our emotional home, so to do something different, to choose a different emotion, would mean abandoning what we know. In your case, it's imperative that you create a new emotional home because the one you are living in isn't allowing you to experience all of life. We don't want to experience only one feeling. People who are happy all the time aren't truly living either. We need to experience the fullness and richness of all our emotions to truly live, and mastering your emotional regulation will be key to your growth.

Guilt has kept me from being truly successful.

Yes, of course guilt has kept you from being successful! This is a brilliant observation because guilt is a major impediment to wealth. This is a great opportunity for you to consider who you have been surrounded by or who you were following on social media that you might have been comparing yourself to. Sometimes we feel as though we're not doing enough because we're looking at other people who appear to be doing more than we are. And sometimes that's not accurate; it can simply be a portrayal of who they are on the outside or who they have practiced being. Grasping what it is you're truly capable of doing, instead of limiting yourself to only what you are doing now, and figuring out how to focus on making tiny shifts so that you can see the progress you make will be imperative to healing this block. Instead of always looking at what everybody else is doing, try to stay focused on what it is *you* are doing and what you *can* do. Celebrate every little milestone along the way.

I tend to think in terms of "right" and "wrong" when it comes to finances.

When we attribute morality to money, it becomes easy to make people out to be good or bad, or financial decisions to be right or wrong. But money is not moral. It's not immoral. It's simply a tool. And while your relationship with money will be meaningful, *you* are the one who defines that meaning. You are missing out on many wealth-building opportunities by trying to make everything fit into your black-and-white box. To heal this block, you'll want to stay entirely open to those shades of gray. Your healing will come from practicing asking, without judgment, a lot of questions of people who are doing financially better than you are. Consider the mindset these questions invoke: Is there another way? Is there something I'm missing? What can I learn from this person? Having financial conversations with *that posture* will begin to heal the block.

I have acted against either my personal beliefs about money or what society has deemed acceptable financial behavior.

Now this is where morality comes into play. If you have acted outside your moral code in the financial realm, you could be hurt in more ways than a dip in your wallet. In order to heal, you'll need to have a lot of self-compassion, but in the meantime, we need to really look at the root cause of these actions. If you were in a state of financial desperation and have since recovered, you might be better able to offer yourself grace for those decisions you made that you are not proud of. If you acted more out of selfishness or ego, then of course those impulses need to be healed, but that healing will come through changed behavior. Taking a ruthless personal inventory of who you are and what your standards for your own life will be, and then acting within this character shift until it becomes conditioned (there's that identity work again!) will be what changes you and heals this block.

I have used my spending to demonstrate my moral beliefs.

Using your spending to demonstrate your moral beliefs is not a detrimental block, but it's worth being mindful of. The old saying "we vote with our dollars" is helpful because we have choices when it comes to our money. We do, however, want to watch that we aren't spending outside our budget to make a point. You still have a personal responsibility to your own life goals to make sure you can make a long-standing difference. So be mindful that in the heat of a moment you don't put yourself in distress.

Money has divided family members or people close to me.

It is certainly true that a lot of families have been divided by money, but this doesn't have as much to do with money as it does with the expectations we have or the meaning that we give money. And when we expect other people to behave the way that we would behave with money, we will always be disappointed. We often assume that the way we handle money is the way everybody handles it, and then we are disappointed when that doesn't happen. Some people use money to control others. Others use it wastefully. Some use it very responsibly. But your *definition* of these terms can vary widely, so even if you are using the same language you might actually be talking about different things with the people you love. Clarify. Clarify. Clarify. If these are relationships that you want to mend, then you'll have to do this mending without any expectations that the financial circumstances will change. If you don't want to mend them, then forgive and move on. You don't need the other party to agree to forgiveness for it to happen. Going forward, this block will be healed with open communication, great boundaries, and airing any unspoken expectations.

I have felt bad about some of the internal thoughts I've had about people and their money.

It's OK that you've had negative thoughts about people and their money. Odds are they've had some pretty ugly thoughts about you, too. Life just works that way! In all honesty, it's OK to have thoughts you aren't proud of, but let's make sure your behavior and your treatment of other people isn't affected by your judgment. There's an old saying that goes, "We aren't responsible for our first thought, but we are responsible for our second" (same with actions!) so it's important to know that the second thoughts, the ones we have a little more control over, are the ones we share with others, if appropriate. As Ram Dass says, "We are all just walking each other home."

Chapter Nineteen

NAKED MONEY MEETINGS FOREVER

Congratulations on doing the work that will forever change your relationship with money! You now have a deeper understanding of what
might be holding you back financially, and also of what your partner may be
struggling with. Where those two places intersect has likely been a place of
friction for you, and now you have the tools to show up lovingly and kindly
in a new, heart-centered way for the person you love the most.

When you catch yourself falling back into an old pattern, don't think
that you have failed. The fact that you catch yourself and are aware means
that you have the capability to change the pattern and choose a new outcome or response. Remember that grace and kindness need to be at the
center of all this work, especially because a majority of the financial industry
is built on feelings of lack and shame.

You may now feel an obligation to be a loving example to other couples in your sphere. When you hear a couple arguing in IKEA, you will
understand on a deep level that neither partner is right nor wrong. (Unless
it's about tea lights. No one needs that many tea lights.) They are simply
arguing because their money blocks have intersected and are causing friction
where something isn't healed.

From now on, whenever you hear people talking about money, you'll be able to recognize how their beliefs about money are affecting their decisions. You will show up for people with more compassion than ever. You will make sure that your financial decisions are aligned with your beliefs. You will build greater self-trust. You will gain competence and confidence, and since you are on such a tremendous trajectory of growth, you might as well open up to experiencing Level Five intimacy in your own life!

Let's make sure that our naked money meetings always have a clear agenda, and our loving, unconditional relationships do not.

Here's to love.

Recommended Reading

Coelho, Paulo. *The Alchemist.*
If you haven't read this book, someone you know has! It's a classic. It explores the idea that you have a destiny to pursue that exists outside of other people and challenges you to consider the obstacles along the way.

Katie, Byron, and Stephen Mitchell. *A Mind at Home with Itself: How Asking Four Questions Can Free Your Mind, Open Your Heart, and Turn Your World Around.*
Truthfully, any of Byron Katie's books are worth investing in. I've chosen this one to reference here because it so clearly exemplifies "the Work," which is transforming your life through self-inquiry and asking yourself four very profound questions when you feel stuck but want a powerful breakthrough.

Christiansen, Julie. *The Rise of Rage (formerly: Anger Solutions)*
I reference this book in a chapter, but it's great reading in general when it comes to learning how your emotions affect you and others. Julie is hands down one of my favorite people. Articulate, funny, brilliant, and wise, Julie will change the way you see yourself and remove the shame around anger so that you can truly heal.

Kern Lima, Jamie. *Believe IT: How to Go from Underestimated to Unstoppable.*
If you are struggling with your belief systems, this is an excellent book that tells a compelling real-life story of overcoming self-doubt while giving you exceptional tools to work through obstacles in your own life. I keep a

few extra copies on hand to give to people who are in a challenging phase, because the shelf life of this book is better than flowers, and the content inside is tremendously valuable.

Hendricks, Gay. *The Big Leap: Conquer Your Hidden Fear and Take Life to the Next Level.*
This book actually has nothing and yet everything to do with much of what we talked about in this book. It will help you understand why you might be engaging in self-sabotage, and it's a great book to read every year between Thanksgiving and New Year's before you try to set any resolutions.

Ruiz, don Miguel. *The Four Agreements: A Practical Guide to Personal Freedom.*
This is one of those books that seems to continually resurface in memes, but going a little more in depth by reading the book will be helpful if you want to understand how to end most of your own suffering.

Chapman, Gary. *The Five Love Languages: The Secret to Love That Lasts*
I reference the five love languages in various parts of the book with the assumption that you are not living under a rock and have a familiarity with this book and Dr. Chapman's work. If you don't, then let me be the first to introduce you to a book that you will be referencing for the rest of your life!

Bulitt, David, JD, and Julie Bulitt, LCSW-C. *The Five Core Conversations for Couples: Expert Advice about How to Develop Effective Communication, a Long-Term Financial Plan, Cooperative Parenting Strategies, Mutually Satisfying Sex, and Work-Life Balance*
David is a divorce lawyer, and Julie is a family therapist. They created this book to help couples navigate the most difficult conversations around the most sensitive topics. This book is packed with expert advice from two loving people who care.

Stanley, Thomas J., PhD, and William D. Danko, PhD. *The Millionaire Next Door: The Surprising Secrets of America's Wealthy.*

If you have only ever believed that millionaires had yachts and gold teeth and custom Bentleys, then this book will give you a look at how most millionaires actually live, and how they created their net worths.

I've also prepared some free downloadable resources for you here:

Acknowledgments

This book was written by an entire community. When you share your stories with me, message me on social, call into the podcast and leave your questions or your stories, hire me to speak, and so on, you are contributing to my life's work. Our stories are now intertwined. This book would not be possible without the *Get the Hell Out of Debt* online community and those members' commitment to encouraging each other. I've shared your stories in these pages (sometimes I've changed details or blended similar stories together for brevity) because of the way you've inspired me. Thank you for your trust. I am committed to honoring and respecting you always.

Aidan. Thank you for your unwavering support and kindness. I love that you are interested in financial freedom. Every adult who reads my books wishes they had taken the steps you are taking now, so know that while the road will sometimes feel bumpy, the overall journey will be much smoother because of your incredible habits. I love you.

Anderson. The level of care and consideration you give to social causes, the earth, humanity, and your family is far beyond the maturity level of most people your age. I learn so much from you when you share your thoughts. Most people only like to have conversations with people who agree with them, but when we can share our ideas and listen to other people whose opinions differ from ours, and we do it in a healthy, kind way, we all grow. I love everything about you, but especially your heart.

Avery. You are brilliant and creative and one of your secret superpowers is your sense of humor. Promise me you will always show up as you. The greatest challenge we all face is not allowing other people to decide who we are. I will always have your back. Club Jibbetz Forever. I love you to the moon and back.

Becca Fields. I love you and your big DINK energy. Thank you for being a calm voice of reason. Your badass boundaries. For being the type of woman who has high standards and continually makes things better. I only ever want to book vacations at the same time as you so I never have to work a day when you aren't there.

Cynthia Amaro. I *knew* I saw something magical in you when I spotted you in the audience that day. I'm so grateful for how you've poured into the people who cross our paths, and for how you continue to show up in every day with grace, compassion, and humility. I cannot thank you enough for how you've helped inspire the *Get the Hell Out of Debt* community, the UHPW community, and the staff at that St. Louis hotel to get their sh*t together. I love you to pieces.

Dani. You are the most creative person I know. Thank you for always thinking about inclusiveness and encouraging the rest of us to carefully consider who might not be included. I love that you are a corporate badass but also a nature-loving free spirit. I love getting things done with you. I love laughing with you. I love figuring out the world with you. I feel so lucky to be your friend.

Darami. Thank you for being the kind of woman who champions other women. Thank you for everything you taught me, including the importance of choosing to rip a rotisserie chicken apart with your bare hands in a hotel room at night instead of abandoning goals and ordering room service. I am forever grateful for the impact you had on me. Here is to big dreams.

Debra Englander, Heather King, Ashlyn Inman, Anthony Ziccardi, and the entire team at Post Hill Press. Thank you for your unwavering support and for letting this wild Christ-loving author run free with words and ideas. I hope you are all drinking sufficient water to wash down this salty language. I love you all so much.

Diane Sette Arruza. We talk often about how impeccable you are: in character, in style, and in leadership. I once took a fancy etiquette program at a finishing school, and I remember they said, "The top mark of etiquette is how someone makes others feel when they miss protocols," and I think this most describes you. You continually set a better standard, and you encourage that for everyone you know, yet you still operate with grace. I learn so much from you, not simply from what you say, but mostly from who you are.

Eloise Macapagal. Thank you for being a faithful friend. I believe in you, and I have learned so much about caring for others by watching you in action. The world needs your voice. You are absolutely perfect.

Emily Prest. I have yet to meet anyone who can manage all the details you do while still remembering that people are at the heart of those details. The way you consciously care for everyone using details (and emojis!) lets them know that you hear them, and that they matter. I remember once hearing Oprah say, "Love is in the details," and I think of that phrase when I think of you.

God. Thank you for the gift and the experience of this life. Thank you for second chances, and seventy-seven chances, and also for the abundant joy and laughter that I experience daily. May this life serve to be an act of love from you, always.

Instagram. Thank you to Roxanna, Milla, Angela, Kaylie, Ana, Natasha, Lauren, Pamie, Michelle, Claire, Chrissy, Vanessa, Sarina, Kristi, Kimber, Nicole, Harmonie, Desiree, Gayla, Erenee, Jen, Simonne, Tara, Tisha, Dawn, Cobie, Rebecca, Dana, Yvette, Ginger, Louise, Kim and everyone from my IG community for jumping in to help with that last minute edit crunch. A community built this book. I love you so much.

Jamie Kern Lima. Your intelligence and your humanity intersect in the most powerful and impactful way. Thank you for going above and beyond. For getting to know Debs name. For showing up for every sound check. For overdelivering. But mostly for being you. My favorite thing to tell people is: "she's the same person off-stage as you see on-stage," and this is why your life's work is so transformational. It's built with love.

Jessie Schwartzburg. You are the absolute *queen*! I will forever be your biggest fan. You are the expert at creating magical moments for people. Your work is the stuff that lifetime memories are made of, and I'm so grateful for all the magical moments you have created in my life too.

Jerde. I love you As-Is.

Julie Gwinn. Thank you for taking a chance on a new author a few weeks into the pandemic. What a risk-taker you are! I will be forever grateful to you. Here's to you and your beautiful family, a lifetime of health, laughter, and great antique shopping.

Karissa Kouchis. You inspire me daily. You are the human embodiment of Constant and Never-Ending Improvement, and also radical love and acceptance. You are made entirely of magic, and I am so grateful for all the ways you've inspired me to raise my standards, play full out, and not let myself go gray. What you created and what you are building are going to blow even you away in the next decade.

Keri Blakeney. You are the absolute best thing that has ever happened to me and to everyone else you meet. You have always had your priorities in the right order, and I cannot ever find the words to thank you enough for this lifetime friendship, and also for coming on these ridiculous adventures, the outcome of which we aren't sure of when we start.

Kiera Baron. If there is a *Love Is Blind* season for publishing where authors blindly match with their editors, I hope I always match with you. You'll know it's me because I'll be saying wildly offensive things from my pod, and I'll know it's you because you will be lovingly and kindly encouraging me to raise my standards. Thank you for caring about my readers as much as I do.

Lucy VanBerkum. I lucked out when you were assigned to edit this book because your comments were equal parts thoughtful and hilarious, and those are my favorite kind of words. (Wow. I just changed that from a BRW for you right now, so you'll be pleased to know that while I am a little slow, I can learn.) I am honored your wisdom touched these pages. *Enseñar y entretener.*

Production. You are my family. Promise me you'll yell "oh!" at Chin and Cello every time you hear a double entendre. Promise me you'll advocate for Debs. Swear to me that you'll send me videos of Josh and Jeff dancing with each other and Gray dancing with TR, and Gabby dancing with the invisible energy in the room. Make sure there are tots for Shipley. Hugs to

Sam and Rhythm. Say hi to Luke on LaFishSticks and Murph on Heads for me. I love you all for life.

Rob. Thank you for sitting through hundreds of hours of podcasts and Audible audio and still treating every detail as though it might be the one that is the most profound. Thank you for bleeping out the naughty words. And singing the theme song. And all the other things you do that have impacted thousands of lives for the better through your work.

Sarah Witt. You legitimately changed my DNA from our first interaction with your extra-abundant generosity. You have the sweetest, most thoughtful heart, and my heart smiles every time I see your face.

Siri. I have a love-hate relationship with you, but you have helped me tremendously while writing this book, even though we nearly missed catching when I said "egotistical" and you wrote "eagle testicle." You are the worst listener, but it's probably because you have a money block.

Stygar. I am so grateful you said that one that time that "I think the problem is we don't understand how other people operate with *their* money blocks," or whatever you said that made me have that giant *aha!* moment. Thank you for Wingspan, epic walking tours of St. Louis, hilarious Marco Polos, and putting up with me editing videos or copy at the dinner table.

Mr. & Mrs. Robbins. The impact you've had on me is difficult to describe because it's woven into every fiber of my being over the last few decades. A few random miracles and unexpected but divinely guided opportunities have given me a life beyond my wildest dreams. My work family has become my real family, and I am madly in love with every one of them. Thank you for it all.

UHPW. To the women of Unleash Her Power Within, thank you for being a community of women who do the work, support each other, laugh together, and create a safe space the world over. UHPW is not simply an eight-week course; it is a global movement that empowers people to step into an outstanding life, and that's entirely because of how you step up each week.

Veronica Friedman. We worked together for all of eight seconds but since we are trauma-bonded for life (*cue Duncan Sheik*) I wanted you to know that I will think of you anytime I wear someone like a bracelet in the future. You are joy in human form, and thank you for being the kind of person who puts the important stuff before the urgent stuff.

Weston. I love you wholly and completely. The hardest seasons of our life are the seasons we grow the most. Your ability to handle challenges while continuing to push toward your goals shows your incredible depth of character. I'm sorry that I will not be able to help you in AP math as you now have not only grown taller than me but you are also way smarter. You were always destined for something greater than even I could ever dream for you. Follow your instincts.

You. Thank you for reading this book. Thank you for showing up for you. Thank you in advance for the rave review online. Thank you most importantly for being the kind of person who is committed to showing up better every day, loving with your whole heart, and empowering yourself financially. This is how we change the world.

About the Author

Photo by Nicole Dypolt

Erin Skye Kelly is an award-wining and bestselling author who has helped thousands of people pay off millions of dollars in consumer debt, and ultimately, change their lives.

In spite of her terrible stage fright and general Canadian awkwardness, Erin has shared the stage with legendary success strategists such as Tony Robbins, Phil Town, and Gary John Bishop.

Erin's seminars and workshops are judgment-free zones made up of equal parts personal growth, rock concert, and love. She is hired to work with ordinary humans who want to achieve extraordinary things, and because of her track record helping people create a trajectory of success, the phrase she most often hears when people meet her for the first time is, "Wow. I thought you'd be taller."